THE YEAR OF GRACE OF THE LORD

THE YEAR OF GRACE OF THE LORD

A Scriptural & Liturgical Commentary on the Calendar of the Orthodox Church

by

A MONK OF THE EASTERN CHURCH

Translated from the French by Deborah Cowan

ST VLADIMIR'S SEMINARY PRESS
CRESTWOOD, NEW YORK

Library of Congress Cataloging-in-Publication Data

Moine de l'Eglise d'Orient, 1893-1980.
  [An de grâce du Seigneur. English]
  The year of grace of the Lord: a scriptural and liturgical commentary on the calendar
of the Orthodox Church / by a Monk of the Eastern Church; translated from the French
by Deborah Cowan.
    p. cm.
  Previously published: London: Mowbray, 1980.
  Includes bibliographical references.
  ISBN 0-913836-68-0
    1. Church year meditations. 2. Spiritual life—Orthodox Eastern Church.
  3. Orthodox Eastern Church—Liturgy. I. Title.
  BX376.3 .M6513 2000   00-062558

THE YEAR OF GRACE OF THE LORD

Previously published in French in two volumes
under the title *L'An de Grace du Seigneur*

ST VLADIMIR'S SEMINARY PRESS
575 Scarsdale Road, Crestwood, New York 10707
1-800-204-2665

ISBN 0-913836-68-0

PRINTED IN THE UNITED STATES OF AMERICA

Contents

PREFACE

The Fellowship of Saint Alban and Saint Sergius (London) and the Young Orthodox Movement (Beirut) have provided the time and the means that made the writing of this book possible. We wish to express our deep gratitude to both of them.

The aim of this work is to help the faithful — be they Orthodox or Roman Catholic of the Byzantine Rite — to know the calendar of this Rite, and to understand its inner meaning, and secondarily, to help introduce western Christians who are interested in eastern Christianity to a liturgical cycle which is different from theirs.

We have not tried to produce either a theological or a historical work. Information that concerns particular developments in one or other of these two fields has been excluded from the text and relegated to the notes. This book is as brief and simple a 'companion' to the liturgical texts as possible, nothing more. It neither replaces the text themselves, nor is it a complete calendar. It is neither a learned commentary, nor yet a scholarly popularisation. It is inspired above all by the practical concern of wanting to bring the faithful into the presence of the words that they hear in their churches Sunday after Sunday, feast day after feast day.

The calendar which is followed is that of the Church of Constantinople. It will not be surprising, therefore, to find no mention made of feasts that belong to other Orthodox Churches, for example to the Russian or Serbian Church. In this calendar, some of the data met with are certainly of a legendary nature: this will be clearly stated. There is an absolute duty to search out and state what is true. Nevertheless, it is possible to venerate, in the form of legend, profound spiritual truths which find expression through symbols. As to the scriptural texts, we reproduce them here as the Church has received them and expounds them. This is not the place to enter into discussions of textual criticism and exegesis which, moreover, do not affect the substance of the scriptural message.

It is this scriptural message which forms the centre of the present work. The texts of the Old and the New Testaments read in the course of the services embody the highest expression of the meaning which the Church attributes to each Sunday and to each feast day. This book is largely, therefore, a straightforward explanation of the gospels, epistles and other biblical texts that form part of the services. These texts take priority over the chants and, even more than they, need commentaries. Our chief wish is to make the biblical message which the Church gives us to hear both more understandable and alive. To introduce believers to the liturgical year is to introduce them not only to the daily Eucharist, but also to the daily Word of God.

As the material dealt with in these pages is not technical, but devotional and pastoral, it has not seemed necessary to give a bibliography. We would advise any readers wishing to know the original texts, their translations (which exist in French, English and German), and the works written about them, as well as the text of the three eucharistic liturgies, to have recourse to the kind offices of the Monks of the Benedictine Priory of Chevetogne (Belgium), or to the Fellowship of St Alban & St Sergius, 52 Ladbroke Grove, London W11 2PB.

The Lebanon,
Christmas 1971

Chapter I
ENTERING THE YEAR OF GRACE

SUMMARY

The Significance of the Liturgical Year. The First Day of the Liturgical Year. The Challenge of St Simeon Stylites. The Vineyard and the Husbandmen (13th Sunday after Pentecost). The Wedding Feast (14th Sunday). The Great Commandment (15th Sunday). The Talents (16th Sunday). The Canaanite Woman (17th Sunday). The Miraculous Draught (18th Sunday). Loving one's Enemies (19th Sunday). The Widow of Nain (20th Sunday). The Sower (21st Sunday). Dives and Lazarus (22nd Sunday). The Gadarene Swine (23rd Sunday). The Nativity of the Virgin Mary (8 September). The Exaltation of the Cross (14 September). St Michael and all the Holy Angels (8 November).

The Significance of the Liturgical Year

Each year, at the beginning of September, the Churches of the Byzantine Rite lead their congregations into a cycle of prayers and commemorations that constitutes the 'liturgical year' or the 'church year'. What does this liturgical year mean, exactly?

One could think of the liturgical year as if it were a picture of the services and feast days during a cycle of 365 days, from September to September: in short, the liturgical year could be reduced to a practical diagram, to a calendar. The liturgical year is, in fact, expressed as a calendar, but simply to identify it with a calendar would be totally inadequate. One could also say that the purpose of the liturgical year was to bring to the minds of believers the teachings of the Gospel and the main events of Christian history in a certain order. That is true, but this educational, pedagogical, function does not exhaust the significance of the liturgical year. Perhaps we could say that its aim is to orient our prayer in a particular direction and also to provide it with an official channel which is objective, and even, in a certain way, artistic. This, too, is true, but the liturgy is more than a way of prayer, and it is more than a magnificent lyric poem. The liturgy is a body of sacred 'signs' which, in the thought and desire of the Church, have a present effect. Each liturgical feast renews and in some sense actualises the event of which it is the symbol; it takes this event out of the past and makes it immediate; it offers us the

1

appropriate grace, it becomes an 'effectual sign', and we experience this efficacy to the extent that we bring to it a corresponding
inclination of our soul. But still, this does not say everything. The
liturgical year is, for us, a special means of union with Christ. No
doubt every Eucharist unites us intimately with Christ, for in it he
is 'both he who offers and who is offered', in the same way that
every prayer, being the prayer of the members of the mystical
body, shares in the prayer of him who is the head of the body and
the only one whose prayer is perfect. But, in the liturgical year,
we are called to relive the whole life of Christ: from Christmas to
Easter, from Easter to Pentecost, we are exhorted to unite
ourselves to Christ in his birth and in his growth, to Christ suffering, to Christ dying, to Christ in triumph and to Christ inspiring
his Church. The liturgical year forms Christ in us, from his birth
to the full stature of the perfect man. According to a medieval
Latin saying, the liturgical year is Christ himself, *annus est
Christus*.

It is not only the commemoration of the events in the life of the
Lord Jesus that forms Christ in us. In addition to the cycle of
feasts that bear directly on our Lord, the liturgical year includes
the cycle of feasts of the saints[1]. These two cycles, however,
should not be thought of as two strands that run parallel to, or
separate from, each other, for the saints are the glorified
members of the body of Christ. Their sanctity is but an aspect, a
shining ray of the holiness of Christ himself. To celebrate the
feast of a saint is to celebrate a special grace that flows from
Christ to that saint and so to us; it is to celebrate that aspect of
our Lord which is specially evidenced by the saint, it is to enter
(for our profit) into the relationship of prayer which unites that
saint to Christ. It is still more. In the same way that the feasts of
our Lord in a mysterious way renew the events of his life, so the
feasts of the saints make their lives, their merits and their deaths
mysteriously actual, in as much as they participate in the life, the
merits and death of the Lord Jesus. Thus commemorations of the
martyrs somehow renew the grace of their violent deaths, so that,
as these were a participation in the passion of Christ, it is this passion which is relived in remembering the martyrs. The liturgical
year has but one and the same object, Jesus Christ; whether we
contemplate him directly, or whether we contemplate him
through the members of his body.

Great graces and great spiritual opportunities are offered us
during the course of the liturgical year. It provides a frame and

support for Christian piety; it gives it a style which is sober and objective; it maintains a bond of unity among believers. And, above all, it communicates an inspiration, it transmits a life. One should, however, beware of excessive 'liturgicalism' which would seek to enclose prayer in ritual frames. The liturgical way is not the only way. Saints and mystics have sometimes reduced outward forms to a minimum; solitaries have done without them altogether. Liturgical life is not an end in itself; it is but a means — amongst other means — of reaching the kingdom of God which 'is within us'. Our taking part in the liturgical year is empty and illusory if the outward cycle is not matched by an inner cycle, and if the events of Christ's life that each feast represents do not find themselves mysteriously renewed in our soul. The liturgical year acquires its true meaning to the extent that it becomes an adoration in spirit and in truth.

The First Day of the Liturgical Year

The Byzantine liturgical year starts on September 1st[2]. A quick look at the texts which are read during the services for this day will show us the inner attitude that the Church wishes to instil in us at the start of the year.

During vespers for September 1st (which, according to the Byzantine custom are celebrated in the evening of the previous day — therefore, on August 31st), we hear three lessons from the Old Testament. The first is taken from the prophet Isaiah (61. 1-9): 'The Spirit of the Lord God is upon me; because the Lord hath anointed me . . .' etc. This is the passage that our Lord read — and which applied to himself — in the synagogue at Nazareth, just as we will hear it in the liturgy[3] on the morning of September 1st. Some words of Isaiah's[4], which do not come into the passage quoted by our Lord, are nevertheless worthy of special attention: 'And they shall build the old wastes, they shall raise up the former desolations, and they shall repair the waste cities'. In this there is a message of hope for those who are aware of bringing to the threshold of the new year a soul full of desolations and of waste: our spiritual waste can be salvaged during the year which is starting. The prophet also tells us what God will do for the afflicted: he will give them 'beauty for ashes, the oil of joy for mourning, the garment of praise for the spirit of heaviness'.

The second lesson for vespers is taken from Leviticus (26. 3-12, 14-17, 19-20). This is a serious warning that God gives to his people, whose destiny will be very different depending on whether the covenant between God and Israel is honoured or violated. From this comes the antithesis: 'If ye walk in my statutes, and keep my commandments, and do them . . . . But if ye will not hearken unto me, and will not do all these commandments; And if ye shall despise my statutes . . .'. In either case, the divine answer will affect the material well-being of the people – well-being that is expressed in terms of agricultural prosperity or scarcity: 'I will give you rain in due season, and the land shall yield her increase, and the trees of the field shall yield their fruit . . . Your strength shall be spent in vain: for your land shall not yield her increase, neither shall the trees of the land yield their fruits'. God is the creator and the master of physical nature, as he is of souls; our material life depends on his goodness, and he does not leave the just without bread or a roof. Moreover two verses of the same text promise us much more than our daily bread: 'I will set my tabernacle among you . . . and I will walk among you and will be your God'.

The third lesson is taken from the Wisdom of Solomon (4. 7-15). In it, the unknown author[5] reacts against the Jewish concept which more or less identified moral perfection with longevity: 'For honourable age is not that which standeth in length of time, nor that is measured by number of years'. To be old, in the best sense, was to have known how to please God. 'He pleased God, and was beloved of him': for 'an unspotted life is old age'. At the threshold of the new year, we are thus invited to meditate on a concept which is no longer material, but purely spiritual, of time and age.

At matins for September 1st, we hear one of the gospel texts of the resurrection which are read at matins every Sunday. The chosen text is Luke (24. 1-12). Perhaps the reason for this choice lies in the words relating to the holy women: 'The first day of the week, very early in the morning, they came unto the sepulchre . . .'. We, too, are invited to turn our thoughts to the risen Lord at the break of day, at the first light of the year which is beginning, *on the first day of the week* – the week, in this case, being the year.

The epistle read at the liturgy on September 1st (1 Tim. 2. 1-7) reminds us of the duty we have to pray for our brothers: 'I exhort therefore, that, first of all, supplications, prayers, intercessions, and giving of thanks, be made for all men'. It is particularly suitable that, on this first day of the year, we should bring to our Lord's heart all those whom justice or charity bind to us. Let us look at the words 'giving of thanks'. St Paul wrote them here, at the end, with a definite purpose. Perhaps we do pray often enough for the needs of others; but most believers rarely think of thanking God for the individual graces he bestows on our brothers.

The central scriptural text for this day is the gospel read at the liturgy (Luke 4. 16-22). Jesus, returning to Nazareth, enters the synagogue. He is asked to read the portion of Scripture appropriate to that sabbath. He opens the scroll of the Prophet Isaiah and reads: 'The Spirit of the Lord is upon me, because he hath anointed me to read the gospel to the poor; he hath sent me to heal the brokenhearted, to preach deliverance to the captives, and recovering of sight to the blind, to set at liberty them that are bruised, to preach the acceptable year of the Lord'. Jesus folds up the scroll, sits down and says: 'This day is this scripture fulfilled in your ears'. Jesus addresses this same solemn declaration to us at the start of each year. I am poor – perhaps materially, but certainly spiritually. I am captive – captive of my egoism and of my sin. I am blind – for my eyes do not know how to perceive the divine light. I am wounded – perhaps by the external circumstances of my life – but much more so by my repeated spiritual failures. And all the time, Jesus is there in front of me, and offers me deliverance. He, himself, is the embodiment of all deliverance and of all forgiveness. If at this moment I accept his word, his salvation, everything can become new for me. *Today*: on the first day of the year this offer is made to me. I have heard this divine promise so many times already, at the start of so many years: and have abused this grace so many times, wasting in sin those opportunities opened for my conversion. But, in spite of this accumulation of infidelities, Jesus still renews his offer to me; this year which is starting can still be for me 'a year of grace of the Lord'. I do not know if I shall have the strength and the grace to persevere; but at least, on this first day, I can look towards our Lord in a spirit of faith and consecration. The gospel says: 'And the eyes of all them that were in the synagogue were fastened on him'. Would that on this first day of the year my eyes might turn away from the defilements in which they take pleasure and fasten themselves on Christ – and remain fixed on him. For, if I have the courage to keep my eyes on Jesus alone, if I do not turn them aside, I shall no longer fall. Lord Jesus, I look at thee. I have listened to thy promises. Let me now hear, in a way that is totally personal and intimate, the assurance: 'This day is this scripture fulfilled in *thy* ears'.

The Challenge of St Simeon Stylites

The Byzantine calendar assigns to September 1st, as 'saint of the day', the earliest and best known of the 'stylites' — those ascetics who, on top of a pillar, lived a life separated from the world[6]. Such was the extraordinary life of Simeon in the 5th century. The Church seems to throw down a challenge to the world deliberately in inviting us, on the first day of the year, to contemplate a case so extreme that it constitutes a paradox. For the life of a stylite appears to be a negation of all the values honoured by 'reasonable', 'civilised', 'modern' man. The history of Christian sainthood is full of such cases, which are in some way a scandal. Of course, sainthood adapts itself to the conditions of each age and usually takes on some of the features of contemporary life. But it is good that, from time to time, a voice cries in the desert and sends out a strong call to renunciation and penitence. This call has never ceased being heard, and even in our day, hermit life still has a number of followers[7]. In honouring Simeon the Stylite on the first day of the year, eastern Christianity takes a clear stand; it shows that it neither disowns nor abandons heroic forms of sainthood. The world does not understand; it either jeers or is indignant. For these belong to the kind of things Jesus spoke of when he said: 'I thank thee, O Father, Lord of heaven and earth, because thou hast hid these things from the wise and prudent, and hast revealed them unto babes'. (Matt. 11. 25).

The Vineyard and the Husbandmen

About ten Sundays fall between the start of the liturgical year and the beginning of Advent. The word 'about' must be understood in its approximate sense here, for each year the answer to the question of *how many* Sundays and *which* Sundays fall into this period varies, depending on the date of Easter[8]. One could say that usually the Sundays between the 13th and the 23rd after Pentecost are those which fall between the first day of the liturgical year and the first day of Advent. We shall try to indicate the spiritual content of each of these ten Sundays, as it appears from the passages of Scripture read at the liturgy.

The gospel for the 13th Sunday after Pentecost (Matt. 21. 33-42) consists of the parable of the vineyard and the wicked husbandmen[9]. A man who had planted a vineyard and dug a winepress in it went into a far country, leaving it in the care of the husbandmen. Several times he sent servants to receive its fruits, but the husbandmen ill-treated or killed them. Then the owner decided to send his son; the husbandmen, eager to get hold of the inheritance, killed the son. What can the lord of the vineyard do but destroy these wicked men and let out the vineyard to others? Jesus intends this parable primarily for the Jews, who, like the wicked husbandmen, have killed those sent by the owner, and will kill the son himself (one notices how well the words 'they caught him, and cast him out of the vineyard, and slew him' apply to Jesus's Passion, when he was taken and crucified outside the holy city), so that the work in the vineyard — that is to say in the establishment of the messianic kingdom — will be entrusted to the Gentiles. But the parable also applies to us personally. Have we, who are his husbandmen, worked selflessly in the Father's vineyard? Have we not all too often despised the repeated messages and calls from the lord of the vineyard — indeed, his Word itself, and the ministry of the angels, and the example of the saints? Each time we sin, do we not share the guilt of the Jews in the murder of the Son? Have we not deserved to be excluded by God from his service and his Kingdom? This is the severe warning that the gospel brings us.

The same warning is sounded in the first sentence of the epistle (1 Cor. 16. 13-24): 'Watch ye, stand fast in the faith', and by one of the last sentences: 'If any man love not the Lord Jesus Christ, let him be Anathema Maran-atha'[10]. Often the epistles for the liturgy have no direct connection with the gospel of the same day[11], but the 'eyes of faith' sometimes can discern certain subtle spiritual links. In the epistle for this Sunday, Paul speaks with praise of the house of Stephanas and Fortunatus and Achaicus; he mentions the church which is in the house of Aquila and Priscilla[12]. These Greek fellow-workers of the apostle show us, by contrast with the wicked husbandmen in the gospel, what good labourers in the vineyard can be like. Finally, we are left with these words, as the central message of the epistle for this Sunday: 'Let all your things be done with charity'. All that really matters is the quality of love in our actions.

The Wedding Feast

It is the same warning – the danger of being unfaithful to the divine summons – that the gospel for the 14th Sunday after Pentecost brings us (Matt. 22. 1-14). A king has prepared a feast for the occasion of his son's marriage; he sends his servants to call those that were bidden, but they excuse themselves under one pretext or another; their business negotiations, their farm, etc.; some of them ill-treat and kill his servants (the analogy with the gospel for the previous Sunday is striking). The king destroys the murderers and, instead of the unworthy guests, sends his servants out into the highways to gather all those they can find. The house is filled. However, the king notices the presence of one guest who has no wedding garment. He has this too presumptuous guest bound and thrown into outer darkness[13].

The general meaning of this gospel is clear. Jewish tradition frequently compared the messianic kingdom to a feast. Here we are concerned with that great and continual feast which is the union – the marriage – of the Son of God with our human nature. All of us are bidden to take part in this union. Woe betide us if we prefer the things of this world to the 'wedding of the Lamb'[14] or if, carried away by a real hatred of God, we kill the messengers of the king! Strangers will take the place of those unworthy guests. But here begin certain difficulties of interpretation. If the king brings all the people from the street into his house – 'as many as they found, both bad and good' – he cannot expect all of them to be equipped with wedding garments (these evidently symbolise the spiritual preparation necessary to enter into the eternal kingdom): consequently, how can he punish someone for this reason? And what exactly is the significance of the last phrase: 'For many are called, but few chosen'? One could assume that there is a certain interval in time between the invitation and the feast. The king sincerely desires that all should come to his feast: 'As many as ye shall find, bid to the marriage'. He can therefore say: 'Many are called'. But he expects his guests to make use of the facilities that he offers them in his own house to prepare themselves for the feast, which will be the final outcome, and to fulfil the conditions of admission. A poor person encountered in the street cannot be expected to have a wedding garment; but, once in the house, he can, he must, get hold of one. In other words, God does not expect us, sinners, to come to him on our own merits (for we have none); he brings us into his house, his

Church, purely through his own grace and mercy, and opens to us opportunities for purification and communion with him; it is for us to make use of these opportunities and to prepare ourselves to take our place, repentant and pardoned, at the table of the Lord. In this way only can we clothe ourselves in the wedding garment and, having been invited, be chosen. But few men, even from among those whom this king has so generously brought into his house, prepare themselves for the feast. We have been called: shall we be amongst the chosen?

This same idea of a distinction between a first call and a definite choice is found in another form at the beginning of the epistle for this Sunday (2 Cor. 1. 21-2. 4). The greater part of the text refers to personal difficulties that St Paul experiences with certain members of the Church of Corinth[15], but the two first verses remind us that God 'hath anointed us . . . hath also sealed us, and given the earnest of the Spirit in our hearts'. These three metaphors – unction, a seal, and a pledge – express the same idea of a beginning, of a point of departure. Someone who has received these signs of being called is already admitted to the house, but does not yet belong to it definitively. He possesses, if one can so express it, the 'first instalment' of eternal life. But the climax is still to come, and he must prepare himself for it.

The Great Commandment

The Gospel for the 15th Sunday after Pentecost (Matt. 22. 35-46) is made up of two quite distinct parts.

First of all, a lawyer or a scribe[16] comes to Jesus, and, to test him, asks which is the great commandment of the law. Jesus answers 'Thou shalt love the Lord thy God with all thy heart, and with all thy soul, and with all thy mind. This is the first and great commandment. And the second is like unto it, Thou shalt love thy neighbour as thyself'[17]. And he adds: 'On these two commandments hang all the law and the prophets'.

'Thou shalt love . . .'. This precept flows from the very nature of God. 'God is love' (1 John 4. 8): that is why we must love. It is through loving that we go in the same direction as life and that, in our own feeble way, we imitate God. We will love God, which means that we shall love love – 'the Lord thy God'. This Lord-love, this God-love, is not an impersonal sentiment or some metaphysical entity. It is a living person who freely communicates his life of love to all creatures; he is that emotion of love which comes from a heart that is infinitely loving and multiplies itself. If loving God means loving love, it would seem that nothing could be simpler and easier than the great commandment. Yes, from a certain point of view, loving God is simple and easy: but what is required of us is a total love; it is to love God with *all* our heart, with *all* our soul, with *all* our mind, and this word *all* marks the difficulty and, somehow, the heroism of such a love. For it involves pruning away everything which is against, or not connected with, God, and the consecration to him of our whole being without reserve – permitting in ourselves only what can be integrated into his love and sanctified by it. God asks for our heart: in Hebrew, as in Greek, the word 'heart' does not have the sentimental connotations that it has in modern languages, but it denotes the most noble part of the human person, the seat of the intellect and the will. God asks for our soul: the Hebrew word[18] here is deeper and richer than the term we use, for it denotes at the same time the soul, life and blood; so that for Jesus and those Jews listening to him, loving God 'with all one's soul' carried in it, already, although obscurely, the connotation of immolation and sacrifice. God asks for our mind, our thought: our human logic, our science, our culture must become transfigured through him. This, then, is the first and great commandment: Jesus makes it quite clear that the priority is love of God. Love of God and love of one's neighbour cannot be put on an equal footing, for love of one's neighbour flows from loving God. This love of God is the fountain-head, so all humanitarianism must find itself condemned and rejected. But Jesus, even if he does not identify the two loves, proclaims that love of one's neighbour is a commandment which is 'like unto' the precept to love God, and it is in bringing these two commandments together that he shows himself, with regard to the Jewish law, as an innovator and also as supremely original. He is this, again, by the new meaning he gives to the word 'neighbour'. Jewish tradition restricted the use of this word to Jews and their proselytes, whereas Jesus, as the parable of the good Samaritan will show, gives the word a limitless extension. The love of one's neighbour, such as Jesus commands it, is no less total than the love of God: it involves loving one's neighbour *as* oneself, and this word *as* makes us measure the whole difficulty of the commandment[19].

By adding that from these two commandments hang all the law and the prophets, by making love the very essence of divine life and of human life, Jesus goes decisively beyond the whole Jewish tradition. And he gives us a criterion against which to measure our spiritual life at every moment (we could say: with which to take our spiritual temperature). We need only ask ourselves: in allowing this thought, in saying that word, acting in such a way, can I sincerely and humbly say that I love God with all my heart and my neighbour as myself?

In the second part of the gospel for this Sunday, Jesus asks the Pharisees what they think of Christ and whose son they think he is. If the Messiah is, as they say, the son of David, how is it that David, in Psalm 110, calls him 'Lord'[20]? The learned doctors are reduced to silence and do not dare to interrogate Him any more. Our Lord quite often takes the same attitude with regard to us, when we approach him in meditation and intimate prayer. Often he puts a question to us or raises difficulties to which he seems to offer no solution, because he wants us to go as far as our thought, helped on by grace, can take us, so that we should find for ourselves the solution that he did not voice.

In the present case, the Pharisees did not dare to draw the conclusion and say that the Messiah was the son, not only of David, but also of God, and they preferred not to ask Jesus anything else. This will not be our attitude; even when the questions put by Jesus (which generally belong to the practical order and call for a decision on our part) embarrass us, we shall not take refuge in a sullen or rebellious silence, but we shall try loyally to answer, without shielding our secret wounds from the full light of the Saviour.

The epistle for this Sunday (2 Cor. 4. 6-15) describes most movingly the trials, sometimes very painful ones, that go with the apostolic ministry, and also the hope which never abandons the apostle: 'We have this treasure in earthen vessels . . . . We are troubled on every side, yet not distressed; we are perplexed, but not in despair; persecuted, but not forsaken; cast down, but not destroyed'.

Certain words of the epistle apply not only to the life of Paul or of an apostle, but to every life that is given for Jesus Christ: 'Always bearing about in the body the dying of the Lord Jesus, that the life also of Jesus might be made manifest in our body . . . . We which live are alway delivered unto death for Jesus' sake . . . . So then death worketh in us, but life in you'. It is not only the supreme sacrifice of the martyrs which is of concern here, but also the sort of sacrifice which finds expression in the 'little' (but often very big) practical things of life, which can occur every day.

The Talents

On the 16th Sunday after Pentecost, in the reading from the gospel, the Church gives us the parable of the talents. A man, on leaving for a far country, entrusts the care of his goods to his servants. When he returns, he calls them to account for their stewardship. He praises those who, having received five talents or two talents, went out and doubled the sums. But he rebukes and casts 'into outer darkness' the servant who buried his talent in the earth and imagined he had fulfilled his duty sufficiently by giving back exactly the one talent he had received.

The goods which the master entrusts to his servants signify the natural gifts granted by God to his creatures: health, intelligence, riches, etc . . . All these exist through God and for God; we are no more than the keepers charged with administering these divine assets. But the talents signify above all the supernatural gifts, the communication of divine life to men and the graces with which we are showered at every instant. The parable[21], it must be admitted, is fairly frightening. For which one of us can say that he has so much as kept intact the capital of natural and supernatural gifts received from God? Have we not abused these graces, have we not profaned them and wasted them? Still more, which one of us would dare to say that he has made the best use of the amount entrusted to him, or that he has doubled or trebled it? This parable brings us a message both of severity and of goodness, and we have no right to suppress either one or other of these aspects. Three sentences in the parable express this duality well, and serve to strengthen in us both fear and filial trust. First of all, there is the insulting remark of the bad servant: 'Lord, I knew thee that thou art an hard man, reaping where thou hast not sown . . . . And I was afraid'. The master reproves him in these words: 'Thou wicked and slothful servant, thou knewest that I reap where I sowed not'. It seems that the servant's mistake is not so much that he failed to make his talent bear fruit as that he harboured deformed, hostile and cruel ideas about his master. What the words suggest, without saying as much, is that if the servant had spoken differently – if he had said: 'Lord, I know that thou art a merciful master who alone knows how to harvest where I did not know how to sow . . . and that is why, despite my serious mistake, I come to thee with trust' – then the master would have pardoned him. Another very importance sentence is this: 'Unto every one that hath shall be given

. . . but from him that hath not shall be taken away even that which he hath'. Many people find these words hard and incomprehensible, but the meaning is simple. One misdeed leads to another misdeed; one good deed leads on to another good deed; if you give in to sin once, you will become weaker, you will give in another time, and still more times, and you will find yourself slithering down a slope on which it becomes increasingly difficult to stop − and you will lose even the little you had. By contrast, the smallest effort towards God, no matter how small, will make other efforts easier and, the more you strive, the more grace abounds and will be given to you. And, lastly, let us look at these words: 'thou good and faithful servant . . . thou hast been faithful over a few things, I will make thee ruler over many things'. Faithfulness in the small things is the first step on the road, it is the necessary condition for faithfulness in the great things. If I am not capable of great things, I shall at least try to do the small things. If I have squandered the talents that were entrusted to me, I shall begin again humbly, patiently, to be faithful in the very small things: to be honest, pure and willing in every day life. On this first foundation of small things, God will be able to build something larger, and one day perhaps I shall hear the invitation: 'Enter thou into the joy of thy lord'.

The epistle for this Sunday (2 Cor. 6. 1-10) continues to develop the theme of the epistle from the preceding Sunday. In it St Paul again describes the suffering and power of an apostle: 'in afflictions, in necessities, in distresses. In stripes, in imprisonments . . . as dying, and, behold, we live . . . as poor, yet making many rich; as having nothing, and yet possessing all things'. But the first verse of this epistle could provide an appropriate conclusion to the parable of the talents: 'We then . . . beseech you also that ye receive not the grace of God in vain'. The following verse (and also the last verses of chapter 5, which are not included in the epistle for this Sunday) makes clear what he means by grace: the mediation of Christ, the reconciliation with God through Jesus who made Himself 'sin' so that we might become 'righteousness'. Truly − and in this lies our only hope − he will substitute himself for us in order to bring to the Father, with overflowing plenty, the talents which we have not known how to make fruitful. But he will only take care of our talents when we know him to be the supreme talent, the unique talent, whose acquisition and growth in us provides the condition of our salvation.

The Canaanite Woman

We have reached the 17th Sunday after Pentecost, and now, in
some way, the perspective and the tone change. The gospels for
the four Sundays that we have so far considered are taken from
the last teachings of Jesus. The Messiah is coming to the end of
his earthly life; by and large, his word has been rejected, consequently the declarations he makes during this period are striking
in their severity. The tone of the last chapters of the gospel
according to St Matthew is, as we have seen, stern. But today we
go back almost to the middle of the gospel of Matthew. We return
to episodes of mercy, of healing and of pardon. The Church,
having set before us the last and solemn warnings of Jesus, in their
intransigence, wants to bring us back gently to the comforting
aspects of the good news.

The gospel for this Sunday (Matt. 15. 21-28) describes how a
Canaanite woman comes up to Jesus in the region of Tyre and
Sidon. Her daughter is possessed with a devil, and she implores
Jesus and cries out to him; but Jesus does not answer, and his
disciples want him to tell her to go away. Jesus then says that he
has only been sent to the lost sheep in Israel; but still the woman is
not discouraged and keeps on insistently. Jesus answers her with
apparent hardness: is he to take the bread from the children to
cast it to the dogs? Truth, Lord, says the woman humbly, but the
dogs themselves eat the crumbs which fall from the table. 'Great
is thy faith' Jesus, says to her: let it be done unto this woman
according to her faith. And her daughter is immediately made
whole.

This episode is probably reported by Matthew to show how the
mission of the Messiah, at first destined for the Jews, is graciously
extended to the Gentiles [22]. Spiritually, this gospel shows what intense faith, and prayer which is humble and insistent can achieve.
Jesus seems to be silent. He seems to say hard things (but,
perhaps, when he spoke of the children's bread that is not cast to
the dogs, this hardness was tempered by a smile). Our Lord acts
in this way when he wants to test the strength of our faith. But he
does not refuse his grace to someone who is humble enough to
compare themselves to a dog feeding on crumbs fallen from the
table. Let us look at the Canaanite woman's reaction when Jesus
says that he has only been sent to the lost sheep of Israel: 'Then
came she and worshipped him, saying, Lord, help me'. It is often
at the very moment when Jesus seems to put up a decisive refusal

that we must redouble our faith, come near to him, worship him and beg for his help. The formula 'help me' is always acceptable to the Lord, even if the particular form of help we are seeking is not that which he desires to give us. 'Lord, Thou dost say "no" to me. I come to Thee and adore Thee: help me as Thou dost judge it good'.

The first sentence of the epistle for this Sunday (2 Cor. 6. 16-7. 1), 'what agreement hath the temple of God with idols?' – belongs very much to the same atmosphere as the gospel. For, in different terms, it poses the question: what is there in common between the Jewish Messiah and a Canaanite woman, between Israel and the Gentiles? However, the train of the apostle's thought is different. Paul emphasises the fact that we are the temples of the living God, as God himself has declared – 'I will dwell in them, and walk in them'[23] – and that we must therefore keep ourselves apart from idols. The whole history of Israel shows how much God detests all compromise between idols and his house[24]. So we must leave pagan surroundings and separate ourselves from them. This does not imply physical emigration, but a withdrawal on the moral plane. 'Come out, come out!' It is the cry which resounds throughout scripture[25]. In the virtually pagan society in which we live, are we attentive enough to this duty of separating and purifying in relation to the 'impure things' which surround us? Paul reminds the Corinthians of several sayings from the Old Testament: 'Touch not the unclean thing; and I will receive you, And will be a Father unto you, and ye shall be my sons and daughters'[26]. These last words, adding 'daughters' to 'sons', show how the religious thought of Israel had progressed since its origins – and how Christianity has built upon this progress[27]. And so the word 'daughter', on this Sunday, reminds us of the Canaanite woman to whom Jesus had shown mercy; he admitted her, too, as a daughter of God. The epistle ends with the injunction not only to be pure from all defilements of the flesh and spirit, but also to strive towards '. . .perfecting holiness in the fear of God'. Is this not aiming too high? How can we, who constantly fail even to avoid defiling ourselves, aspire to this holiness? We are incapable of it, except by putting on the holiness of Jesus Christ, through an act of faith and union with him; and we shall certainly fall and lose this holiness, yet, each time, we must get up and again put on Christ, who is perfect holiness. Our sanctification is a long process of total consecration to Jesus – often interrupted, but always to be taken up again and renewed.

The Miraculous Draught of Fishes

The gospel for last Sunday marked, as we pointed out, a change of perspective. Instead of the stern warnings given in the last chapters of St Matthew we found ourselves back, near the middle of the book, amidst the Saviour's miracles and works of mercy. On the 18th Sunday after Pentecost, this change is still evident. We leave the gospel of Matthew, and start on that of Luke, from which readings will be taken for several Sundays to come. St Luke is, pre-eminently, the evangelist of healing (whether of body or of soul) and of grace. Today, we read in Luke's gospel the account of the miraculous draught of fishes (Luke 5. 1-11).

Simon, James and John have spent the whole night fishing on the lake without catching anything. Jesus gets into one of their ships, and from it, teaches the multitude which has gathered on the shore. Then he tells Simon to launch the ship out into the lake and to let down the nets. Simon objects that the night's fishing has been fruitless, but that, all the same he will obey. 'At thy word I will let down the net'. A great multitude of fishes is taken; the nets break; the ships themselves, under the weight, begin to sink. Peter begs Jesus to go away from him, for he is a sinful man, and Jesus tells him not to be afraid, for, from now on he will be a fisher of men. Peter and the sons of Zebedee obey this call, and having brought the ships back to land 'they forsook all, and followed him'.

This episode draws our attention to several points. There is the calling of the apostles. On the one hand, Jesus chooses these three men in the very midst of their work and at the moment when this work is particularly fruitful: to leave everything at such a moment implies a decisive and courageous rupture: Jesus never calls a future apostle at a time when he might be idle and, consequently, ready to accept a new venture as a possible occupation. And, on the other hand, Jesus has involved himself closely with the work of the three fishermen; he has guided their actions, and before calling them, wanted to enter at depth into their daily and professional life; and it is thus that Jesus acts most often with the men he calls. This gospel also shows us just what wonders obedience founded in faith can accomplish: 'At thy word . . .', says Peter. He who hears a word spoken by Christ and who takes some sort of risk to obey this word, will obtain results quite out of proportion to anything he could have hoped for − for Peter had neither asked for the nets to break nor for the ships to sink under the weight of fishes. There may also, perhaps, be a symbolic element in this episode: near the shore, fishing brought no result; in the deep, it is superabundant; thus the effort of the apostles will fail in their natural element, amongst the Jews, but will succeed further out, amongst the Gentiles. Finally, the gospel for today allows us to witness a process of profound transformation take place in Peter's soul. This transformation shows itself in the way that Peter addresses Jesus. At the beginning of the episode, he calls him 'Master', at the end, he calls him 'Lord'. The first term implied that Peter recognised in Jesus a special authority, a superiority[28]. The second term implies that Jesus has a certain sovereignty, a power over Peter himself, and also expresses the humble dependence that Peter feels towards Jesus. When someone who has accepted Jesus as 'master' then accepts him as 'lord', great spiritual progress has been effected. Peter, falling to his knees before Jesus, says to him: 'Depart from me; for I am a sinful man'. The miracle produces in Peter a very vivid awareness not only of the power, but also of the holiness of Jesus: for Jesus could not perform such works were he not very close to God. Peter has had personal experience, in his everyday life, of Jesus's goodness and purity, and the miracle somehow consecrates this impression of holiness. Jesus must withdraw from him, Peter is not worthy of being so close to him. It is not that the holiness of Jesus constitutes a danger – it is the contrast between this holiness and Peter's sinfulness which is too intense; it is like an intolerable burn. Peter's case differs from that of Gideon and Manoah who expected to die because they had seen an angel of God face to face (Judges 6.22 and 13.22): his situation is more like that of Daniel: 'I opened my mouth, and spake, and said unto him that stood before me, O my lord, by the vision my sorrows are turned upon me, and I have retained no strength. For how can the servant of this my lord talk with this my lord?' (Dan. 10. 16-17). Contact with absolute holiness cannot but cause a sinner moral agony; for, as with the woman taken in adultery, the silent presence of this holiness is, in itself, a judgement and a condemnation. If very few Christians have a lively and agonising awareness of their sins, it is because Jesus is not truly present to them. We touch here on a point which is important, and that concerns 'evangelisation' and 'conversion': one does not progress from the consciousness of sin to the presence of Jesus, but, on the contrary, it is from the presence of Jesus that one becomes conscious of sin. It is the way we look at Jesus (or, rather, our awareness of the way that Jesus looks at us) which produces repentance in us.

The epistle for this Sunday (2 Cor. 9. 6-11) contains some general considerations on the giving of alms: give generously and joyfully, and God, in his turn, will show himself bountiful towards you; the more you sow, the more you will reap. This passage can be better understood if it is seen in its full context, that is, in the setting of the whole of chapter 9 of the second letter to the Corinthians, in which St Paul speaks of the collection which he is organising on behalf of poor Christians in Jerusalem. Paul (writing from somewhere in Macedonia) has already boasted to the Macedonians of the Corinthians' generosity: he has told them that the Corinthians have been preparing this collection for a year already. He would be sad if the Corinthians let him down now by their avarice − and even covered him with confusion before the brethren of Macedonia. Two sentences from the epistle today bring us a very practical message. Paul writes: 'Every man according as he purposeth in his heart, so let him give . . .'. Alms must not be given without due thought, or in an improvised way depending on the hazard of circumstances or feelings; to give alms is a form of 'ministry'(9. 1); it is necessary, therefore, to think in advance of what one can, of what one ought to give, in order to make the best use of the money that we manage for God: let us prepare our alms in our heart. Then, when the decision has been taken, let us give without regret, and even with joy; 'for God loveth a cheerful giver'. Here Paul cites from the Old Testament[29]; but, whether he is quoting from memory and the exact text escapes him, or whether he has deliberately wished to change the text, he writes that God 'loveth', where the original text has God 'praiseth'. We will not complain at this alteration, which, moreover, is an improvement. God loves those who give with joy, not only when it involves alms, but each time that we offer to God which has been costly for us, each time that, for him, we accept a painful trial, each time that we resist a temptation: let us therefore give 'not in a downcast and constrained manner', but with the spontaneity and smiling alacrity which are born of affection.

Loving one's Enemies

The 19th Sunday after Pentecost takes us back to the very first teachings of Jesus in Galilee, and, in particular, to the Sermon on the Mount in St Luke's abridged version of it[30]. The very short gospel read today (Luke 6: 31-36) deals with loving one's enemies. Do unto others as you would that men should do unto you. If you love only those who love you, if you do good only to those who do good to you, if you lend only to those who lend to you, you act no differently from sinners themselves, and nothing more. It is your enemies you must love, you must do good to them, and lend to them, for only in this way will you show yourselves to be children of God, who himself extends his goodness to those who are evil.

The idea of not doing to others what we would not wish them to do to us was familiar to Jesus's Jewish contemporaries, and was part of rabbinical teaching[31]. But Jesus goes beyond this negative precept and requires us to treat others as we would like to be treated by them. However, this new commandment, this positive commandment, risks being misunderstood by us. We might be led into doing good to others in the hope that they would respond by doing good to us, and that there would be some sort of reciprocity between our attitude and theirs. This is why Jesus immediately insists on the principle of disinterestedness. Our love must be freely given and go out to those from whom we expect nothing in return. The climax of today's gospel is the saying: 'Be ye therefore merciful as your Father also is merciful'. Here, we are very far from a trite moral injunction such as: love other people without hoping for reward. For this phrase confronts us with all that is absolute and − though one hesitates to say so − inaccessible in the Christian duty to love. To be merciful *as* the Father is merciful does not mean that our mercy could ever reach to the infinity of divine mercy; but, that in our own small measure, we should be inspired by the same feelings as the Father; it is from the ocean of the Father's mercy that the minute drops of water which are our acts of mercy must come, and it is into this ocean that they must finally flow. We are not able to perform the merciful acts of the Father, but we can share in his spirit of mercy. A first sign of this spirit is never to think of a man as utterly lost. 'Love ye your enemies ... hoping for nothing again', today's gospel tells us. This is not a humanitarian and superficial optimism: after all, a man is never entirely bad; he can change. And another thought can inspire our attitude: if God never ceases to do good to a sinner, if he is always ready to open his arms to him, who am I to dare to be stricter than God? Even in the greatest sinner, the most hardened criminal, the 'image of God' is still present. What is important is to know how the 'image of God' in me can meet the 'image of God' in my enemy – or in a wrong-doer. The epistle which is read this Sunday (2 Cor. 11. 31-12.9) is of a specially personal and autobiographical nature. St Paul, who knows that he is talked about and perhaps opposed by certain members of the church of Corinth, sets out the titles on which his authority is based. He has been persecuted: because of this he had to escape from Damascus by being let down over the wall in a basket[32]. Not only has he suffered for Christ, but – if he has to glorify himself (although, says Paul, he would prefer not to) – he has had visions and revelations from the Lord. He knew a man (and there is no doubt that here the apostle speaks of himself) who was carried up to paradise where he heard unspeakable words. Nevertheless Paul will not glorify himself in such things, but rather in his infirmities. Thus, so that the greatness of these revelations should not exalt him, he has been given a thorn in the flesh – 'the messenger of Satan to buffet me'. Three times he has asked God to take this trial away from him, but God has answered: 'My grace is sufficient for thee: for my strength is made perfect in weakness'.

In saying this, Paul lifts the veil which covers his deepest inner life. We will not try to lift this veil any higher than Paul himself does. The nature of the visions, how he was transported to paradise, what exactly paradise is, even the 'third heaven' he speaks of, or what the words he heard were: all these things will never be known in this world. Nor will we know more about what his 'thorn in the flesh' was: perhaps an illness[33], perhaps a persistent temptation. And, in any case, these details have very little spiritual importance for us. What does matter is the eternal teaching that they convey. Let us not take pride in the privileged manifestations of the divine which may be accorded to us (the feeling of the presence of God or of Christ, inner words, etc.) – and which are frequently accorded to sinners and those who are newly introduced to spiritual life. Even the highest ecstasies of the mystics are irrelevant to true spiritual progress, which lies in conforming our human will to the divine will. Let us thank God, rather, that his power is able to penetrate into our weakness; let us thank him for the occasions when, with the help of his grace, we have patiently and successfully borne the thorns which may have been put into our flesh. If sometimes these thorns seem too painful for us and God does not seem to hear our prayer when we ask him to deliver us from them, let us remember that the grace of God is sufficient for all things, and that these trials are perhaps

the condition necessary for our advance on the road to the
kingdom of the Father: this is especially true of certain temptations and certain humiliating illnesses. Lord Jesus, may thy
power be fulfilled in my weakness.

The Widow of Nain

On this 20th Sunday after Pentecost, the Church shows us Jesus's
compassion triumphing over death. Jesus is passing through the
city of Nain; there he meets a funeral procession for the only son
of a widow. Moved by the sight of the mother's grief, he tells her
not to weep; then, touching the bier, he commands the young
man to rise. The dead man sits up, and begins to speak. Jesus
restores him to his mother, and the people, seized by fear, give
glory to God (Luke 7. 11-17).

The theme of this reading, as we have said, is Jesus's compassion. It is quite accidental that Jesus meets this funeral procession. He is a stranger in Nain, a stranger to the family that has
been struck by bereavement. There is, it seems, no special reason
why Jesus should wish to manifest his power in Nain. Or rather,
there is a reason, an only reason: it is that Jesus, seeing the sorrow
of the mother 'had compassion on her'. The first word that Jesus
speaks is not the command given to the dead man, but his word of
consolation to the mother: 'Weep not'. And, when the young man
rises, the gospel does not tell us that Jesus spoke to him (although
no doubt he did speak to him), but we read that Jesus 'delivered
him to his mother'. (We notice that the gospel says 'delivered
him', and not 'restored him'. Jesus, in raising the young man has
acquired a special right of possession over him, and it is a gracious
gift that he now makes to the mother.)

The gospels tell of three resurrections carried out by Jesus: that
of the widow of Nain's son, that of Jairus's daughter, and that of
Lazarus. In each of the three cases, it seems that it is the compassion that Jesus feels for the sorrowing relatives which is the
foremost cause of the miracle. The three cases show us Jesus,
loving and compassionate. If this element of compassion is the
first to be emphasised, it cannot be ignored that the miracles of
resurrection have another cause, too: they demonstrate that the
Messiah has all power over life and death. Some details of today's
gospel throw light on this power: there is the authority with which
Jesus, by a sign, stops the procession; then the solemn and
imperative form of the words 'I say unto thee, Arise'; and the fact

that the evangelist, who, in the first verses of the same chapter
speaks simply of 'Jesus', now uses the word 'Lord', for this is an
encounter in which the Lord of life meets death and human grief.
We also notice that the three cases of resurrection reported in the
gospels cover all the successive physical aspects of death. Jesus
raises the daughter of Jairus when she is still lying on her bed, he
raises the son of the widow of Nain while he is being carried in a
bier, he raises Lazarus who is already buried and decomposing:
Jesus's lordship over death is absolute. This applies just as much
to different degrees of spiritual death as it does to those of
physical death, and the gospel accounts of resurrection indicate
symbolically how Jesus restores life to sinners. Also, not enough
attention is generally paid to the part played by women in the
cases of resurrection. Here, it is the mother's grief which moves
Jesus (and it could be said that the widow of Nain has a more
important place in today's gospel than her son). The wife of Jairus
joins her tears to those of her husband. Martha suggests to Jesus
that he could raise her brother. The same thing is found outside
the gospels. Peter raises Dorcas on the entreaties of the widows of
Lydda (Acts 9. 36-41). Elijah brings the son of the widow of
Zarephath back to life because of his mother's grief (1 Kgs. 17.
18-23). It is also because of the mother that Elisha raises the son
of the Shunammite woman (2 Kgs. 4. 18-37). The author of the
epistle to the Hebrews therefore has reason to say: 'Women
received their dead raised to life again' (Heb. 11. 35). Perhaps
these passages (like today's gospel) throw a veiled light on one
aspect of the spiritual ministry of women. The conversion of sinners is similar to raising from the dead, for the prayer of women,
and especially of mothers[34], and of women whose lives are entirely offered and consecrated to God, often has intercessory value of
remarkable efficacy, and, in this way, a hidden and contemplative life can be an apostolic life[35].

The epistle for today is taken from the letter of St Paul to the
Galatians (1. 11-19)[36]. The apostle declares to the Galatians that
the 'gospel' he preaches derives from no human tradition, but
that he has received it by direct revelation from Jesus Christ. His
calling to be an apostle is due, not to election by the twelve, but to
an immediate grace from God. After his conversion, he did not
confer 'with flesh and blood'; he did not go to Jerusalem to make
contact with the other apostles, but lived for three years in Arabia
and Damascus. Only after these three years did he go to
Jerusalem to see Peter; moreover, then he only stayed with him

for fifteen days and saw none of the other apostles except James. Paul's insistence on the immediate and personal nature of his apostolic calling was necessary. Certain Christian circles, especially those which were most under the influence of the 'apostolic' Church of Jerusalem, were contesting Paul's apostolate and setting up the authority of the twelve in opposition to it. This conflict had reached the Galatians and was raising divergent views with regard to practical questions, for example that of circumcision. Paul vehemently asserts his rights as an apostle. This vindication has lost nothing of its importance, for the same conflict is frequently renewed during the course of the centuries. The epistle read today reminds us how vigilant we must be never to allow the institution to extinguish the Spirit.

The Sower

The parable of the sower, which is the gospel read for the 21st Sunday after Pentecost (Luke 8. 5-14), is one of the best known of the gospel texts. But this parable may perhaps be better known in its negative aspects (the instances of the seed that does not grow) than in its positive aspect. Generally speaking, we know that the seed grows if it falls on 'good ground', but we may not see precisely and concretely enough the conditions set out in the gospel for its germination.

Jesus explains to his disciples — he did not say this to the crowd — that the sowing represents the word of God. The sower, that is to say God himself or his Son, casts the seed. Sometimes the seed falls by the side of the road, but the passers-by tread on it and the birds eat it; thus those who are at the roadside receive the word, but the devil comes along and takes it out of their heart. Sometimes the seed falls on a rock, and from lack of moisture dries up and withers; thus those who have received the word with joy, but have no roots, lose what they had received when temptation comes along. Sometimes the word falls among thorns, and the thorns choke it: thus worldly cares, riches and pleasures suffocate the word which had begun to take root. And sometimes the word falls 'on good ground', and it produces a hundred times for one: thus is it with those who have received it with a sincere heart and cling to it with patience.

It is not enough for the word to fall 'on good ground'. The reasons why the sowing did not bear fruit in the other instances show the conditions that are necessary for true spiritual life. We must not stand at the roadside within range of passers-by; a certain withdrawal from the world, a certain silence, a certain contemplation (which vary in each case, but are necessary in *all* cases without exception) will protect what has been divinely sown. The ground on which the seed falls must have moisture in it, it must be frequently and regularly watered; this means that we must have constant and regular recourse to prayer and to other sources of grace, without depending on moments of emotion or 'inspiration'. We must not lightly reject a fixed framework, such as timetables and rules of life: they may constitute a useless hindrance to the free flight of eagles, but most often they are a help to the children and cripples that we are. We must not allow the thorns, that is to say the attractions and distractions of the world, to suffocate the word: these are not only reprehensible passions, or earthly riches or ambitions; often entertainments which are not necessarily harmful in themselves (travels, parties, the theatre, novels, etc.) hinder an intimate relationship between God and us. The 'good ground' is a mixture of natural gifts and of grace (and grace can, moreover, make up for the deficiencies of nature). But, even where 'good ground' exists, no spiritual life is possible without *daily* and patient effort, without repressing certain things, without a certain regularity and stability, as much in material life as in mental life (the 'roots'), without meditation and examination of conscience (the terms may be modern, but the Desert Fathers practised these things). In short, the seed of the word cannot grow in us without a certain asceticism. Asceticism is not in fashion: people prefer talking about mysticism. But no true mystical life exists without a serious ascetic foundation: the word of God will not take possession of our soul if we have not cultivated the ground and cut back the thorns.

Our Lord says to the disciples that he speaks in parables so that for others 'seeing they might not see, and hearing they might not understand'. These words do not necessarily mean rejection and final condemnation of those to whom it is not given 'to know the mysteries of the kingdom of God'. On the contrary, our Lord exercises a merciful condescension towards those who are not yet ready to receive his teaching with sympathy. He therefore teaches in symbols, in a veiled way. Those spirits who are ready to hear — and desire to hear — will understand the mysterious meaning of the parables. The others will hear in a purely literal way, without understanding; and, by leaving them in the dark, Jesus spares them the sin which would result from their conscious rejection of the divine message. But they are not excluded from the declaration of the message. Because of its striking form, of its vivid images, the parable will make a powerful impression even on those who do not understand it, it will be engraved on their memories and perhaps a day will come when they, too, will be ready to understand and when, under the impression of the letter which they remember, the spirit of the message will be made clear to them.

The epistle which is read today (Gal. 2. 16-20) follows on, in a way, from the one which was read last Sunday. Paul, as we saw then, had to defend his apostolic authority against a certain 'judaising' faction. This faction taught that salvation was obtained through works and through the observance of the law, whereas Paul taught that salvation came through faith and grace. Today, we hear Paul state in the clearest terms: 'man is not justified by the works of the law, but by the faith of Jesus Christ . . for by the works of the law shall not flesh be justified'. He hastens on to counter the harmful consequences that some people might deduce from a doctrine of justification by faith: it in no way implies that we are free to sin. On the contrary: 'I through the law am dead to the law, that I might live unto God: I am crucified with Christ: nevertheless I live; yet not I, but Christ liveth in me'. In these last words — the substitution of a living person for a written law — we find condensed the whole essence of Paul's 'gospel'. The person of Jesus living in me at once both fulfils and abolishes the whole body of the law, in the same way that a river flowing into the sea is at the same time both totally conserved (from one point of view) and totally eliminated (from another point of view), or that a man, in leaping over a certain obstacle instead of going round it step by step, eliminates and fulfils the whole distance in one movement. If, from now on, I carry out some actions and avoid others, it is no longer (or it is no longer only) because the old, written, law prescribed or prohibited them, but because Jesus Christ lived and died in a particular way. The living person of Christ has become my law. The faith that Paul speaks of, faith that justifies, is faith in this living person of Jesus: 'I live by the faith of the Son of God, who loved me and gave himself for me'. That is why this faith must be a living faith, that is to say a faith which results in works; and from there on we begin to understand Paul's teaching on salvation and faith. We are justified by faith, not by works, but the faith which justifies is not a dead and sterile faith: it is always accompanied by works which are good, and these constitute the fruit and the necessary sign of true faith. Where faith and works are both present, it is faith (which does not mean a simple intellectual acceptance, but a total consecration to the person of Jesus Christ) which saves: works do not save. But, if the works were not there, the faith which saves, and is the mainspring of the works, would also be absent[37]. Faith — like the sowing of the word of God — must bear fruit: and so we rejoin the parable of the sower.

The Rich Man and Lazarus

On the 22nd Sunday after Pentecost, the Church brings us the parable of Lazarus and the rich man (Luke 16. 19-31). This parable is, in a way, unique in its mixture of realism and of symbolism. It is the only parable in which Jesus names one of the characters[38], so that some have questioned whether it is perhaps an account of a real event. The parable establishes a striking contrast between a certain sumptuously dressed, sumptuously fed, rich man and a beggar who lay at his door, covered in sores which the dogs licked, and who desired to be fed with the crumbs which fell from the rich man's table. Both Lazarus and the rich man die, but their fate is very different. The rich man, tormented in Hades[39], begs Abraham to send Lazarus — now in heaven — who, with his finger dipped in water, could refresh the tongue of the wretched man now suffering in the flames. Abraham answers gently that this is impossible: in his lifetime, the rich man had all the good things and Lazarus all the sufferings; now the situation is reversed and, moreover, there is an impassable gulf between the two men. But the rich man persists: let Lazarus at least be allowed to go and warn his father and five brothers against such a fate as his. That too is useless, answers Abraham, for, if they have not listened to Moses and the prophets, even the voice of one coming from the dead will not persuade them.

This parable is in quite a different tone from the accounts of healing and mercy which are so frequent in the gospel of Luke. It is a severe warning. Egoistic enjoyment in this world will be paid for in the next world by suffering; by contrast, the poor will know plenty. The general meaning of the parable is so clear, so simple, that it needs no explanation. Some of the details, however, are worth looking at more closely. 'A certain beggar . . . was laid at his gate'. The world of misery and of suffering is not an unreal, faraway, world. God himself lays this misery at my gate, at my own door; he will not ask me whether I had pity, in an abstract way, on all that far-distant misery which I can do nothing real to relieve, but he will ask what I did to help 'a certain beggar' — an actual person in need, who is very real and present — "named Lazarus", whom he had specially chosen so that I might show mercy on him. What this Lazarus may be in need of — money, care, moral help — is irrelevant. What does matter, is that my eyes notice him who lies at my door (that is to say: the one whom God has specially given me the chance of meeting), and that I should do something for him. We notice that the rich man does not seem to have been particularly hard-hearted or cruel: he sinned through negligence, he simply paid no attention to Lazarus. God will not necessarily reproach me for closing my heart to unfortunate people; he will reproach me for being too careless and too egoistic to think of opening it to them. The contrast between the ends of these two lives is striking: 'The beggar died, and was carried by the angels into Abraham's bosom: the rich man also died, and was buried'. The one was 'carried by the angels'; the other was 'buried' — Oh! doubtless with all the pomp that is due to a rich man, but also with all that the word 'buried' implies of finality and of contrast to being transported by angelic hands. 'Carried by the angels' or 'buried': these two destinies, taken in a spiritual sense, are not reserved for the dead; already in this life a person can be carried towards God by the angels or can let himself be buried and covered over by the dust which is the only thing he has attached himself to. The opposition between these two destinies is strongly emphasised: 'Between us and you there is a great gulf fixed . . . so that they that would pass . . . cannot'. Is this an affirmation of the irrevocable and eternal nature of the sufferings of the 'damned'? We will not touch on this theological question now, for we shall have occasion to speak about it again. But we do notice that the rich man, even in Hades (whatever the nature of this Hades is), does not seem at all repentant — there is no question of God refusing to show mercy to someone who now regrets his old attitude towards Lazarus and condemns his own egoism: there is simply no trace of such regret. What we read is only that the rich man desires, in the first instance, relief from the torments he endures and, then, that his own family should not suffer such a fate. Finally, we can look at the expression: ' . . . neither will they be persuaded'. God wishes us to be 'persuaded' to repentance: the repentance he desires is the fruit neither of acceding to outside authority, nor of the shock that a miraculous sign such as the raising of a man from the dead might cause (indeed, when Jesus did raise another Lazarus from the dead, the Pharisees did not repent). This repentance must be the fruit of an inner persuasion, of a long and inevitable working of the Spirit on our spirit − for, in spiritual life, everything must come from the Spirit.

The epistle for this Sunday (Gal. 6. 11-18) − which begins with the moving sentence 'Ye see how large a letter I have written unto you with mine own hand'[40] − sets out in a straightforward and concrete fashion the principal question on which St Paul and the 'judaisers' were opposed. This conflict has already been touched on in the epistles for the previous two Sundays: it is about circumcision. Paul's adversaries want to force the Galatians to be circumcised. But, what is circumcision except a mark 'in the flesh'? The mark of being Jesus's disciple is not circumcision, but the cross of the Saviour. 'But God forbid that I should glory, save in the cross of our Lord Jesus Christ'. The apostle once again affirms that the life of a Christian is something entirely spiritual and does not depend on certain physical facts such as circumcision: 'For in Jesus Christ neither circumcision availeth anything, nor uncircumcision, but a new creature'. Then, once again, Paul introduces a moving and very personal note, whose meaning remains mysterious to us: 'From henceforth let no man trouble me: for I bear in my body the marks of the Lord Jesus'[41].

The Gadarene Swine

The gospel for the 23rd Sunday after Pentecost (Luke 8. 26-39) describes the healing, in the country of the Gadarenes, of a man possessed by devils. Sometimes this man had to be bound in chains, sometimes he ran away into the desert and lived among the tombs (surely a life which is dominated by the spirit of evil is already a tomb). Seeing Jesus, the possessed man falls down before him and begs not to be tormented, for Jesus had commanded the demon to come out of the man (and the man now speaks as if he identified himself with the demon). The demon, knowing it is going to be expelled, asks Jesus at least not to send it 'into the deep' − that is to say to Hades where, following the Jewish concept, the demons undergo their torments − but to allow it to enter into a herd of swine which were feeding on the mountainside. Jesus consents to this. The demons (rather than the demon) abandon the man they had possessed, enter into the swine, and the whole herd throws itself into the Lake of Galilee. The man who had been possessed is now healed, and sits at Jesus's feet. But the Gadarene people, in fear, beg Jesus to depart from them: is not the presence of Christ always a threat to our private life and our own affairs? Does it not require changes that are too hard for us?

For many readers, this episode of the gospel is not without difficulty. There is, first of all, the question of diabolic possession. Surely all these cases of diabolic possession which we meet with in the gospels are really cases of nervous illness. Do demons exist? Can they possess a man? Science offers no answers to these questions. It is beyond doubt that Jesus believed in a personified spirit of evil, capable of taking possession of individuals. That frequently in the subsequent history of Christianity, diabolic influences have been attributed to what now reveals itself simply as mental pathology, we readily admit. But it would be difficult to cut out from the gospels the cases of possession except by substituting an entirely subjective and arbitrary interpretation. Sending the demons into a herd of swine also seems rather a crude myth to many readers. Doesn't it imply cruelty as well as an abuse of other people's property? Various explanations have been proposed. The episode could be designed to show the sovereign power of the creator over all creatures. Or, perhaps, that Jesus wished to punish the villagers who violated Jewish law by possessing pigs (but were the Gadarenes Jews?). Without claiming to penetrate what will remain a mystery, we incline to look upon the unhappy end of the herd of swine as a 'sign': Jesus suggests that abandonment to the power of evil always leads to death and destruction which, in its last throes, is characterised by a certain fury.

Let us look at some secondary aspects of this episode. Jesus asks the possessed man: 'What is thy name?' There is more in this than a simple question, for these words themselves already initiate therapy. Jesus wishes to bring the man, who had spoken as if he identified himself with the demon, back to awareness of his own identity. He wants to restore to him a sense of his own personality and independence. Whenever a sinner is so sunk in habit that it seems as if he is driven by the power of evil, Jesus, above all, wants him to dissociate himself from these powers and to remember his own name – the name given him by God: 'I have called thee by thy name; thou art mine . . .' (Is. 43. 1). In this name, by which God calls us, is found our true liberty and our true vocation. The possessed man answers Jesus: 'My name is Legion', and the gospel explains, 'because many devils were entered into him'. Perhaps the man had seen a Roman legion, that inexorable force, which is both a multitude and a unity. In the same way, if we give in to sin, we become 'legion'; our instincts, our mental images, all our psychic elements take on a chaotic independence; the will, weakened by each successive fall, is in no state to regain possession of them and to co-ordinate them; our whole personality becomes dissociated and disintegrates. God alone can gather these broken fragments and mend them. 'Unite my heart . . .' we ask of him in Psalm 86.11. Later, when the possessed man is healed, he begs Jesus to let him stay with him; but Jesus tells him to return to his house and to show what God has done for him. And the man returns 'and published throughout the whole city how great things Jesus had done unto him'. The majority of Christians are not called to follow Jesus in the literal sense of the word and to become itinerant disciples; but they all have an ordinary apostleship to practise in their immediate and daily surroundings, in the circles of their family and their work. This apostleship does not consist of 'preaching', it consists rather of bearing personal witness, of sharing with others an authentic experience, of 'declaring' and 'publishing' what Jesus has done for them. Neither eloquence nor great intelligence are needed for this ministry. It is open to the humblest — for all it calls for is a spirit of sincerity and devotion.

This Sunday, we read a passage from the epistle to the Ephesians (2. 4-10). God, so rich in mercy and in love, has brought us back to life when we were dead through sin. (This idea of spiritual death followed by salvation brings the epistle into line with the account of demonic possession in the gospel.) But St Paul stresses that it is not by our own efforts or through our own works that we are saved, it is through grace, through faith, through the gift of God. We are saved in Christ Jesus; with Him we are resurrected and raised to heavenly places; God's goodness to us is manifested in Christ Jesus, and in Christ Jesus we have been created to accomplish certain good works that God has prepared for us in advance. This final formula expresses marvellously the double fact that, on the one hand, it is only by Christ, through Christ, and freely, that we have been saved, and, on the other hand, that we meet in Christ himself the good works which are inseparable from his person and which God has destined us to accomplish.

The Nativity of the Virgin Mary

As we have already indicated, the liturgical year comprises, in addition to the cycle of Sundays and the cycles of the feasts that commemorate our Lord directly, a cycle of feasts of the saints. The first great feast of this cycle of saints to come after the start of the liturgical year, is the feast of the nativity of the Blessed Virgin Mary, celebrated on September 8th[42]. It is appropriate that, during the first days of the new religious year, we should be brought into the presence of the highest example of human holiness that the Church recognises and venerates — that of the mother of Jesus Christ. The texts that are read and the prayers that are sung on the occasion of this feast throw a lot of light for us on the kind of worship that the Church accords to Mary.

During vespers, celebrated on the eve of September 8th, several lessons from the Old Testament are read. First of all there is the account of the night which Jacob spent at Luz (Gen. 28. 10-17). While Jacob slept, with his head pillowed on stones, he had a dream: he saw a ladder reaching up from earth to heaven, and the angels ascending and descending along this ladder; and God himself appeared and promised that he would bless and keep Jacob's seed. Jacob, when he awoke, blessed the stone on which he had slept with oil, and called the place Beth-el, that is to say 'house of God'. Mary, whose motherhood was the human condition necessary for the Incarnation, is, in herself, a ladder between heaven and earth. As the adoptive mother of the adopted brothers and sisters of her Son, she says to us what God said to Jacob: 'I am with thee, and will keep thee in all places whither thou goest . . .'. She, who carried her God in her womb, is truly that place, Beth-el, of which Jacob could say: 'This is none other but the house of God, and this is the gate of heaven'. The second lesson (Ezek. 43. 27-44. 4) refers to the future temple which is shown to the prophet Ezekiel: a phrase from this passage can well be applied to the virginity and to the motherhood of Mary: 'This gate shall be shut, it shall not be opened, and no man shall enter in by it; because the Lord, the God of Israel, hath entered in by it, therefore it shall be shut'[43]. The third lesson (Prov. 9. 1-11) presents us with a personified divine Wisdom: 'Wisdom hath builded her house, she hath hewn out her seven pillars . . . . She hath sent forth her maidens: she crieth upon the highest places of the city'. The Byzantine and the Roman Church have both established a link between holy Wisdom and Mary[44]. She is the house built by Wisdom: she is, in the highest degree, one of the virgins sent forth by Wisdom to men; she is, after Christ himself, the highest manifestation of Wisdom in this world.

The gospel read at matins for September 8th (Luke 1. 39-49, 56) describes Mary's visit to Elisabeth. Two phrases from this gospel express the attitude of the Church towards Mary very well, and indicate why she has, in some way, been set apart from and above all other saints. First, there are her own words: 'From henceforth all generations shall call me blessed. For he that is mighty hath done unto me great things'[45]. Then there are the words spoken by Elisabeth to Mary: 'Blessed art thou among women, and blessed is the fruit of thy womb'. Anyone who wished to take us to task for recognising and honouring the fact that Mary should be 'blessed amongst women' would gainsay Scripture itself — so we shall continue, like 'all generations', to call Mary 'blessed'. Moreover, we shall never separate her from her Son, and shall never say 'blessed art thou' to her without adding, or at least thinking: 'and blessed is the fruit of thy womb'. And, if sometimes it is given to us to feel the gracious approach of Mary, it will be of Mary bearing Jesus in her womb, Mary in as much as she is mother of Jesus, and, with Elisabeth, we shall say to her: 'Whence is this to me, that the *mother of my Lord* should come to me?'

At the liturgy for the same day, we read, joined together (Luke 10. 38-42 and 11. 27-28), two passages of the gospel which the Church repeats at all the feasts for Mary, and to which this repetition itself gives the weight of a particularly important declaration. Jesus praises Mary of Bethany, who is seated at his feet, and listens to his words, for having chosen 'that good part, which shall not be taken away from her', for 'one thing is needful'. It is not that the Lord blamed Martha, who was so preoccupied with serving him, but that Martha was 'troubled about many things'. The Church applies this approval, given to Mary of Bethany by Jesus, to the contemplative life, in as much as it is distinct from (we do not say: opposed to) the active life. The Church also applies this approval to Mary, the mother of the Lord, who is considered the model of all contemplative life, for we read elsewhere in the gospel according to Luke: 'Mary kept all these things, and pondered them in her heart . . . his mother kept all these sayings in her heart' (Luke 2. 19, 51). Let us not forget, too, that the Virgin Mary had previously consecrated herself, like

Martha, and to a much greater extent than Martha, to the practical service of Jesus, for she had nourished and brought up the Saviour. In the second part of the gospel for this day, we read that a woman lifted up her voice and said to Jesus: 'Blessed is the womb that bare thee and the paps which thou hast sucked', to which he answered: 'Yea rather, blessed are they that hear the word of God, and keep it'. These words must not be thought of as dismissal of the praise that the woman accords to Mary, or as under-estimating her holiness: rather, they bring things into exact focus, and show where the true merit of Mary lies. That Mary became the mother of Christ was a free gift, it was a privilege that she accepted, but that her personal will had no part in originating. On the other hand, it was through her own effort that she heard and kept the word of God. It is in this that Mary's true greatness lies. Certainly, Mary is blessed, but not principally because she bore and nourished Jesus; above all she is blessed because, to a unique degree, she was obedient and faithful. Mary is the mother of the Lord; she is the protector of men: but, first and foremost, she is the one who listened to, and kept, the Word. In this lies the 'gospel' foundation of our devotion to Mary. A short verse, sung after the epistle expresses this well: 'Hearken, O daughter, and consider, and incline thine ear' (Ps. 45. 10).

The epistle for this day (Phil. 2. 4-11) does not mention Mary. In it Paul speaks of the Incarnation: Jesus, who 'being in the form of God . . . made himself of no reputation, and took upon him the form of a servant, and was made in the likeness of men'. But it is clear that this text has the very closest bearing on Mary, and has been chosen for this day because of her. For it is through Mary that the descent of Christ in our flesh became possible. We therefore come back to the woman's exclamation: 'Blessed is the womb that bare thee . . . .'. And consequently the gospel that we have read, 'Blessed are they that hear the word . . .', answers and complements the epistle.

One of the troparia for this day establishes a link between the conception of the Christ-light, so dear to Byzantine devotion, and the blessed Virgin Mary: 'Thy birth, O virgin mother of God, announced the joy of the whole world, for from out of thee has come, and shines, the Sun of Justice, Christ our God'.

The feast of the nativity of Mary is, in a way, carried over into the next day, September 9th, by the feast of St Joachim and St Anna, whom an uncertain tradition has made out to be the parents of the Virgin[46].

The Exaltation of the Cross

At the threshold of the liturgical year, we encountered the Blessed Virgin Mary, and there we also encounter the cross of the Saviour. These two themes could not be omitted from our prayer and our meditation with impoverishing them. The Church celebrates the feast of the Exaltation of the Cross (September 14th), a few days after the nativity of Mary. Let us look beyond the wood of the cross, and the historical circumstances which led to the worship of the cross[47], and concentrate on all that is spiritual and eternal in the very idea of the cross of Jesus.

The Church starts to prepare us for the feast of the Cross a week in advance. On the Sunday preceding it, in addition to the epistle and the gospel that are proper to the Sunday, another epistle and gospel are read that have a special connection with the cross. In the epistle (Gal. 6. 11-18), St Paul says that a Christian does not know how to glorify himself 'save in the cross of our Lord Jesus Christ, by whom the world is crucified unto me, and I unto the world'. In the gospel (John 3. 13-17), we read: 'As Moses lifted up the serpent in the wilderness[48], even so must the Son of man be lifted up: That whosoever believeth in him should not perish, but have everlasting life. For God so loved the world, that he gave his only begotten Son, that whosoever believeth in him should not perish, but have everlasting life'.

As the feast of the Cross draws near, it is not useless to remember that the cross which it concerns is the cross on which Jesus Christ was crucified for our salvation. The decision to 'bear our cross' – which is so deeply evangelical, and without which this feast of the Cross would somehow remain an abstract idea – is an essential aspect, though a secondary one, of the mystery of the cross. The principal aspect, is that we are saved by the Passion of Jesus. The attention of eastern Christians, which is given so easily and enthusiastically to the incarnation of Christ, must not overlook the mystery of expiation. Christ is God made man; he is the conqueror, and he who rose from the dead. But he is also the crucified Redeemer. The feasts of the Cross give us an opportunity to meditate on what the Blood of Christ means in our spiritual life, on the death of the Saviour as a reparation for our sins, and on the relationship between the cross and love. They are precious as an opportunity for us to deepen our understanding of that article in the Nicene creed when we confess that Jesus died 'for us men and for our salvation'.

During the vespers that are celebrated on the evening of September 13th, three readings from the Old Testament show us that the shadow of the cross is already cast over the history of Israel. The first of these readings comes from the book of Exodus (15. 22-16. 1). When the Israelites were in the wilderness of Shur, they found there bitter waters which they could not drink; they murmured against Moses. He then 'cried unto the Lord; and the Lord showed him a tree, which when he had cast into the waters, the waters were made sweet'. Thus the tree of the cross, plunged into our bitterness, can make it sweet. The second reading is drawn from Proverbs (3. 11-18). It begins thus: 'My son, despise not the chastening of the Lord . . . . For whom the Lord loveth he correcteth; even as a father the son in whom he delighteth'. These words throw light vividly on Jesus as he bears the punishment for the sins of the world, and on the relationship between the Father's love for the Son and for the Son's cross: they also indicate to us the spirit in which we must accept − and look for − the punishment of our own sins. Then, having praised wisdom, the author of Proverbs[49] concludes: 'She is a tree of life to them that lay hold upon her'. The cross, which seems to the world 'folly', is wisdom herself: it is identified with the tree of life of the earthly paradise[50]. The third reading (Isa. 60. 11-16) is about the glory that is coming to Zion; the passage seems to have been chosen because of a verse in which are mentioned various trees which will contribute to the beauty of the Temple: 'The glory of Lebanon shall come unto thee, the fir tree, the pine tree, and the box together, to beautify the place of my sanctuary; and I will make the place of my feet glorious'. But the true, invisible, wood of the sanctuary is the wood of the Cross.

At matins for September 14th, the gospel which is read (John 12. 23-36) and which is the start of the speech that follows the Last Supper, does not seem to bear directly on the Cross. Yet Jesus's saying: 'The hour is come, that the Son of man should be glorified . . .' has a mysterious link with the Lord's Passion and with today's feast. So do Jesus's words to Peter: 'Whither I go, thou canst not follow me now; but thou shalt follow me afterwards'. Let each one of us find out for ourselves what this phrase contains for us.

After the great doxology for matins, a special rite is performed for this day. The cross which is normally kept on the altar is placed on a salver and surrounded by flowers; the priest, holding this over his head, comes out of the sanctuary preceded by the servers with incense and lights. But today the cross leaves the sanctuary by one of the side doors of the iconostasion, the north door, and not, as is usual, through the central or 'royal' door. This signifies that the way of the cross is a way of abasement and of humility. The procession, having left the iconostasion, stops in front of the 'royal door' and faces the east. The priest proclaims (as is usual during the liturgy, when the book of the gospels is solemnly carried to the altar): 'Wisdom! Stand and attend!'. For the cross, this seeming folly, is the symbol of divine wisdom. Then, the procession turns to the west. The cross is put down on a stand placed in the middle of the church and decorated with flowers. The congregation come up to it, they prostrate themselves, and then kiss the cross. In cathedrals and monasteries, another rite is added to this one. The choir begins to sing the invocation 'Lord, have mercy!' This is repeated a hundred times. The priest, holding the cross, blesses the four cardinal points of the compass, then he bows down very slowly and, as he bows, the choir continues the invocations on a descending tone. When the choir reaches the fiftieth invocation, the priest is bowed very low, very close to the ground, always holding the cross (Oh, that this cross might descend thus towards all those who have fallen the lowest, towards all extremes of misery; and that thus it might come down to me, and into me – gradually being plunged into my heart). Then the priest rises as slowly and, while the choir sings the remaining invocations on a tone which now rises more and more, he lifts the cross, he 'exalts' it ('I, if I be lifted up from the earth, will draw all men unto me . . .'). The priest blesses the people again with the cross, then replaces it on the stand, where it stays until the liturgy.

In this day's gospel for the liturgy (John 19. 6-11, 13-20, 25-28, 30-35), we read a somewhat abridged account of the Passion. In the epistle (1 Cor. 1. 18-24), Paul proclaims the great Christian paradox that we have heard so often that it may, perhaps, no longer give us the vital shock that it should: 'Hath not God made foolish the wisdom of this world? . . . . We preach Christ crucified, unto the Jews a stumblingblock, and unto the Greeks foolishness . . . Christ the power of God, and the wisdom of God . . . . Because the foolishness of God is wiser than men; and the weakness of God is stronger than men'.

Three of the chants for this day call specially for our attention. While the congregation kiss the cross, the choir sings: 'We fall down before Thy Cross, O Master, and we praise Thy holy

Resurrection'. The Church is concerned never to dissociate the cross from the tomb, the crucifixion from the resurrection, death from life. The grief of Holy Friday ends in the joy of Easter. Another chant connects the elevation of Christ on the cross and the shining forth of divine light: 'The light of Thy countenance, O Lord, spreads out over us'. This attitude to the Passion is profoundly Greek and Byzantine. Finally, another chant associates Mary with the cross. For Mary is the 'mysterious paradise' in whom was brought about the growth of Christ, and Christ himself 'planted on earth the life-giving tree of the cross'.

On the Sunday which follows September 14th, the epistle and the gospel consist − as they did for the Sunday preceding it − of passages which have a bearing on the cross. The epistle (Gal. 2. 16-20) has been chosen because of Paul's saying: 'I am crucified with Christ: nevertheless I live . . . .'. In the gospel (Mark 8. 34-9.1), we hear the warning given by our Lord: 'Whosoever will come after me, let him deny himself, and take up his cross, and follow me. For whosoever will save his life shall lose it; but whosoever shall lose his life for my sake and the gospel's, the same shall save it'. In this is found the practical outcome of the feast. It is not to some chosen disciples only that Jesus addresses these words, it is to all of us: 'When he had called the *people* unto him with his disciples also, he said unto them . . . .' Our Lord establishes an instructive gradation, if we know how to meditate on it, between these three acts − of self-renunciation, taking up one's cross, and following Christ. Each one of us must take up his own cross; not the cross of his choice, but the cross − that is to say the portion of suffering and trial − that God has assigned to him especially, and which is one of the aspects of the cross of Jesus himself. In the feast of the Exaltation of the Cross, let us exalt and enthrone in our heart the cross of Jesus, let us apply to the Passion of our Lord, and even to our poor efforts (which are our share in the Passion) this saying, through which the mystery of the cross receives its highest and most complete interpretation: 'Greater love hath no man than this, that a man lay down his life . . . . .'.

St Michael and all the Holy Angels

At the start of the liturgical year, the Church has brought us into the presence of the Cross, that is to say, of the mystery of our salvation through the Passion of our Lord Jesus Christ. It has brought us into the presence of the most Blessed Virgin Mary, who is the height of all human holiness. It is now going to bring us into the presence of a third aspect of spiritual life: the ministry of the angels. It is this aspect that she now invites us to contemplate on the feast of St Michael and all the holy angels (November 8th). The angels are pure spirits, but created spirits who are destined to adore and reflect the infinite divine beauty, and secondarily, who are 'sent forth to minister for them who shall be heirs of salvation' (Heb. 1.14). The Old Testament shows us how frequently they intervened with the patriarchs and prophets; the Hebrews considered angels as the visible manifestation of God, as the bearers of his image and of his power[51]. The gospels show them to us announcing the birth of Jesus, ministering to him in the desert and in his agony, and as witnesses of his resurrection. They are intimately involved in the life of the apostles and in the beginnings of the Church. The belief that a guardian angel is appointed as a guide and protector to each individual soul has never been defined as an article of faith; but this concept, already outlined in the Bible and developed by the Fathers, is certainly in keeping with the spirit of the Church and can be of great assistance in our spiritual life. The Holy Scriptures name only three angels: Gabriel, Raphael, and Michael, whose feast we celebrate today and round whom the Church groups the whole 'body' of angels.

The Hebrew name *Michael* means: 'Who is like unto God'. Michael is mentioned several times in the prophet Daniel, in the epistle of St Jude, where he is called 'archangel'[52], and in Revelation. The veneration of St Michael began perhaps in Phrygia and was particularly developed in Constantinople[53]. Christian tradition above all thinks of Michael as the one who is successful in combating Satan[54].

The epistle to the Hebrews, which we read today (2. 2-10), puts those to whom it is addressed on guard against an exaggerated veneration of angels. There was some danger of this in certain Judaeo-Christian circles. 'For unto the angels hath he (God) not put in subjection the world to come', but to Jesus Christ. The epistle indicates how close man is to the angels: 'Thou madest him a little lower than the angels'. Then too, the epistle tells us that 'the word spoken by angels was stedfast'. This divine word continues to be addressed to us by the angels — but is our personal relationship with them sufficiently intimate to hear their message? The gospel for this day (Luke 10. 16-21) describes the joy of the seventy sent out by our Lord who, on their return said to him: 'Even the devils are subject unto us through thy name'.

And Jesus tells them that he himself had seen 'Satan as lightning fall from heaven'. The disciples had had an experience of the power that the angels exercise continuously, and to an incomparably greater degree. Perhaps, too, this gospel was chosen because of Jesus's saying to them: 'Rather rejoice, because your names are written in heaven'. These words mean that after their earthly life, Jesus's disciples will enter into heaven, which is the dwelling place of the angels, and into the joy of heaven, which is the joy of the angels; and that then human life will become nearer to angelic life. Lastly, this portion of the gospel begins with the words: 'He that heareth you heareth me . . .'. It is not only through the preaching of the disciples and through the apostolic tradition, but also through the secret message of the angels in our soul that we shall be able to hear the word of the Saviour. If we know how to listen to the angels, it is to Jesus himself that we listen.

Today we sing an antiphon of biblical origin, which proclaims that God has made his angels winds and his messengers a flaming fire. Wind and fire: thus the angels are closely connected both with Pentecost and the Holy Spirit.

Notes for Chapter I

1   The celebration of saints' feasts has its origin in the veneration of martyrs. From the first half of the second century, the death of certain martyrs (what was called their 'day of birth') was commemorated, especially in the places where they had suffered and in those where their relics were preserved. The Church drew up official lists of these anniversaries (the 'martyrologies'). Later on, 'confessors', that is to say those who, without having been killed, had suffered imprisonment or torture for their faith, were also commemorated; later on still, 'confessors' who had simply confessed Christ by their heroic virtue or their learning, were admitted to the calendar. These lists, gradually enlarged, resulted in the present saints' calendar. Differing from the movable cycle of Sundays which depends on the annually varying date of Easter, the cycle of the saints is fixed: each feast day for a saint corresponds to a particular day of the year.

2   The modern Jewish calendar also starts in September, but on a variable date. The day of the start of the Jewish year in biblical times remains a controversial question. The history of the Christian calendar is too complex and uncertain for us to try to summarise it here. It will suffice to mention first that, for a long time, each Church (Rome, Constantinople, Antioch, the Goths, etc.) had its own calendar and its own method of calculating time: because the Julian calendar (still followed by some Orthodox Churches) is thirteen days behind the Gregorian calendar (followed by the Roman Church, the Protestant Churches, and some Orthodox Churches), so that September 1st by the Russian ecclesiastical calendar corresponds to September 14th by the Roman ecclesiastical calendar. Then the liturgical year for the Roman Church begins with the first Sunday of (Roman) Advent, which itself depends on the date of Christmas.

3   Here we use the word 'liturgy' not in the western sense of the whole body of ecclesiastical rites (the Roman, the Gallican, the Mozarabic liturgy, etc.), but in the Byzantine sense of the celebration of the eucharist.

4   The book which bears the name of Isaiah is a compilation of the writings of several authors, which results in the critics speaking of a 'second' and a 'third' Isaiah. Only the first thirty-nine chapters of the book seem to have any direct connection with the prophet Isaiah of Jerusalem.

5   The Book of Wisdom is one of those 'deutero-canonical' writings which was not part of the Hebrew Bible of the Jews of Palestine, but was included in the Bible translated into Greek by the Jews of Alexandria. It is unanimously recognised that Solomon was not the author of the book, which seems to have been composed in Egyptian Jewish circles in the third or second century before the Christian era.

6   Simeon Stylites the elder – called this to distinguish him from Simeon Stylites the younger (sixth century) – was born around 388 in Syria and died in 459. He spent thirty-six years on a pillar topped by a narrow platform. Visitors reached this by means of a ladder. There was no covered cabin on the platform. One might be tempted to relegate such an extraordinary life to the realm of legend were there not apparently sound historical documents, relating to Simeon. Moreover, Simeon was in touch with emperors, was concerned with the Council of Chalcedon, and carried on an extended correspondence. This type of asceticism has had numerous followers. Stylites could still be found in the Russia of the fifteenth century.

7   The life of Father Charles de Foucauld in the Sahara was, in the twentieth century, the life of a desert father. Quite a number of hermits still exist in the eastern Churches, on Athos and elsewhere. The Roman Church has organised the life of a solitary, or semi-solitary, in a precise manner (the Carthusians, Cistercians, Camaldolese, etc.).

8   The Sundays between Pentecost and Lent are called 'Sundays after Pentecost'. The date of Pentecost varies, depending, of course, on the date of Easter. Each year, therefore, there will be a greater or lesser number of Sundays after Pentecost, and the correspondence between these Sundays and the fixed dates of the calendar will also vary. The list of Sundays given in this chapter is therefore subject to adaptation. It can be corrected in the light of the church calendar for the current year and by collating it with the lists of Sundays given in Chapters II and VII.

9   The same parable, with some variations, is found in Mark 12. 1-12.

10   The expression *maran atha* belongs to the Aramaic language, spoken by Jesus and His disciples, which had replaced Hebrew as the popular language in Palestine. This expression, which should really be written *marana athah*, can mean either: 'Our Lord comes', or: 'Our Lord is coming', or: 'Our Lord is come', or: 'Come, our Lord!'.

11   It is only on the occasion of certain feasts that particular care has been taken to choose, for the same day, an epistle and a gospel whose meaning converges or coincides. As a general rule, the reading of a specific epistle and a specific gospel is continued Sunday after Sunday, or day after day, without a connecting link being established between the two readings.

12   Stephanus is mentioned elsewhere (1 Cor. 1. 16) as one of the few Christians baptised by Paul himself. We have no information about Fortunatus, nor about Achaicus. Aquila and Priscilla seem to have been a Jewish couple who were closely linked with Paul; banished from Italy under the persecution of

Claudius, they gave hospitality to Paul at Corinth and, like him, plied the trade of tentmakers (Acts 18. 2-4). They also stayed at Ephesus; Paul mentions their presence in this town in his second letter to Timothy (4. 19). Finally they found themselves in Rome with Paul, for whose life, in his own words, 'they laid down their necks' (Rom. 16. 3-4).

13   Luke (14. 15-24) has an analogous parable, but the details differ. The parable in Matthew resembles closely a rabbinic parable attributed by the Talmud to Jochanan ben Zaccai, whose activity as a scribe began around the year 30 of our era. Perhaps both these parables share a common source of popular inspiration.

14   'Blessed are they which are called unto the marriage supper of the Lamb' (Rev. 19. 9).

15   Between the first epistle to the Corinthians (year 54 or 55) and this epistle (year 55 or 56), there is a visit by Paul to Corinth – where he meets lively opposition from the pro-Jewish faction – and a letter of reproach to the Corinthians (which has not been preserved) to be fitted in. The present epistle shows that there is an improvement in the situation, although the clouds have not completely cleared.

16   Originally, the scribes were the actual transcribers of the scrolls of the law. At the time of Jesus, they were the professional students and doctors of the law. They generally belonged to the intransigent party of the Pharisees and therefore were opposed to the priests and to the Saduccees, who were influenced by Hellenism.

17   The first part of the commandment, relating to the love of God, is a quotation from Deuteronomy (6.5). This text constitutes one of the most frequent formulae of the Jewish religion nowadays. The second part of the commandment, relating to the love of one's neighbour, is a quotation from Leviticus (19. 18). The law of love was not, therefore, absent from Judaism. The great commandment is also found in Mark (12. 28-31) and in Luke (10. 27).

18   *Nephesh*. The Hebrews thought of the soul as a principle of life which was inherent in the blood. From this comes the prohibition against mixing blood with food.

19   We are perhaps surprised that Jesus did not command us to love our neighbour *more* than ourselves. Tolstoy, who was moved by this idea, thought that the gospel texts must have suffered an alteration here. But the gospel wants to make two points clear: first that God alone must be loved by us with all our heart, more than any creature, and next that all souls have an equal value in his eyes. That is why we do not have the right to love another soul more than our own, that is to say, to lose our soul or to expose it to loss for the love of a creature, even if (an impossible supposition) by sinning ourselves we could assure the salvation of another soul. But, on the physical plane, it is entirely in keeping with the spirit and the letter of the gospel for us to risk and sacrifice our earthly life for others.

20   In its actual content, Psalm 110 is much later than David. But it is possible that it incorporates fragments from an earlier date that are of Davidic origin. Jesus here is speaking the language of his contemporaries.

21   The same parable is found in Luke (19. 11-28).

22   This episode is also found in Mark (7. 24-30).

23   Here Paul quotes from Leviticus (26. 12).

24   In ch. 8 of the prophet Ezekiel a striking description is found of God's 'jealousy' of all idolatory, and of his hatred of the pagan 'abominations' which

had been imported into the religion of Israel.

25   We should remember the orders given to Abraham, to Lot, to the neighbours of Dathan and of Abiram, etc. Each time, it is a summons to depart brought about by the necessity of separating oneself from iniquity. In Revelation (18. 4), a voice cries from heaven, speaking of Babylon: 'Come out of her, my people, that ye be not partakers of her sins, and that ye receive not of her plagues'.

26   Isa. 52. 11, Exod. 4. 22, 2 Sam. 7. 14.

27   The text from the second Isaiah: 'Bring my sons from far, and my daughters from the ends of the earth' (43. 6) had already introduced a new note into Israel. Before this, only the 'sons' were spoken of. But, even in the Judaism of Jesus's time, women were reduced to a state of effacement and abasement.

28   There is in the Hebrew word *rabbi* something more than in the Greek *didaskalos*. A *didaskalos* is simply a master who teaches, but the literal meaning of *rabbi* is: 'my great'.

29   Paul transforms a text which has already been modified. For the words 'God loveth a cheerful giver' are found in the Septuagint (the Greek version of the Hebrew Bible), as an addition to the Hebrew text of verse 8, chapter 22 of Proverbs. One of the deutero-canonical books, Ecclesiasticus, says: 'In all thy gifts shew a cheerful countenance, and dedicate thy tithes with gladness' (35. 9).

30   The expanded text of the Sermon on the Mount is found in Matt. chs. 5, 6 and 7.

31   Hillel, the grandfather of the Pharisee, Gamaliel, who is spoken of in the Acts of the Apostles, taught that the law 'Do unto others as you wish others to do unto you', contains the whole of the law, and that the rest is simply commentary.

32   Paul's words about this are confirmed by the Book of Acts 9. 24-25. The place where this episode is supposed to have taken place is still pointed out in Damascus.

33   Some commentators on this epistle have suggested epilepsy, others a severe ophthalmia, others malaria. There is insufficient evidence to establish that Paul suffered from any one of these illnesses.

34   St Monica is a special representative of this kind of prayer. St Ambrose, bishop of Milan, speaking to Monica of her son, Augustine, who was not yet con-verted, said that 'the son of so many tears could not be lost'.

35   In the west, this idea held a central place in the prayer of St Teresa of Avila, and in that of St Theresa of Lisieux.

36   We do not know exactly who these Galatians were to whom Paul writes. The word calls to mind the word 'Gaul'. Certain Gallic tribes, after invading Italy, had migrated to the areas which are now Hungary, Yugoslavia and Bulgaria. It is more probable that the people for whom Paul's letter was destined were settled in Asia Minor.

37   There is no real contradiction between the Lutheran doctrine of justifi-cation by faith and the patristic and Catholic doctrine defined by the Council of Trent, but rather a misunderstanding which an attentive reading of the texts dispels. Luther's *pecca fortiter, sed fortius crede* was one of those verbal excesses in which the reformers frequently indulged. But Luther, as much as the Fathers and St Thomas, admitted that the faith which justifies is recognised through works: it not only 'covers', it transforms.

38   This is why Tertullian thought − without sufficient justification − that the story of Lazarus was not a parable, but the account of a real event. Attempts have been made − again with insufficient reason − to identify the Lazarus of

the parable with the Lazarus who was raised from the dead at Bethany; from there to draw from the parable the account of the resurrection of Lazarus is but a step, and there are those who have taken this step in the most arbitrary manner.

39   Hades was not necessarily a synonym for hell (in the present sense of the word). Hades was thought of as a place where all the dead awaited the last judgement; it was both a paradise and a gehenna. In the present case it is clearly the latter which is intended.

40   We know, from other places in the epistles, that Paul usually made use of an *amanuensis* or secretary to write his letters. Here, he has written the last paragraph of the epistle with his own hand. Not only does it thus give the epistle a special ring of authenticity, but it emphasises certain important ideas.

41   This may refer perhaps to physical traces of an illness, perhaps to marks left by some torture or ill-treatment. Or perhaps Paul is speaking in a figurative way. The Greek word he uses, *stigmata*, is the same which has become famous because of certain mystics − such as St Francis of Assisi − who bore in their flesh the imprint of the wounds of the Passion. Should we perhaps look in this direction for the explanation of Paul's words? In any case, Paul, who thought of himself as the servant of Jesus, was no doubt thinking of slaves who were marked (sometimes with red-hot irons).

42   We know absolutely nothing of the historical date of Mary's birth. The feast on September 8th seems to have originated in the sixth century in Syria or Palestine. Rome adopted it in the seventh century. It had already been introduced in Constantinople; there is a hymn by Romanos the Melodist about the Nativity, and several sermons by St Andrew of Crete. The Coptic Church of Egypt and the Church of Ethiopia celebrate the Nativity of Mary on May 1st.

43   We know that the Orthodox Church, like the Roman Church, rejects the hypothesis according to which Mary, after the birth of Jesus, had several children by Joseph. This theory, which was upheld in the fourth century by Helvidius, was contested by St Ambrose, St Jerome and St Augustine.

44   This link has nothing to do with the 'sophiological' doctrines which certain Russian philosophers and theologians, such as Soloviev, Bulgakov, etc., have upheld.

45   We do not overlook the fact that certain modern critics attribute the *Magnificat* to Elisabeth and not to Mary. This attribution does not seem to us in any way proven. Whether the words of the *Magnificat* were in fact literally spoken by Mary is another question: it is enough that this hymn should give faithful expression to Mary's feelings.

46   The canonical gospels tell us nothing about Mary's father and mother. The legends about Joachim and Anna have their origin in the apocryphal gospels, notably in the gospel attributed to James, which the Church has rejected and which are rightly held suspect. It is not impossible, however, that certain authentic details, which are not mentioned in the canonical gospels, found a place in the apocryphal gospels. The legend according to which Anna, at an advanced age, gave birth to Mary, seem to have been influenced by the biblical account of Anna, the mother of Samuel. Nothing indicates that the mother of Mary can be identified with the Anna who prophesised in the Temple about Jesus (Luke 2. 36-38). But we do know that from the fourth century, the memory of Mary's parents, under the names of Joachim and Anna, was honoured in Jerusalem. Whatever may be the historicity of these names and biographical details, the honour paid to the father and mother of the most holy Virgin is

surely legitimate.

47   We have no historical information about what, after the Passion, became of the cross to which Jesus was nailed. The accounts which tell of the discovery or 'invention' of the cross by Helena, the mother of Constantine, are so imprecise and contradictory that they belong to the realm of legend. What is historically certain is that in 335 the Basilica of the Holy Sepulchre, built in Jerusalem by order of Constantine, was completed. It was dedicated on September 14th. In 347 a relic, considered to be wood from the cross, was venerated there. The feast of the Exaltation of the Cross was celebrated in Constantinople from 614, on September 14th. When the Persians conquered Jerusalem, they carried away the 'wood of the cross', but the imperial army recovered it in 628. The relic only returned to Jerusalem for a short time. Heraclius took it finally to Constantinople in 633. We do not know exactly what became of it; moreover it was divided into tiny fragments which were sent to various churches. The feast of September 14th at Constantinople was preceded by four days of solemn preparation; the two Sundays between which it fell were also dedicated to the cross. The Roman Church also venerates the cross on September 14th. In addition to this feast, the Churches of the Byzantine rite dedicate the third Sunday in Lent and August 1st to the veneration of the cross.

48   The twenty-first chapter of the Book of Numbers tells how, when the Israelites were bitten by serpents in the desert, God commanded Moses to make a serpent of brass and to fix it to a pole: after that, anyone who had been bitten by a serpent, and who looked at the serpent of brass, was healed.

49   The Book of Proverbs carries the name of Solomon as its author. It is possible that certain passages of the book trace back to this king, but the majority of modern exegetes consider that the book is a collection or compilation of maxims subsequent to the exile.

50   Following the account given in Genesis (chs. 2 and 3), the tree of life was found in the centre of the garden; its fruits imparted physical immortality. It must not be confused with the tree of the knowledge of good and evil, whose fruit Adam and Eve ate. These descriptions must not be understood literally: they are deep spiritual symbols.

51   In the biblical episodes such as the visit of the three angels to Abraham, and the struggle of Jacob with the angel, the angel takes the place of God; the spirit of the narrator swings constantly between the idea of God and the image of the angel.

52   Nowhere in the New Testament is there a classification of the categories of angel. Only in the sixth century, under the influence of the writings of the Pseudo-Dionysios the Areopagite, did ideas relating to the celestial hierarchies (cherubim, seraphim, thrones, dominions, etc.) become established. These concepts do not belong to defined Christian dogma, but they express an effort, which is far from unacceptable, to distinguish degrees in the glory and the ministry of the angels.

53   In Constantinople, Michael was specially honoured as the celestial doctor, who brought healing to the sick. In Rome, his feast has been celebrated from the sixth century, on September 29th.

54   The Greek liturgical texts call Michael the 'archi-strategus'. Jude (v. 9) mentions the fight over Moses's body between Michael and the demon; this refers to a Jewish legend. In Revelation (12.7), Michael and his angels fight the dragon in heaven.

Chapter II
THE TIME OF ADVENT

SUMMARY

He who comes. Jairus's Daughter (24th Sunday after Pentecost). The Good Samaritan (25th Sunday). Thy Soul shall be required of Thee (26th Sunday). Healing on the Sabbath Day (27th Sunday). The Great Supper (28th Sunday). The Presentation of Mary in the Temple. Saint Nicholas. The Ancestors of the Lord (2nd Sunday before Christmas). The Geneaology of Christ (Sunday before Christmas). Christmas Eve.

He who Comes

On November 15th, the Byzantine Churches start the 'Christmas Fast'. It is also called the 'fast of St Philip' because it is immediately preceded by the feast of this apostle (November 14th). This time of expectation and of preparation corresponds to the Roman Advent[1]. There is no disadvantage, therefore, in calling the Christmas fast 'Advent-tide'. Like Great Lent, which precedes Easter, this lasts forty days, but it does not involve the same liturgical restrictions and the same strictness in fasting as does Lent.

The central idea of Advent is that it is the 'coming' of the Lord Jesus. One might perhaps feel that this term 'coming' is purely symbolic, for in fact Christ comes to us at all times, and even lives in us. Nevertheless, this approach and this presence of Christ, both of which are eternal, take on a special character at Advent-tide; they somehow acquire an 'intensity'. A special grace of the 'coming' of the Lord is offered us. The Lord Jesus is already present to us; but the grace of Advent allows us a more vivid, and quite new, awareness of this presence. Jesus is near us and in us. All the same, he makes himself known to us, during this period, as 'He who comes', that is to say he makes himself known as wanting to be with us, and as if adapting us better to his intimacy.

Christian prayer during the time of Advent might be summed up in one word: 'Come'. It is the 'Come, Lord Jesus' with which the Book of Revelation ends[2]. If we utter this call for help with sincerity and fervour, it becomes a true ascesis, and the hope and anticipation of the Lord in fact fill an increasing place in our soul. Each day of Advent, this 'Come!' fills us more and is said with greater power, so that it drives away those thoughts, images and passions which are incompatible with the coming of Christ. This 'Come!' purifies and enflames us. It should give our prayer a special meaning. May we utter this call less and less imperfectly, on each successive day of Advent.

We have already said that the term 'coming' points here to an intensification, the becoming objective of an approach and a presence which, themselves, are eternal. Our prayer at Advent, 'Come', could therefore be interpreted thus: 'Oh, let me be aware of thy presence in me – May the whole world feel thy presence'.

He who comes, or rather, he whose presence we desire to be more conscious of, can appear to us under differing aspects during Advent. The west, by preference, seems to await the King, the Messiah, both ruler and liberator. There is in this a very fruitful idea which follows on from the synagogue's Messianic expectation. This view entails that, in order to prepare ourselves to receive Jesus as King and Messiah, we must above all, during Advent, develop an attitude of inner obedience: may my own will no longer prevail, but let me rather be under orders; may he, who is stronger than I and whom I recognise as Master, come! The east has seen Advent more as a time of awaiting the light which will shine forth. The celebration of Jesus's birth coincides with the victory of light over darkness in the physical world – from Christmas on, daylight lengthens. In the same way, our interior darkness will be dispelled by the coming of him who is the Light of the world. The Byzantine Advent above all looks to Epiphany, 'the feast of lights', whereas the Roman Advent concentrates especially on Christmas, the feast of the coming of the Lord in our flesh. In order to prepare for this victory of light we must, during Advent, open ourselves more and more to the light 'which lighteth every man that cometh into the world'[3]. We must examine ourselves under this inner light, and let this light 'which is in our deepest self' guide our daily actions. We must live in an atmosphere of gentleness, of truth and of sincerity.

Advent also has an important eschatological significance. It reminds us of the Second Coming at the end of time, and of the transitory nature of the things of this world. But eschatology is only fruitful if we interiorise it and let its implications affect our personal life. The glory of the Second Coming must first be prefigured by the coming of Jesus into the individual and by the day breaking through our own dark night.

Jairus's Daughter

We have already said that the series of Sundays after Pentecost continues quite independently of the fixed feasts (like Christmas) and the liturgical seasons that are linked to them. One must not look for a link between the Sundays of the pentecostal cycle which fall in Advent and Advent itself. In addition, this independence of the cycle of Sundays makes it impossible to calculate how many Sundays, and which Sundays, will find themselves included in Advent: this varies each year according to the dates of Easter and, therefore, of Pentecost. If we assign to Advent roughly those five Sundays which fall between the twenty-fourth and the twenty-eighth after Pentecost, we will probably not be far off an average chronology. It is possible that a Sunday may have to be added or taken off this list; in this case − and we will know if it is the case by consulting the current liturgical calendar − the adjustment is easy: it is enough to refer to the series of the Sundays in the chapter which precedes this one and to the series in the chapter which follows it.

The gospel for the twenty-fourth Sunday after Pentecost teaches us to trust even in cases which seem hopeless. This gospel (Luke 8. 41-56) brings together two episodes. A woman, who for twelve years had suffered from an issue of blood which long medical treatment had been unable to alleviate, touches Jesus and is healed. The ills which affect our bodies and souls are therefore not incurable, however serious and long-established they may be. Even where apparent spiritual death is concerned, still, one must hope against all hope. The daughter of Jairus, a ruler of the synagogue, seemed dead, and when Jesus said that she was not dead but asleep, the people ridiculed him. But he, taking the young girl by the hand, commanded her to arise, and she arose. Thus we must not despair, either for oneself or for others, even when the appearance of spiritual death has set in. One must never say: 'For me, or for this or that person, nothing can be done'. In such extreme cases, one can no longer count on human intervention: one must allow Jesus alone to work in a sinful soul. 'And he put them all out, and took her by the hand . . .'. This great message of hope, which coincides more or less with the beginning of Advent, shows that portions of the Scriptures which are fixed quite independently of it can harmonize with this liturgical period. The gospel for today also speaks, in its own way, of the victory of light over darkness.

The epistle (Ephesians 2. 14-22) proclaims that Christ 'is our peace', and that he comes to 'reconcile (us) unto God'. Three verses especially merit our attention. First of all: 'He . . . preached peace to you which were afar off, and to them that were nigh . . .'. Even if I am not near to God, even if I am 'afar', I can take courage, because Jesus has come precisely in order to preach peace to sinners like me. And then: 'Through him we both have access by one Spirit unto the Father'. This verse expresses most concisely the parts played by the three divine Persons in our spiritual life; it expresses the essence of all spiritual life: access to the Father through the Son by the Spirit. And lastly: 'Ye are builded together for an habitation of God through the Spirit'. Here, once again, the scriptural text can have a connection with our special preoccupation during the time of Advent. We are concerned with preparing in ourselves a dwelling for the God who is about to be born, and it is only through the Spirit that we can obtain this indwelling of God. I shall not be able to share in the blessing of Jesus Christ's coming in the flesh if I do not first of all open my soul to the Spirit of Jesus Christ.

The Good Samaritan

The gospel for the twenty-fifth Sunday after Pentecost (Luke 10. 25-37) gives us the parable of the Samaritan who had compassion on a Jew after he had been attacked and wounded by thieves on the road between Jerusalem and Jericho. The parable is introduced through reference to the two great commandments. We have already come across and commented on them in connection with the gospel for the fifteenth Sunday after Pentecost (see the preceding chapter). It is the second of these commandments which gives a lawyer the opportunity to ask Jesus: 'And who is my neighbour?' The meaning of this parable is not to contrast the inhumanity of the priest and the Levite who pass by with the generosity of the Samaritan who tends and takes charge of the wounded Jew, nor to condemn the ethnic and religious antagonism between the Jews and the Samaritans[4], but to proclaim this general truth: that my neighbour is not exclusively someone connected to me by blood, or country or creed, but that my neighbour is, at each instant, someone whom God has brought near me, has put in my path; my neighbour is the person I become close to through serving his need, even if he is a stranger or an enemy. It depends very largely on me whether this or that man does or does not become my neighbour. I can try to act in such a way that every man becomes my neighbour. On another plane, the Samaritan represents Jesus himself, who pours wine and oil on the wounds of the human race and makes himself the neighbour of every man. 'Which . . . thinkest thou was neighbour unto him that fell among the thieves? . . . He that shewed mercy on him'.

In the epistle (Eph. 4. 1-17), St Paul recommends us to 'keep the unity of the Spirit in the bond of peace', because there is one body, and one Spirit, one Lord, one God. Paul's advice must be taken in a very literal sense, and applied to the circumstances and to the difficulties of our daily life. What good does it do to work out lofty ideas about unity in Christ, or the unity of the Church, if first of all I pay no attention to safeguarding 'the unity of the Spirit' and the 'bond of peace' with members of my family, with those who live in my house, with those with whom professional, economic or civic life bring me into contact each day. 'The unity of the Spirit' and the 'bond of peace': these two great sayings will only become true in my life when I give them practical effect in the small details of the day in the kitchen or the office. Thus the epistle for this Sunday is in harmony with the gospel, for it is only through the unity of the Spirit and the bond of peace that another man can become my neighbour.

Thy Soul Shall be Required of Thee

The gospel for the twenty-sixth Sunday after Pentecost (Luke 12. 16-21) is a serious and stern warning. Jesus describes the state of a rich man who 'layeth up treasure for himself, and is not rich toward God'. This rich man builds barns in which to store his harvests and his fruits. He says to his own soul: 'Take thine ease, eat, drink, and be merry'. But God says to him: 'Thou fool, this night thy soul shall be required of thee: then whose shall those things be, which thou hast provided?'. This parable faces each of us with a searching question − if, this very night, my soul were to be required of me, in relation to whom would I be found rich? Would I be rich for myself, or rich for God?

The epistle (Eph. 5. 8-19), although set independently of Advent, is essentially an Advent epistle. 'Awake thou that sleepest, and arise from the dead, and Christ shall give thee light[5] . . . because the days are evil. . . . Walk circumspectly, not as fools, but as wise, Redeeming the time'. Once again, our attention is

drawn to the contrast between our own darkness and divine light.
The expression 'redeeming the time' means: seizing and putting
to the best use the present moment, as if in some way buying it
and exploiting it so that it produces the best fruits possible. St
Paul makes the nature of these fruits clear: 'For the fruit of the
Spirit is in all goodness and righteousness and truth'. It is not
without point to remember that, wherever there is a little
goodness, a little justice, and a little truth − on whatever side
they are found − we are in the presence of the fruits of the Spirit.
In certain modern religious circles the reaction (which is often
necessary) against 'humanism' and 'moralism' is pushed so far
that these simple elementary virtues tend to be underestimated.
Yet all spiritual effort is illusory if it does not start by seeking out
goodness and honesty. These things are not in any way human attributes. They entail the goodness and the truth of Our Lord. It is
much easier to hold forth about the Incarnation or about grace
than to strain with all one's heart after the goodness, truth and
righteousness of Jesus. The last words of this Sunday's epistle
'Singing and making melody in your heart to the Lord' evoke an
admirable concept of spiritual life.

The Healing on the Sabbath Day

A woman who has been bowed down with an infirmity for eight-
een years is healed on the Sabbath day by Jesus, in a synagogue
where he is preaching. The ruler of the synagogue gives vent to
his indignation at the day of rest being violated by this work of
mercy. Jesus, to the shame of his adversaries and the joy of the
people, answers that, if no one thinks anything of loosing his ox or
his ass to take it to water on the Sabbath, then there is much
stronger reason to release a daughter of Abraham on this day.
Most of us strongly approve of this lesson from the gospel for the
twenty-seventh Sunday after Pentecost (Luke 13. 10-17); in principle, we are absolutely in agreement with the free attitude of
Jesus towards the Sabbath, and are very ready to accuse the
hypocrisy and legalism of the Pharisees and to take a stand
against them. But, in fact, it often happens that we imitate them.
We are easily shocked by any good work which is not done 'according to the rules' − that is, what we ourselves consider to be
the indispensable rules. If a person or a group whose beliefs differ
from ours, or who belong to a political party of which we disap-

prove, or that we judge to be morally inferior, achieve some results that are objectively good, but that we did not expect to come from that side, our first instinctive reaction (which is often concealed) is one of scepticism, of resentment or bitterness. Church people are especially prone to the temptation to denigrate and condemn all that is not of 'their' orthodoxy. Let this gospel teach us, therefore, to become humble enough, amenable enough to all light from above to admit − with joy and gratitude − the good that can be done through other channels than those which, rightly or wrongly, we consider 'proper'. May God make us able, when faced by any 'healing on the Sabbath', to feel what the people who surrounded Jesus felt: ' . . . all the people rejoiced for all the glorious things that were done by him'.

In the epistle for this Sunday (Eph. 6. 10-17), St Paul exhorts Christians to 'put on the whole armour of God'. He makes a long comparison between the objects that comprised a Roman soldier's armour − the breastplate, the shield, the helmet, the sword − and those gifts which constitute the spiritual armour of a Christian. This passage is often misinterpreted. Paul is not proposing that we should be inspired by military armour or take it as a model. His message is not: soldiers have a breastplate and a shield, therefore endeavour to equip yourself with a spiritual breastplate and shield. On the contrary, far from trying to establish an analogy between the armour of a soldier and the armour of God, he wants to underline their contrast. In place of (and not: in the manner of, or in imitation of) a belt, take truth. Instead of shoes, the gospel of peace. Instead of a breastplate, take justice. Instead of a shield, faith. Instead of a helmet, salvation. The deep reason for making this contrast is that 'we wrestle not against flesh and blood', but 'against spiritual wickedness in high places'. Commentators generally recognise that here Paul refers to spirits or to the spirit of evil. This is why the essential weapon of the Christian will be 'the sword of the Spirit, which is the word of God'. There is nothing soft or indolent in the disposition of the Spirit. It penetrates, it cuts, it severs. The mistake would be to seek, instead of these purely spiritual weapons which are the negation and the opposite of this world's weapons[6], means that are more or less analogous to earthly ways of doing battle: the result is a holy war, or the suppression of heresy by physical violence[7], or, on another level, the sort of ecclesiastical diplomacy which allows for intrigue and lies. All that, we can reject. We have no other weapon than the Spirit.

The Great Supper

The gospel for the twenty-eighth Sunday after Pentecost (Luke 14. 16-24) tells us again, in a slightly abbreviated form, what the gospel for the fourteenth Sunday told us (Matt. 22: 2-14). It is the parable of the supper to which many were invited. They excuse themselves for a variety of reasons, and the master of the house invites the poor and the crippled to take their place. 'None of those men that were bidden shall taste of my supper.' For the interpretation of this parable, we would refer the reader to the preceding chapter.

The epistle (Col. 1. 12-18) develops two ideas. The first is that we must give thanks to the Father because he has saved us from the powers of darkness (here again, we find the conflict between darkness and light), brought us into the kingdom of his Son, and cleansed us of our sins through the blood of the Redeemer. The second comprises objective reflections on the glory of the Son. He is the image of the invisible God; all has been created by him and for him: 'For by him were all things created . . . . He is the head of the body, the church'. We find powerfully condensed in this passage what might be called the christocentricism, or the pan-christicism, of Paul, were it not dangerous to attempt to transform the great intuitions lived by the apostle into intellectual systems. Contemporary theology has, with predilection, developed the theme of the Church as the body of Christ (thereby excluding all pantheism, and all identification of the created with the uncreated). These high speculations, which were familiar to the Fathers, open up the vastest horizons: the air there is somehow intoxicating. But increasing comprehension of the 'cosmic' role of Christ as King and upholder of the whole universe − of the total Christ, of whom we are members − must not weaken in us the vision of Jesus, compassionate and humble of heart, who remains our earthly model, or lessen the effort to unite our will with his [8].

The Entry of the Most Holy Mother of God into the Temple

Some days after the beginning of Advent, the Church celebrates the feast of the Entry of the Holy Virgin into the Temple. It is fitting that, at the start of this time of preparation for Christmas, our thought should turn to the Mother of God, whose humble and silent expectation should be the model of our own expec-

tation during Advent. The nearer we draw to Mary through our
prayer, our obedience and our purity, the more will be formed in
us he who is about to be born.

That Mary, as a very small child, was presented to the Temple
in Jerusalem to live there, is something that nowadays is recognised as belonging to the realm of legend, not to that of history[9].
But all the same, this legend forms a graceful symbol from which
we can draw the deepest spiritual insights.

At vespers in the evening of November 20th (therefore at the
start of November 21st, as liturgical time is reckoned), the three
readings from the Old Testament relate to the Temple. The first
lesson (Exod. 40) tells of the orders given by God to Moses about
the building and interior arrangements of the tabernacle. The
second lesson (1 Kgs 7. 51-8. 11) describes the dedication of the
Temple of Solomon. The third lesson (Ezek. 43. 27-44. 4),
already read for the feast of the Nativity of the Virgin on
September 8th, speaks of the door of the sanctuary, closed to all
men and by which God alone enters. These three texts symbolically have as their object the Mother of God herself, who is the
living and perfect temple.

The gospels read at matins and at the liturgy are those which
were read for the feast of September 8th. In the preceding
chapter, a brief commentary on the gospel for the liturgy will be
found at this date. As for the epistle read for today (Heb. 9. 1-7),
it speaks of the arrangement of the sanctuary and of the 'holy of
holies': this text too refers symbolically to Mary.

The spiritual meaning of the feast of the Entry of the Mother of
God is developed in the various texts for the services and the
liturgy. The two principle themes that we find there are the
following: first, the holiness of Mary. The small child who is
separated from the world and brought to live in the Temple
evokes the idea of a life set apart, consecrated, 'presented to the
Temple'; a life of intimacy with God: 'Today the All Pure and All
Holy enters the Holy of Holies'. It is clear that here the Church
makes a special allusion to virginity, but all human life, in its different measures, can be a life that is 'presented to the Temple', a
life that is holy and pure with God. The second theme is the comparison of the Temple made of stone and the living Temple: 'The
most pure Temple of the Saviour . . . today is led into the house of
the Lord, bringing with her the grace of the divine Spirit'. Mary,
who will bear the God-Man in her womb, is a holier temple than
the sanctuary at Jerusalem; it is fitting that these two temples

should meet, but here it is the living temple which sanctifies the temple which is built. The superiority of the living temple over the temple of stone is true in a special way of Mary, because she was the instrument of the Incarnation. But, in a more general manner, this is true of every man who is united to God: 'Know ye not that ye are the temple of God . . .?[10] . . . Know ye not that your body is the temple of the Holy Ghost . . .?[11].

Still other thoughts, which the liturgical texts do not voice explicitly, are suggested to us by this feast. If our soul is a temple where God wishes to live, it is fitting that Mary should be 'presented' to it: our soul must be open to Mary so that she may dwell in this temple − our own personal temple. Then again, because the whole assembly of the faithful is the body of Christ and the Temple of God, let us think of today's feast as the Entry of Mary into this temple − the holy, universal Church. The Temple, which is the catholic Church, today pays homage to the Temple which is Mary.

Saint Nicholas

During the time of Advent, we celebrate the feasts of saints about whom we are much better informed than we are about Nicholas of Myra: saints whose service to the Church seems to have been far more outstanding: for example, the apostle St Andrew, or St John of Damascus, the great Syrian doctor, or St Ambrose, bishop of Milan. But one could say that none of the saints of Advent hold as high a place in popular devotion as does Nicholas Thaumaturgus, bishop of Myra in Lycia. The Church itself surrounds his feast (December 6th) with a special solemnity. And meanwhile we know almost nothing about him. The incidents of his life for which he is best known do not belong to history, but to legend[12]. However this legend, this veneration, this figure, have a spiritual meaning which we shall try to bring out.

One of the responses from the service for the saint shows precisely where the worth and originality of St Nicholas lie: 'Thy practical virtues, O Father clothed by God, have made the beauty of thy priestly robes shine with yet greater splendour'. These lines say all, and put it perfectly. He is the ideal type of 'hierarch' who would not only be a pontiff or a doctor, but who would also be actively involved in the secular world, doing good there. He wears 'priestly robes', but on him, these 'shine with yet greater splendour' than on so many others, because he combined them with 'practical virtues'. The legends attached to the name of Nicholas always represent him as engaged in bringing help to some urgent case of human distress. This 'saintly life', which cannot pretend to be historical (but which might have some historical foundation, orally transmitted and enlarged upon) expresses an ideal of charity. It is what the chants of the service for the saint repeat several times: 'Called upon from all sides, thou didst hasten to help those who sought the shelter of thy protection . . . appearing to them in faith by day and by night, saving them in their destitution and their trials . . . . Who, seeing thy infinite condescension, would not marvel at thy patience and at thy joyous mercy towards the poor and thy compassion towards the afflicted . . .?'. Today, still, crowds of Orthodox willingly shelter under the patronage of Nicholas who is a healer of the sick, the liberator of captives, the treasure of the poor, consoler of the afflicted and the guide to travellers. He is a living symbol of the Saviour's mercy and love towards men. For, in the final analysis, it is to Jesus himself, that the popular devotion accorded to St Nicholas reaches.

The gospel for matins is that of the Good Shepherd (John 10. 1-9). The epistle for the liturgy takes up the theme of obedience to those in authority and above all to Jesus Christ 'that great shepherd of the sheep' (Heb. 13. 17-21). The gospel for the liturgy is that of the Beatitudes (Luke 6. 17-23). May this feast bring us a message of 'practical Christianity' and of hope in divine goodness.

The Ancestors of the Lord

The Sundays of Advent-tide, as we have already said several times, belong to the cycle of the Sundays after Pentecost and have no direct connection with the mystery of the coming of the Lord Jesus expressed by Christmas. This is why the Church, in wanting to prepare the faithful for the great feast of the Incarnation, has added to the readings and to the prayers of the two Sundays which precede Christmas (whatever these Sundays may be in the order of Sundays after Pentecost) other texts which do have a direct bearing on Advent. These, then, are the two 'Sundays before Christmas' which are in some way superimposed on the two Sundays after Pentecost with which they coincide. In principle on these two Sundays the epistle and gospel for the Sunday after Pentecost should first be read, then the epistle and gospel which are added because of Christmas. Often the texts for the

Sunday after Pentecost are omitted, and we restrict ourselves to the readings and prayers that prepare us for the Nativity of Our Lord.

The first of these two Sundays is called 'Sunday of the Ancestors of the Lord'. It is celebrated on the second Sunday before the 25th December – this falls between December 11th and the 17th.

The 'Ancestors' are the Patriarchs and the Prophets of the Old Covenant, from Adam to John the Baptist. The Church sings: 'Let us rejoice together, we who are friends of the Fathers, in commemorating their memory . . .'. One wonders whether these words correspond to any genuine feeling on the part of the majority of believers. Many among us have lost touch with the Old Testament, and neither read nor understand it, and so do not take into account that Jesus Christ is present, though veiled, in all the events and all the texts of Hebrew Scripture. All is centred on him. Many do not recognise in Abel the first martyr, and the prototype of the Good Shepherd as well as the Sacrificer; in Melchisedek the type of the eternal priest; in Abraham the spirit of faith and the type of the Father; in Isaac the spirit of sonship and of sacrifice, in Jacob free election, patient service and conversion; in Joseph the great features of the Passion and of Christ's redemptive work. They forget that through the reading of the Prophets the voice of Jesus himself speaks to our heart. They are not really 'friends of the Fathers' and they do not delight in remembering them. Let us ask our Lord, on this Sunday, to open our understanding to the message of the Old Covenant and to teach us, as He taught the disciples at Emmaus: 'O fools, and slow of heart to believe all that the prophets have spoken; . . And beginning with Moses [13] and all the prophets, he expounded unto them in all the scriptures the things concerning himself' [14].

The epistle read at the liturgy for this Sunday, 'When Christ, who is our life, shall appear . . .' (Col. 3. 4-11), is the one assigned for the 29th Sunday after Pentecost (see the following chapter). The gospel is that for the 28th Sunday after Pentecost: 'A certain man made a great supper . . .' (Luke 14. 16-24), that we have already spoken about in this chapter. These texts bear on the Nativity of Christ rather than on the Ancestors. The chant called the *kontakion* also makes a direct allusion to Christmas: 'On this day, and beyond all telling, the Virgin gives birth to the Word in a cave . . .'.

A special feature of this Sunday is the frequent mention made

in the chants of the prophet Daniel and also of the three young
men, Shadrach, Meshach and Abed-nego who, thrown into the
furnace for refusing to worship the image of the king,
Nebuchadnezzar, were miraculously saved from death[15]. This is
explained by the fact that the feast of Daniel and the three young
men falls on December 17th, and will thus fall very close to this
Sunday. The liturgical texts themselves bring out the symbolic
meaning of the episode. On the one hand, the three young men
(like the three angels who appeared to Abraham) represent the
Trinity: 'The young men of God came and went in the fiery furnace, rejoicing in the dew of the Spirit which refreshed them, and
representing the mystery of the Trinity . . .'. They represent the
victory of faith over death: 'By their faith they quelled the power
of the fire'. Finally they represent – and here is found the link
with Christmas – the new burning bush, the fire of the divine
presence which does not consume: 'Thy young men, O Christ,
when they were in the furnace which was to them like dew,
mysteriously figure thy birth from the Virgin, which has illumined us without burning us'. We are reminded that, as the
Bible tells us, the three young men were not alone in the furnace:
'Lo, I see four men loose, walking in the midst of the fire . . . and
the form of the fourth is like the Son of God'[16]. These last words
shed light on the problem of human suffering. The Son of God
himself is always there to be with men in the midst of the
furnace.

The Genealogy of Christ

The second Sunday which is specially consecrated to the preparation for the Nativity is that which immediately precedes the
feast of Christmas. It is called 'Sunday of the Fathers or of the
Genealogy'. It falls between December 18th and 24th.

'Turning our thoughts to Bethlehem, let us lift ourselves in
spirit to contemplate the great Mystery which is taking place in
the cave . . . . Now that the time of our salvation draws near. . . .
Prepare thyself, O Bethlehem . . .', the choir sings during the service, and mention is made of the patriarchs, the prophets, the
holy women of the Old Covenant who 'through faith shine like the
stars'. The Church's idea, this Sunday, seems to be to bring the
righteous who lived before Christ into the joy of the Nativity 'inviting them all by praises and divine songs to prepare for the birth
of Christ'.

The gospel read at the liturgy (the whole of Matt. 1) traces back the genealogy of Jesus according to the flesh: 'The generation of Jesus Christ, the son of David, the son of Abraham. Abraham begat Isaac; and Isaac begat Jacob; . . .'. And it continues up to Joseph 'the husband of Mary, of whom was born Jesus, who is called Christ'[17]. We have read or heard this genealogy many times. We may have the impression that this reading is of purely historical and documentary interest. What can this list of names bring us that has any spiritual import? But each one of these names does have a particular meaning, if we remind ourselves of the story of the person who bore it. What needs to be clearly understood is that the ancestors of Jesus were not all just and holy men. Amongst them are also sinners; those who have committed incest, adultery, murder; an alien woman: the names of Judas, of Thamar, of David and Ruth are filled with spiritual significance. Jesus wanted, humanly, to be linked with 'all that', and to 'all those'. He wanted to clear a way for himself through the sins and crimes of men. And so it is the history of each one of us that he takes upon himself and overcomes. For each one of us has some of the features of those of Jesus's ancestors who are the furthest from holiness. In each of us can be found, either dormant or awakened, the sins of the patriarchs and of their children. All the same, however, Jesus must be born in us. We must, in ourselves, overcome and go beyond the misdeeds that certain names in the genealogy of Jesus represent. It is necessary for us to live this genealogy, for us to acquire a personal experience of it, so that through falling and starting afresh we shall eventually reach Joseph and Mary. This does not mean sinning deliberately so that we can identify ourselves more closely with the genealogy of the Lord, but simply means recognising certain elements of this genealogy in the sins that we do commit, and of uniting ourselves in spirit to the progressive purification which prepared for the birth of Jesus. Thus the genealogy of Christ will become an integral part of our own lives.

The gospel for this Sunday goes on to describe, in a way which is both very precise and very sober, Joseph's doubts, the message brought to him by the angel and his confident obedience[18].

The epistle (Heb.11. 9-10,32-40) praises the faith of the patriarchs: 'By faith he (Abraham) sojourned in the land of promise . . .'. Isaac, Jacob, Gedeon, Samuel, David, and others are mentioned. The logical conclusion is not reached in this reading, but is found in the first sentence of the following chapter: 'Wherefore seeing we also are compassed about with so great a cloud of witnesses, let us lay aside every weight, and the sin which doth so easily beset us, and let us run with patience the race that is set before us, looking unto Jesus the author and finisher of our faith . . .' (12: 1-2).

The Eve of Christmas

The day of December 24th presents very interesting liturgical characteristics which, at first sight, are somewhat disconcerting. On the one hand, the vigil of the Nativity is the culminating point of the hope and expectation of Advent. On the other hand, the services for this day anticipate the feast of Christmas itself: not only do we ask with fervour for the coming of Christ, but the Church already gives us accounts of the Nativity from the gospels. This fusion of two elements – penitence in the expectation of an event, and the announcement of that event as having already taken place – is explained by the play of liturgico-historical factors rather than by any deliberate doctrinal or pedagogical design. (This has also happened on Holy Saturday). What does matter is that we should know how to use to the best advantage the double meaning thus given to December 24th. The fact that, by Christmas eve, we have heard read the scriptural texts which recount the story of the Nativity and have sung hymns of thanksgiving does not invalidate the joyful prayer of December 25th. On the contrary, it prepares and facilitates this prayer. The services for Christmas eve are longer than those for the feast day itself; during these services, we hear biblical accounts of the Nativity which are more detailed than those which we hear the next day. In this way on December 24th the Church sets before us the whole panorama of the Nativity; each point of detail has been mentioned and explored; a complete picture has been established in our spirit. On Christmas Day itself, the Church does not go over everything that has already been said; it is assumed that we know it, and have meditated on it. The services for the feast are shorter than those of the vigil. The Church focuses our attention on points; she offers us the opportunity, not just to learn and develop intellectually, but to taste and savour as spiritual fruits the words of life which we already know. December 24th speaks to us of the same things as December 25th, but the 24th is a preparation, an instruction, a praise which 'welcomes' the event;

the 25th is the fulness, the fruition, the praise which crowns an accomplished fact.

On the morning of December 24th the 'canonical hours' (which, on this day are given the name of 'royal hours'[19]) are celebrated with particular solemnity. Each of these hours includes, in addition to the psalms and various hymns, a lesson from the Old Testament, and readings from an epistle and a gospel. At Prime, a passage from the prophet Micah (5. 2-4) is read which refers to Bethlehem, little among the thousands of Judah, but out of which will come the future ruler of Israel; the epistle (Heb. 1. 1-12) says that God, having spoken to us through the prophets, has finally spoken through his Son, who is so much better than the angels; the gospel (Matt. 1. 18-25) is the same as for the Sunday before Christmas, and describes the perplexities of Joseph and how they were set at rest. At Terce, a text from the prophet Baruch (3. 36-4: 4)[20] proclaims that God 'did . . . show himself upon earth, and conversed with men'; the epistle (Gal. 3. 23-29) declares: 'The law was our schoolmaster to bring us unto Christ . . . . But after that faith is come, we are no longer under a schoolmaster . . . . For as many of you as have been baptized into Christ have put on Christ'; the gospel (Luke 2. 1-20) tells of the birth of Jesus at Bethlehem and of the adoration of the shepherds. At Sext, the prophet Isaiah (7. 10-16, 8. 1-4, 9-10) announces the Nativity: 'A virgin shall conceive, and bear a son, and shall call his name Immanuel. Butter and honey shall he eat, that he may know to refuse the evil, and choose the good . . .'[21]; the epistle (Heb. 1. 10-2.3) again speaks of Jesus being superior to the angels[22] and gives us a serious warning: 'How shall we escape, if we neglect so great salvation'; the gospel (Matt. 2. 1-12) tells of the journey and adoration of the Magi. At Nones, we hear Isaiah (9. 5-7): 'For unto us a child is born, unto us a son is given . . . and his name shall be called Wonderful, Counsellor, The mighty God, The everlasting Father, the Prince of Peace'; the epistle (Heb. 2. 11-18) tells us the reason for the Incarnation: ' . . . in all things it behoved him to be made like unto his brethren, that he might be a merciful and faithful high priest in things pertaining to God, to make reconciliation for the sins of the people. For in that he himself hath suffered being tempted, he is able to succour them that are tempted'; the gospel (Matt. 2. 13-23) narrates the departure of the Magi, the flight into Egypt, and the massacre of the Innocents.

The 'royal hours' are immediately followed by vespers. During these, we hear three readings from the Old Testament: the account of the creation of the world (Gen. 1. 1-13), that creation which the Incarnation of God was designed to perfect; then the message: 'Unto us a child is born, unto us a son is given . . .' (Isaiah 9. 6-7); and finally the prophecy: 'A virgin shall conceive, and bear a son . . .' (Isa. 7. 10-16, 8. 1-4, 9-10). We have already heard these last two lessons during the 'royal hours'. After the third reading from the Old Testament, vespers somehow merges into the liturgy: the celebrant recites a short litany, then goes immediately on to the prayer which follows the 'Little Entrance'. The *Trisagion* is sung; then the epistle and the gospel of the liturgy are read: the epistle is that for Prime, and the gospel that for Terce; we have already mentioned them in speaking of the 'royal hours'. The liturgy then continues in the normal way[23].

The chants which accompany the 'royal hours', vespers and the liturgy are already songs of triumph: 'Come, let us rejoice in the Lord, in proclaiming this mystery . . . Light of light, brightness of the Father, thou dost fill with joy and illumine all creatures . . . . We glorify thy Nativity, O Christ . . . .'

All the same, this Christmas vigil does not lose its penitential character. The fast for this day should be observed particularly strictly. In Russia, the custom exists of fasting until the first star appears. This brings to mind both the star which led the Magi to Bethlehem and Christ who is the true light. May this day also be a day of fast in our souls: let us abstain from all bad or useless thoughts and speech, and await in silence and composure the Saviour who is coming to us. Darkness falls. Soon the first star will rise and mark, according to the Church calendar, the start of the new day and of the great feast of Christmas. With the rising of this star, may the light of Our Lord rise for us so that, in the words of the apostle Peter, 'Ye do well that ye take heed, as unto a light that shineth in a dark place, until the day dawn, and the day star arise in your hearts'[24].

Notes for Chapter II

1   We do not know precisely at what date the celebration of Advent was introduced into the Church. Documents establish that, towards the end of the fourth century, the Nativity of Christ was celebrated by some on December 25th and by others on January 6th. The Council of Saragossa, in Spain, decided (in 380) that, from December 17th till Epiphany, no one could absent himself from services. In Gaul, in the sixth century, a sort of Lent was observed from November 11th until Christmas. Advent was celebrated in Rome, under the pope St Gregory the Great, towards the end of the sixth century. It seems to have

come into the practice of the Churches of the Byzantine rite much later. In the ninth century, the Greeks fasted from November 15th until Christmas, but nothing in the liturgical life of those forty days implied any sort of preparation for the feast of the Nativity. Present day Byzantine custom seems to have become established in the seventeenth century, under circumstances of which we know nothing. The Roman Church now begins Advent on the nearest Sunday to the feast of the apostle St Andrew (30th November), and their Advent comprises four Sundays.

2 Rev. 22. 20.

3 John 1. 9.

4 The conflict between the Jews and the Samaritans began at the time of the return from exile; its origins are almost unknown. This conflict was intensified and became crystallised when Sanballat, the Persian governor of Samaria, obtained from Alexander the Great permission to built a temple on Mount Gerizim which would rival the temple in Jerusalem. The high priest of this temple was Manasseh, the brother of the high priest of the Jews, and Manasseh had married Sanballat's daughter: the Jews considered him a turncoat and an apostate.

5 This same theme of spiritual awakening and illumination is found in the epistle to the Romans (13: 11-14). The Roman Church takes these five verses as the epistle for the first Sunday in Advent.

6 It is not without point to remember here that, until the fourth century, the prevailing opinion in the Church was that the Christian faith and the carrying of arms were incompatible. Not only do several disciplinary documents and theological writings from this period protest against Christians taking part in military service, but we possess the 'Acts' of several martyrs who were put to death, and venerated by the Church, for their 'conscientious objection'. This was not only in certain cases where this objection was provoked by military customs tainted with idolatry, but stemmed from the conviction that someone who bore the sign of Christ had no right to use actual weapons, even in a 'just war'. Although some Fathers of the Church (for example St Basil and St Martin of Tours) remained faithful to this view, the Church as a whole became reconciled to military service after its alliance with the empire of Constantine. From then on until our day, we have seen popes, bishops, priests and ministers of all sorts of confessions provoking wars, encouraging the combatants and blessing arms. Only small minority sects (the Waldensians, Anabaptists, Quakers and Russian sects, etc.) have been opposed radically to the use of arms. The last wars, of 1914 and of 1939, however, seem to have confronted Christian consciences with this question even more acutely. Protestantism has given rise to a considerable number of 'conscientious objectors'. In the Roman Church, several theologians, notably those at the heart of the Dominican Order, have openly doubted whether, given the circumstances of modern warfare, the requisite conditions for a 'just war' can ever be realised nowadays. Perhaps it is time for these questions to be posed and examined seriously by the Eastern Churches.

7 We are not only alluding to the Crusades and the Inquisition. Anglicanism, Protestantism, and Orthodoxy have all, at different times in history, been persecutors. All the ecclesiastical hierarchies have, at some time, deserved the rebuke that the disciples received from Jesus when they wished to make fire come down from heaven upon a Samaritan village (Luke 9. 55).

8 The theology of the Church as the mystical body of Christ has been

especially developed in the Roman Church during the last sixty years. The Anglican and Protestant Churches became keenly interested somewhat later. Similarly, the Orthodox Churches are now deepening the rich heritage of the Greek Fathers on this subject. This theological movement everywhere seems to be more or less linked with liturgical and ecumenical movements. The theology of the mystical body of Christ has, to a certain extent, renewed the concept of the Church, substituting the idea of a living organism for that of a juridical organisation, and a fervent collective consciousness, for individualist tendencies; it has, on the other hand, deepened the intimacy of believers with the person of Jesus Christ, showing them that they do not only live with Christ and through Christ, but *in* Christ. This theology, if it is treated with more enthusiasm than wisdom, is liable to certain distortions. It was this, in the heart of the Roman Church, that provoked a real 'crisis' in the theology of the body of Christ and led to several official statements by Pope Pius XII. While he defended the Pauline assertions that the Christian is a member of Christ, the Pope reprimanded the sort of christology which ignored the difference in the natures of the God become man and created man, the sort of ecclesiology which denied the visible and apostolic structure of the Church, quietism which disdained ascesis, and a liturgical attitude which belittled the importance of individual prayer. We shall have several opportunities of returning to this theme of the mystical body.

9   According to the apocryphal gospels (the pseudo-James, the pseudo-Matthew, etc.), Mary was taken to the Temple by her parents, at the age of three, and remained there. The feast of the Entry was first celebrated in Syria (which is precisely the country of the apocryphal gospels) towards the end of the sixth century. In the seventh or eighth century, Greek liturgical poems were composed in honour of the Entry. Nevertheless, in the seventh century, the menology of Constantinople does not yet mention this feast. It was, however, celebrated in Constantinople by the eleventh century. The popes at Avignon in the fourteenth century introduced the Entry to the Latin West. It was in vain that, in the sixteenth century, Pope Pius V, who was more concerned about historical truth, removed it from the breviary and from the Roman calendar — Pope Sixtus V, in the same century, replaced it.

10   1 Cor. 3.16.

11   1 Cor. 6.19.

12   The only certain historical facts are that Nicholas was bishop of Myra and that he died around the middle of the fourth century. According to legends which were collected and edited in Greek by Metaphrastus, during the tenth century, Nicholas made a pilgrimage to Palestine, took part in the Council of Nicaea and was imprisoned under Diocletian. A large number of miracles are attributed to him as well as striking acts of charity. He is credited with the setting free of captives, with saving schoolboys from death and young girls from dishonour. His cult is particularly strong in Greece and in Russia. His name is mentioned in the liturgy attributed to St John Chrysostom. By the sixth century, a church had already been dedicated to him in Constantinople. In 1087, Italian merchants stole his body from Myra (in Asia Minor) and transported it to Bari (in Italy), where he still is, and continues to work miracles. In addition, his veneration was introduced to Germany by an empress of Greek origin, Theophano, the wife of Otto II, in the tenth century. Portrayals of Nicholas are as numerous in western art as they are in eastern iconography. We know that in germanic countries and in North America he has been turned into Santa Claus.

13   The evangelist does not mean here that Jesus took as his starting point the Book of Exodus, in which Moses is mentioned for the first time, but that he started with the Book of Genesis, for the first five books of the Bible (or the Pentateuch) were called 'the book of Moses'. Also, before going on to what are commonly called the prophets, Jesus must have spoken to the two disciples of the books which we call 'historical' (Samuel, Kings, etc.) and that the Jews called 'the Prophets'.

14   Luke 24. 27.

15   This story is told in Daniel, chapter 3. The Septuagint (the Greek version) and the Vulgate (Latin version) intercalate in this chapter the prayer of Azarias and the song of the three children, which the Hebrew Bible does not contain. Ananias, Misael and Azarias are the Greek names of the three children; they, in the Hebrew Bible and the majority of the English versions, are called Shadrach, Meshach and Abed-nego. The traditional view, according to which the Book of Daniel was written by the prophet Daniel during the exile of Israel in Babylon (sixth century before Christ), today has few supporters. For historical and linguistic reasons, it is now thought more probable that the book was written by an unknown author during the time of the Maccabees. The episode of the three children is connected, in all likelihood, with the literature that was inspired by the religious persecution of the Jews by Antiochus IV Epiphanes (175-164 BC).

16   Daniel 3. 25. In certain Greek versions, one finds: 'a son of God'. The original Aramaic version (for this portion of the Book of Daniel is written in Aramaic, not Hebrew) gives: 'son of the Gods'. Jewish exegesis saw this mysterious being as an angel. Patristic Christian exegesis has generally identified it with the second person of the Trinity. From the point of view of literal and historical exegesis, this identification is no doubt inexact, but could find support on a spiritual level.

17   The genealogical table contained in the first chapter of the gospel according to Matthew in no way claims to be of strict historical exactness. It is quite evident that it is an arrangement which is in part artificial; the author intends, not to draw up a complete list, but rather to call attention to certain names and to those characteristics that they evoke. The division into three groups of fourteen generations is, it seems, inspired by certain symbolic considerations: perhaps it is related to the waxing and waning of the moon (each lasting approximately fourteen days), which a Jewish belief saw as a sign of the destinies of Israel; perhaps it is due to the fact that the Hebrew name of David consisted in three letters whose total numerical value is fourteen. The gospel according to Luke (3. 23-38) also gives a genealogy for Jesus, going back from Joseph all the way to Adam; this genealogy agrees at some points (after Abraham) with that of the gospel according to Matthew, but it differs on others. Luke, like Matthew, wanted to underline certain features rather than to establish a strictly historical list. Matthew wrote for the Jews: it mattered to him to show that the Messiah was of the race of Abraham and of the house of David. Luke wrote for the Gentiles as well as for the Jews: in recalling that Jesus was descended from Adam, the 'son of God', he indicated that Jesus is the brother of all men. One wonders how these two evangelists, who affirmed the virgin birth of Jesus, thought they were linking Jesus to David in making use of Joseph as an intermediary. Perhaps they thought that the legal paternity of Joseph implied, through the same legal fiction, Davidic descent. Perhaps it is necessary to admit that the genealogy given by Luke is, in reality, the genealogy of Mary, who would then have been a

kinswoman of Joseph's, but that the name of Joseph had been substituted for that of Mary by virtue of the legal marriage. In any case, the Fathers of the Church admitted Davidic descent not only for Joseph, but also for Mary. The apostle Paul taught that Jesus is 'made of the seed of David according to the flesh' (Rom. 1. 3) and that 'Jesus Christ of the seed of David was raised from the dead' (2 Tim. 2. 8).

18   The account of the Nativity of Christ according to Matthew is written more from the point of view of Joseph, whereas the same account according to Luke is more from the point of view of Mary.

19   In liturgical terms, the adjective 'royal' as in 'royal hours' and 'royal doors' (of the iconostasion) does not imply a greater intrinsic dignity in some particular service or architectural feature. The origin of the term must be looked for in the imperial ceremonial of Constantinople. The 'royal hours' are those during which the emperor was present the whole time. The 'royal doors' are those through which the emperor, alone of all the laity, had the right to pass on certain occasions.

20   The Book of Baruch belongs to the apocryphal or deutero-canonical writings of the Old Testament. This origin does not mean that they did not have a sacred or inspired character.

21   In this text from Isaiah, the word 'virgin' translates exactly the Greek word used in the Septuagint; but the Hebrew word used in the original could equally well be rendered by 'young woman'. No Jewish tradition presupposed a virgin birth for the Messiah and so this would not have influenced the authors of the Greek version. The reasons why they deliberately chose the term 'virgin' remain a historical mystery. Their reasons must have been very strong, for the translators were scholars who were trained to be well aware of the slightest nuances in the text. A Christian will have no difficulty in admitting that the Alexandrine translators must here have been guided by a divine light.

22   One of the aims of the epistle to the Hebrews − which seems to have been written if not by St Paul, at least by one of his close disciples − is to combat certain tendencies towards adoration of angels and the worship of 'intermediaries' in Christians of Jewish origin.

23   If Christmas Eve falls on a Saturday or a Sunday, the liturgy is that of St John Chrysostom. If the vigil falls on another day of the week, the liturgy of St Basil is celebrated, because of the analogy between Advent and Great Lent (during which this liturgy is often used). When December 24th is on a Saturday or a Sunday, the 'royal hours' are said on the Friday morning; vespers are then dissociated from the liturgy of the vigil and postponed till Saturday evening; in this case, they undergo some modifications, which take account of the fact that the feast itself has already started.

24   2 Pet. 1. 19.

Chapter III

CHRISTMAS AND EPIPHANY

SUMMARY

The Feast of the Nativity. Meditation on Christmas. The Day after Christmas. David, James and Joseph (Sunday after Christmas). St Stephen, Protomartyr (27 December). The Holy Innocents (29 December). The Circumcision of Our Lord (1 January). The Sunday before Epiphany. The Vigil of Epiphany. The Feast of Epiphany (6 January). Meditation on Epiphany. The Precursor (7 January). Sunday after Epiphany. The Three Hierarchs (30 January). The Presentation of Our Lord in the Temple (2 February). The Grateful Leper (29th Sunday after Pentecost). The Rich Ruler (30th Sunday after Pentecost). The Blind Man of Jericho (31st Sunday after Pentecost). Zacchaeus (32nd Sunday after Pentecost).

The Feast of the Nativity

The celebration of the birth of Christ was introduced into the ecclesiastical calendar at a relatively late date[1]. During the first centuries, the Church concentrated on Epiphany, the first and glorious manifestation of the Lord, rather than on his birth, an event which seemed somehow private and as if wrapped in shadow — even though this shadow was shot through by rays of divine light. In the liturgical life of contemporary eastern Churches, Epiphany still has pre-eminence over Christmas, and this pre-eminence is noticeable also in popular devotion. The Roman west officially assigns a place to Epiphany which is not inferior to that of Christmas; but the devotion of the faithful has definitely concentrated on this last feast; it would even seem that, for the majority of Roman Catholics, Anglicans and Protestants, Christmas has become more important than Easter. However, being faithful to the early tradition, we consider Epiphany to be the highest and most complete celebration of the coming of our Lord amongst men. We shall be careful, though, not to underestimate the inspiration by which the Holy Spirit has impelled the whole Christian community to contemplate Jesus's birth itself and honour it better. We shall strive to receive the message and the grace that Christmas brings with our whole heart. We shall consider the period which lasts from Christmas to Epiphany as an indivisible feast, of which Christmas is the starting point and

66

Epiphany the culmination. The prolongation of this celebration offers increased possibilities for our conversion to him who comes.

Matins for Christmas are celebrated either on the evening of December 24th or on the morning of December 25th. At these the gospel account of the angel's message to Joseph (Matt. 1. 18-25), which has already been read during the 'royal hours' of December 24th, is read again; the angelic hymn: 'Glory to God in the highest, and on earth peace, goodwill toward men . . .' and the odes proper to the Nativity are sung. During the liturgy for Christmas[2], instead of the *Trisagion*, the antiphon formed on the words of St Paul is repeated: 'All ye that are baptised into Christ have put on Christ'[3]. It is from the same letter to the Galatians (4. 4-7) that the epistle for this day is drawn; 'When the fulness of the time was come, God sent forth his Son, made of a woman . . . . And because ye are sons, God hath sent forth the Spirit of his Son into your hearts, crying Abba, Father'. The gospel (Matt. 2. 1-12), already read on the eve, is that of the adoration of the Magi[4]. The final blessing of the liturgy is altered to start in the following way: 'Christ, our true God, who, for our salvation, was born in a cave and laid in a manger . . . .'.

We shall quote some of the words sung at matins for Christmas, to show what spirit animates the Church at this feast:

'All things are filled with joy today . . . . Let all the earth acclaim its God.'

'Rod of the root of Jesse, and flower that blossomed from its stem, O Christ, Thou has sprung from the Virgin.'

'To those who are caught in the night straying into the works of darkness . . . grant, O Christ, thy blessing.'

'I was pierced by the arrows of the tyrant, but found refuge in Thee, O Christ, who hast overcome the evil one . . . .'

'Having beheld those lightless figures and the shades that have turned away from the Word, now, O most pure Mother, that He has issued from the door that was closed and that we are judged worthy of the light of truth, we bless thy womb . . . .'

'Our Saviour, the Dayspring from on high, has visited us, and we who were in shadow and in darkness have found the truth . . . .'

We notice here, once again, the tendency of the Byzantine Church to think of Christ in terms of light. Byzantine Christians certainly do not forget that the Word became a small child who was laid in a manger; but, while Western Christians seem, since the middle ages, to cling with pleasure to this flesh and blood child, the East sees above all in the Incarnation the coming of light, its triumph over darkness, and our own conversion from the night of sin to the divine radiance. The East wants to contemplate the eternal reality to which the historical event gives expression. This spiritualisation of Christmas evidences a very different state of mind from that (which is no less legitimate) of most Western Christians[5], and it finds its perfect formulation in the troparion for the Nativity:

'Thy Nativity, O Christ our God, has shone upon the world with the light of knowledge: for thereby they who adored the stars through a star were taught to worship Thee, the Sun of Righteousness, and to know Thee, the Dayspring from on high. O Lord, glory to Thee.'

Meditation for Christmas

We will interrupt the description of the Nativity services for a while so that we can reflect on some of the words from the gospels which the Church has brought to our attention during this feast.

'The shepherds said one to another, Let us now go even unto Bethlehem, and see this thing which is come to pass, which the Lord hath made known unto us.'[6] Let us, too, go even to Bethlehem. In spirit, let us climb that hill 'unto the hills, from whence cometh my help'[7]. Climbing up to Bethlehem implies an effort; but shall we let such a great occasion slip by?

'Joseph also went up from Galilee, out of the city of Nazareth, into Judaea, unto the city of David, which is called Bethlehem . . . . To be taxed with Mary his espoused wife, being great with child . . . .'[8] It is no longer Caesar Augustus, but the King of kings who decrees that 'all the world should be taxed . . . every one into his own city'[9]. Each person must declare sincerely which city he has chosen, to which group he allies himself. Some will choose Rome; others Athens. Shall I choose riches, or power, or intelligence? No. Those cities are not for me. I shall not even choose Jerusalem, the place where God manifests his glory. During my earthly life, I wish to be a citizen of Bethlehem, and to have that humility and that poverty as my share; with Mary, with Joseph and with Jesus, I would like my name to be enrolled in that little town which may be despised or ignored by men, but is so great before God.

'Behold, I bring you good tidings of great joy . . . unto you is born this day . . . a Saviour . . . .'[10] The birth of Jesus at Bethlehem is not a far-distant historical event which is of no concern to me. And, if it does concern me, it is not merely because I am a member of the great human collectivity. The message of Christmas is not addressed to humanity in general, it is addressed to each person in particular. It reaches each soul in a way that is unique and exceptional. This joy is announced to me in a different way than to any one else; it is to me and for me that a Saviour is born. Let us recognise the Nativity of Christ as a very personal gift. Let us receive this gift with faith and thankfulness.

'And lo, the star, which they saw in the east, went before them, till it came and stood over where the young child was.'[11] The Magi followed the light which was given to them faithfully: being obedient to this light, they were led by it to the child. If I try to be faithful to the full measure of light that God has given me, if I have the courage to leave all to follow the star, if I decide to be true and obedient to my conscience (whatever may happen), and ready to 'bear witness of the Light . . . that was the true Light, which lighteth every man that cometh into the world'[12], the divine light will not fail, despite my ignorance, to lead me − not in any abstract way, but through all the concrete circumstances of life, and whenever it is needed − right up to the Child in whom I have placed all my hope.

'And she brought forth her first-born son, and wrapped him in swaddling clothes, and laid him in a manger; because there was no room for them in the inn'[13]. This birth in a manger declares that Jesus wants to be counted among the poorest, among the most humble; he will be found among the disinherited, the sick, the prisoners, the sinners. I would rather be poor with Jesus than be rich without Jesus. I prefer to be in a cave with Jesus, Mary and Joseph than in the inn where there is no room for them. Then, too, we must accept the fact that, for those who love Jesus, there is no place in this world. 'The Son of man hath not where to lay his head'[14].

'And this shall be a sign unto you; Ye shall find the babe wrapped in swaddling clothes . . . .'[15] I seek a God and a Lord, and I find a tiny child. The message of Christmas is a message of childhood: 'Verily I say unto you, Whosoever shall not receive the kingdom of God as a little child shall in no wise enter therein'[16]. God does not ask us to renounce the adult knowledge and discretion needed to accomplish our earthly tasks, but, in our relations with him, he wants us to return to the trusting simplicity of a child. The child has faith in his father; he walks hand in hand with him; he knows that his father will lead him where he needs to go, he knows that his father will protect him, feed and shelter him; he allows himself to be led by his father, eyes shut, without the least anxiety. When he speaks to his father, he does not try to use any complicated formula, he says quite simply and affectionately what he wants to say. And this is what the little child of Bethlehem symbolises for us[17]. Furthermore, Jesus's childhood is more than a model to be imitated; it is one of those mysteries of the Saviour's life which, although they are historical and transitory, also have an eternal reality; Christmas is a favourable time at which to honour the mystery of Jesus's childhood.

'They saw the young child with Mary his mother, and fell down, and worshipped him: and when they had opened their treasures, they presented unto him gifts; gold, and frankincense, and myrrh.'[18] Like the Magi, we offer our treasures and we offer the little child the most precious things we have. In spirit we offer gold, the sign of Jesus's sovereignty over all riches and all created things, a sign also of our own detachment from earthly goods. In spirit we offer incense, the sign of adoration, for Jesus is not only the king of the universe, he is our God. We offer in spirit myrrh, the spice with which we honour in advance the death and burial of Jesus and through which too, is represented our own renunciation of bodily pleasures. Lord Jesus, accept my offering.

'And the shepherds returned, glorifying and praising God for all the things that they had heard and seen . . . .'[19] Lord Jesus, before we leave Bethlehem, or come to the end of this feast of the Nativity, allow us to see something of what the shepherds saw, to hear something of what they heard, and to receive in our hearts the message which is preached to us from the manger.

'Ye are the body of Christ, and members in particular.'[20] The feast of Christmas is the feast of the mystical Body, for it is through the Incarnation that men have become members of Christ. Whatever theological interpretation we give to this great scriptural and patristic affirmation of our incorporation into Christ[21], we must believe that with the Incarnation, an ineffable union — that passes all understanding — began, in human flesh, between Jesus Christ and men. Beyond the particular historical event which took place at Bethlehem and through which the Son of God took on a visible human body, another event took place that concerns the whole human race: God, in becoming incarnate, in some way weds and assumes the human nature which we all share and creates between himself and us a relationship which, without its ever ceasing to be that between the Creator and his creature, is also that between the body and its members. There is union without confusion. Christmas allows us to become most deeply conscious of what is our true nature, human nature, regenerated by Jesus Christ[22].

'And the Word was made flesh'[23]. These words summarise and express the feast of Christmas perfectly. If we give them their full meaning, we will understand that they do not only concern the mystery by which the Son and Word of the Father became man: this formula also carries an implication of a moral and practical order. Our flesh is often a source of temptation and sin to us. May the Word of God therefore become flesh in us, may it enter into our body. May the power of this Word (for there can be no question of its being an Incarnation in substance) pass from the exterior to the interior, and so, into our bodies; then the law of the Spirit will prevail over the law of the flesh. Christmas will have a true meaning for us only if our own flesh becomes transformed, changed and ruled by the Word made flesh.

The Day after Christmas

December 26th is called the 'synaxis' of the Blessed Virgin Mary. Here, the word 'synaxis' has a double meaning. On the one hand, it invites believers to gather in honour of the Mother of God[24]. On the other hand, it recalls the fact that Mary has a central place amongst the glorified saints; we venerate her today as surrounded by all the saints and all the angels; the heavenly gathering corresponds to our earthly gathering. It is fitting, therefore, that having celebrated the nativity of Christ our thoughts should turn first to his Mother, towards the person who is the link between God become man and humankind[25]. The epistle (Heb. 2. 11-18), that we heard first on Christmas Eve, at the office of Nones, contains a phrase which could have been placed on Mary's lips: I and the children which God hath given me'[26]. Here, indeed, is Mary, and here, with her, the children whom God has given her, that is to say first of all Jesus, then all men − the adopted brothers of Jesus. The gospel for this day is the same as for the Sunday after Christmas, of which we shall speak later.

David, James and Joseph

The Sunday which follows December 25th is dedicated to the commemoration of three members of Christ's earthly family: the prophet David; the apostle James, 'brother' of the Lord; and St Joseph, the husband of Mary, and foster-father of Jesus.

David is not only an ancestor of Christ. As a shepherd, he prefigures Jesus the Good Shepherd. As King, he mysteriously announces the royalty of Christ. As an adulterer and murderer, he is the type of the repentant sinner. As the author of the psalms (or, at any rate, some of them), he has bequeathed to the synagogue and to the Christian Church a type of prayer, of adoration in spirit and in truth, that Jesus Himself used, and in which all generations have found expression for the deepest longings of their souls.

James, 'brother' of the Lord[27], was head of the first Christian community in Jerusalem. His name reminds us of the link which connects us with the Church of Jerusalem, with that of the first century as much as with that of the twentieth century. Antioch and Alexandria, Rome and Constantinople are great and venerable names in the history of the Christian Church; but it is from Jerusalem that we are first of all descended. The epistle for the day is a passage from Paul's letter to the Galatians (1. 11-19), chosen because of one sentence in which Paul recalls that after his conversion he saw 'James the Lord's brother' in Jerusalem. But this feast should inspire us to read the 'catholic' epistle[28] of St James again, in which we find so many precious words, such as these:

'Let no man say when he is tempted, I am tempted of God: for God cannot be tempted with evil, neither tempteth he any man.'[29]

'Pure religion and undefiled before God and the Father is this, To visit the fatherless and widows in their affliction, and to keep himself unspotted from the world.'[30]

'As the body without the spirit is dead, so faith without works is dead also.'[31]

'If any man offend not in word, the same is a perfect man, and able also to bridle the whole body.'[32]

'Ye rich men, weep and howl for your miseries that shall come upon you.'[33]

The person of St Joseph has had less attention and homage paid to him in the east than in the Roman west. We know very few things about Joseph[34]. But the gospel tells us that he was a just man, obedient to the angelic messages, careful to protect Jesus and Mary. We could, with advantage, grant him a greater place in our devotion. He is the most eminent representative of what one might call the holiness of the layman, which is neither the holiness of an apostle, nor that of a bishop or a priest, nor that of a monk — all of whom are so abundantly commemorated in the ecclesiastical calendar — but is that of the head of a family, of the man who plies a trade and earns his daily bread. St Joseph is the natural protector of Christian families, of workmen, of those whose food is not assured. For he fed Jesus and Mary, as formerly the patriarch Joseph, in Egypt, fed his brothers and father in the time of famine. Tradition also links the name of St Joseph with Egypt: the flight into Egypt is the theme of the gospel for this day (Matt 2. 13-23). This episode is not without its difficulties for historical exegesis[35], but we can find in it a very clear spiritual teaching for ourselves. The angel commands us, as he did Joseph: 'Arise, and take the young child and his mother, and flee into Egypt'. That is to say: renounce your sin and your slackness; take into your soul the Jesus you saw at Bethlehem and Mary, whom you must never separate from her son; flee the evil and the temptations that surround you; set yourself a hidden, retired, silent life, a life of intimacy with the small child and his mother — and also with Joseph. May the life of the Holy Family, whether in Egypt, or later on at Nazareth, become an inspiration and a model for us.

St Stephen, Protomartyr

'Yesterday, the King was born in the flesh; and today his servant is stoned and dies for love of Him . . . .' Thus sings the Church on December 27th, in the *kontakion* in honour of the first deacon and first martyr, Stephen. He opens the history, which is so moving and rich, of Christian martyrdom[36]. We will read again the account of the election of the first seven deacons and of Stephen's death in the Acts of the Apostles[37]. Simplicity and the sublime are united in the last words of this account: 'And they stoned Stephen, calling upon God, and saying, Lord, lay not this sin to their charge. And when he had said this, he fell asleep'. Another aspect of Stephen's Passion also holds our attention. During the debate between Stephen and his accusers, 'all that sat in the council, looking stedfastly on him, saw his face as it had been the face of an angel'. And, while his adversaries were gnashing their teeth, 'he, being full of the Holy Ghost, looked up stedfastly into heaven, and saw the glory of God, and Jesus standing on the right hand of God'. We are not Stephen; but, while keeping a due sense of proportion, the attitude of the first martyr in the midst of abuse and contradictions shows what our own attitude should be in the midst of such conflicts as we may be involved in. A Christian, in a discussion, must keep his eyes on heaven, and on the glory of God and Jesus; and his bearing and words must be such that those who contradict him can see his face 'as it had been the face of an angel'. The martyrdom of Stephen already contained a great victory for grace: those who stoned Stephen 'laid down their clothes at a young man's feet, whose name was Saul . . . and Saul was consenting unto his death'. But Saul was already destined to become Paul and the hour was not far off when he was to meet Jesus on the road to Damascus.

The Innocents

On December 29th, the Church celebrates the memory of those children from the region of Bethlehem who were put to death by King Herod in order to do away with the Messiah whom he feared and whose birth had been announced to him by the Magi[38]. Is this episode entirely alien to our spiritual life? Do we not also have on our hands the blood of innocent children whom we have killed? This question must be understood in a spiritual sense. Each time that we may perhaps have seduced or deeply shocked a soul, or that we may have been the cause of someone else committing a sin, we have killed, spiritually. God uses to us the same words that he addressed to the first murderer: 'Cain, Where is Abel thy brother?'[39] Our Lord also says to us: 'Offences will come: but woe unto him, through whom they come! It were better for him that a millstone were hanged about his neck, and he cast into the sea, than that he should offend one of these little ones'[40]. Another massacre of the innocents takes place only too frequently in our own soul. At every moment, God puts 'good thoughts' into our minds, so that they might become 'good desires' in us, but very often we stifle these divine suggestions, killing them as soon as they are born. In this way, we massacre the Innocents, for these thoughts were like children who could have grown and borne blessed fruit. Do we, ourselves, not hear Rachel 'weeping for her children . . . because they are not'[41].

The Circumcision of Our Lord

January 1st is the feast of the circumcision of Jesus Christ; it is also the day dedicated to the memory of St Basil.

Vespers for the circumcision, which are celebrated on the evening of December 31st, include three lessons taken from the Old Testament. The first (Gen. 17. 1-7, 9-14) reminds us of the covenant which God made with Abraham: 'Every man child among you shall be circumcised . . . my covenant shall be in your flesh for an everlasting covenant'[42]. The second and third lessons, taken respectively from the Book of Proverbs (8. 22-30) and the Book of Wisdom (9. 1-5 and other verses), sing the praises of divine wisdom; they are an allusion to the theological work of St Basil. At matins for January 1st, the gospel (John 10. 1-9) — which depicts the relationship of the good shepherd to his sheep — also refers to St Basil, this time in his capacity as a bishop. At the liturgy, the epistle (Col. 2. 8-12) points out the new meaning that circumcision has taken on for a Christian: 'In whom also ye are circumcised with the circumcision made without hands, in putting off the body of the sins of the flesh'. The gospel (Luke 2. 20-21, 40-52) tells of Jesus's circumcision — 'when eight days were accomplished for the circumcising of the child, his name was called Jesus' — and of the episode when Jesus was lost, and found again in the Temple, during his parents' annual pilgrimage to Jerusalem.

The feast of the circumcision of Our Lord — perhaps because it evokes the Jewish and pre-Christian character of the rite, perhaps because it coincides with the first day of the civil year — is one of the feasts which seems to speak least to the soul of modern Christians[43]. However, its spiritual content is very rich. Our Lord, in submitting to the law of circumcision, wants both to humiliate himself in his flesh and to mark that he is the fulness and completion of the Old Covenant: the perpetual sign of the Covenant was on his flesh more than on any other flesh; his circumcision prefigured that other bloody consecration which his body was to receive on the cross. Moreover, even if we no longer have to submit to physical circumcision, we still have to submit to a true spiritual circumcision. Our covenant with God, the new covenant in Jesus Christ, must bring about in us the complete submission of our flesh and of its desires to God, the complete consecration and sanctification of our body and of its natural functions (especially of those connected with the organ submitted to circumcision, which plays such an important part in the ascetic battle). And it is not only our flesh that needs spiritual circumcision; first, and before all else, it is our heart. Circumcision of the heart must reach all our thoughts, all our desires, all our feelings − and excise everything that is in conflict with the search for God. The great commandment: 'Thou shalt love the Lord thy God with *all* thy heart . . .' expresses very well, what this circumcision of the heart means and that it does not take place without very serious effort.

'Today the Lord is circumcised in his flesh, and is given the name of Jesus', the choir sings at vespers in the ninth canticle. The feast of the circumcision is also the feast of the Name of Jesus. It reminds us what a central place the invocation of this name must occupy in our spiritual life, and of the power it possesses[44]: 'Wherefore God also hath highly exalted him, and given him a name which is above every name: that at the name of Jesus every knee should bow, of things in heaven, and things in earth, and things under the earth[45] . . .'. 'Lord . . . by stretching forth thine hand to heal . . . that signs and wonders may be done by the name of thy holy child Jesus'[46].

The last words of the gospel for this day give us the only information that we have about Jesus's hidden life in Nazareth. 'And he went down with them, and came to Nazareth, and was subject unto them[47] . . . . And Jesus increased in wisdom and stature, and in favour with God and man.'[48] If the second part raises an interesting theological problem[49], the first part sets before us the model of a humble and obedient life.

One of the chants for vespers subtly links the memory of St Basil to that of the circumcision: 'O wise Father Basil, thou hast circumcised thine uncircumcision through love of philosophy'. The word 'philosophy' is used here in the sense often given to it by the Fathers of the Church: all searching for divine wisdom, every effort of the mind to find God. In effect, destroying 'every high thing that exalteth itself against the knowledge of God, and bringing into captivity every thought to the obedience of Christ', as St Paul says[50], is a noble form of circumcision. We will not say much about St Basil now, as we shall speak of him again at the feast on January 30th.

The Sunday before Epiphany

The time of Bethlehem and Nazareth is drawing to a close. After about thirty years of hidden life, which were made holy by humble work with his hands and by obedience, Jesus is soon to be revealed to the world. In the same way that, in spirit, we went to the manger at Bethlehem, we shall go, guided by the angels, towards the river where the Father will manifest his Son. 'Go ye, O angelic powers, moving on from Bethlehem to the flow of the Jordan.' This is sung by the Church at matins for the Sunday which precedes Epiphany. Not only does the Church associate herself with the joy of the angels who will be present at the baptism of Christ, as they were present at the Nativity, but she invites men, too, to draw near to the Jordan, and tells them what it is that they will receive there. For, at vespers on the Saturday evening, she sings: 'Let us, the faithful, prepare with just praise for the coming feast of the baptism of our God. Behold he has put on our flesh . . . and asks for the baptism of salvation so that he might regenerate all those who, in purity, have been illumined by faith, all those who share in his Spirit'. And again: 'In truth Christ our God comes to be baptised in the Jordan, and through his coming takes upon himself the cleansing of our sins'. These words indicate briefly and precisely the double purpose of the grace which Epiphany brings to men. On the one hand, it is a grace for purification and for the remission of sins; on the other, a grace for illumination and participation in the Holy Spirit. We draw near to the Jordan desiring and humbly asking for this double grace. We would not, however, be true to the genius of the eastern Church (and of the universal Church) if we reduced the meaning of Epiphany to these gifts of pardon and light which it offers to sinful men. Even before offering us these special graces, it is an objective glorification of Christ. We should be capable of selfless joy in the presence of this mystery of Epiphany. Our hymn of praise must take precedence over our prayer of petition.

The gospel and epistle read at the liturgy for the Sunday before Epiphany are devoted to the memory of John the Baptist and Precursor who, at Epiphany itself, is the one who, in a way, presents Jesus Christ to the world. The gospel (Mark 1. 1-8) brings us the austere figure of John, preparing the way, crying in the wilderness, preaching the baptism of repentance; John, clothed with camel's hair, feeding on locusts[51] and wild honey; John, an-

nouncing that another will come after him, the latchet of whose
shoes he is not worthy to unloose, who will baptise not with water
but with the Holy Ghost. In the epistle (2 Tim. 4. 5-8), the apostle
Paul urges his disciple to watch, to endure afflictions, to do the
work of an evangelist; he reminds Timothy that he himself is
ready to depart, to 'be offered', having fought the good fight and
run his course, and that a crown of righteousness awaits him.
These words are suited to Paul, but they apply just as well to John
the Precursor, whose life will be 'offered', that is to say ended in a
bloody way, soon after he has baptised Jesus. Paul's exhortation
to Timothy: 'make full proof of thy ministry', is also the call that
the Church addresses to John: prepare thyself, Precursor, to accomplish the chief act of thy ministry, which is to baptise Jesus
and to proclaim to the world: 'Behold the Lamb of God'.

We shall come back later − in connection with the feast of
January 7th − to the significance of the person, the message, and
the baptism by St John the Baptist. Today, it is enough to say
this: the best preparation for the baptism that Jesus confers is
John's baptism, in the same way that John's preaching is the best
preparation for Jesus's preaching. 'The voice of one crying in the
wilderness, Prepare ye the way of the Lord, make his paths
straight. . . . The baptism of repentance for the remission of sins
. . . .' Moral uprightness and repentance for our sins, these are
the two lessons that we can learn today at the feet of the Precursor. Austerity and justice in our conduct, inner and outward
penitence, and, also, exultation at the coming of the Saviour −
'There cometh one mightier than I after me' − let us listen to
these themes which make up John's call; let us listen to the voice
which cries in the wilderness.

The Vigil for Epiphany

On January 5th, we celebrate the 'great hours'. These, like the
'royal hours' for Christmas Eve, are the canonical hours, each
one comprising three psalms, antiphons, a lesson from the Old
Testament, an epistle and a gospel. At Prime, the lesson taken
from the prophet Isaiah (35. 1-10) announces that 'in the
wilderness shall waters break out . . . and the parched ground
shall become a pool, and the thirsty land springs of water'. The
epistle, taken from the Book of Acts (13. 25-33), is chosen
because of the allusion that Paul, preaching in the synagogue at
Antioch in Pisidia, makes to John the Baptist in recalling his

words: 'But, behold, there cometh one after me . . .'. The gospel
(Matt. 3. 1-6) tells again of the preaching of John in the
wilderness: 'Repent ye: for the kingdom of heaven is at hand . . .'.
At Terce, another lesson from Isaiah (1. 16-20) speaks of the
water that cleanses. 'Wash you, make you clean . . . though your
sins be as scarlet, they shall be as white as snow'. The epistle (Acts
19. 1-8) gives us St Paul saying to certain disciples at Ephesus that
the baptism by John is not sufficient: they must receive the Holy
Spirit. The gospel is the same as for the Sunday preceding
Epiphany, which we have already spoken about. At Sext, the
lesson from Isaiah (12. 3-6) again touches on the theme of water:
'With joy shall ye draw water out of the wells of salvation . . .'.
The epistle of Paul to the Romans (6. 3-11) deals with the
sacrificial significance of baptism: 'Know ye not, that so many of
us as were baptised into Jesus Christ were baptised into his death?'
The gospel (Mark 1. 9-11) already gives us the account of Jesus's
baptism by John. At Nones, the theme of water is taken up again
in Isaiah (49. 8-15): 'he that hath mercy on them shall lead them,
even by the springs of water shall he guide them': The epistle of
Paul to Titus (2. 11-15, 3. 4-7) speaks of baptism: 'After that the
kindness and love of God our Saviour toward man appeared . . .
he saved us, by the washing of regeneration, and renewing of the
Holy Ghost; Which he shed on us abundantly through Jesus
Christ our Saviour'. The gospel (Luke 3. 1-18), when it has given
the events their historical context ('In the fifteenth year of the
reign of Tiberius Caesar, Pontius Pilate being governor of
Judaea, and Herod being tetrarch of Galilee . . . Annas and
Caiaphas being the high priests'), goes on to describe the mission
and the preaching of John the Baptist.

The 'great hours' are immediately followed by vespers. During
these, we hear three lessons from the Old Testament. The first
(Gen. 1. 1-13) recalls how, at the time of the creation, 'The Spirit
of God moved upon the face of the waters'. The second (2 Kings,
or, following the numeration of the Septuagint, 4 Kgs. 2. 6-14)
shows us Elijah dividing the waters of the Jordan with his mantle
and crossing the river-bed, and Elisha repeating this miracle later
on with the mantle of his master. The third lesson (4 Kgs. 2.
19-22) presents us with Elisha casting salt into the waters which
were carriers of sterility and death, and making them healthy.
Here, vespers merge into the liturgy[52]. The service continues with
the reading of the epistle for the liturgy (1 Cor. 9. 19-27); perhaps
the choice of this text is explained by a phrase in which St Paul

says: 'Though I be free from all men . . . to them that are under the law, (I became) as under the law'; this saying can be applied to our Lord, who submitted to the baptism of John without being in any way obliged to. The gospel for the liturgy is the same as that for Nones, of which we have already spoken. The liturgy follows its normal course.

After the liturgy, the blessing of the waters takes place. The clergy move in procession to a basin or vessel filled with water. The prophecy of Isaiah, which was read at Terce, is read again, then another lesson from Isaiah (the whole of chapter 55) which begins thus: 'Every one that thirsteth, come ye to the waters . . .', and finally the lesson from Isaiah which was read at Sext. A passage from the first epistle to the Corinthians (10. 1-4) is added; Paul recalls that 'our fathers . . . were all baptised unto Moses in the cloud and in the sea . . . and did all drink the same spiritual drink; for they drank of that spiritual Rock that followed them: and that rock was Christ'[53]. The biblical readings end with the same portion of the gospel as was read at Sext. A litany follows, during, or at the end of which, the priest reads a secret prayer desiring our Lord to 'sprinkle us . . . with pure water, the gift of thy tenderness of heart'. Then the priest reads two long prayers aloud, in which are gathered numerous biblical references to water, to the Red Sea, to the Jordan. He entreats God to hallow the water in front of him, and with his hand, traces on this water the sign of the cross. He plunges the cross itself into it, holding it upright, and then lifts it out: this gesture symbolises Jesus receiving baptism by immersion in the Jordan. Finally, the priest sprinkles all the congregation with the water. The choir sings, 'Let us therefore draw this water with joy . . . for to those who draw of it, the grace of the spirit is given invisibly'.

The vigil of Epiphany should be observed as a day of strict fast, in the same way as Christmas Eve.

The Feast of Epiphany

January 6th, the day of Epiphany, or of the Theophany is − after Easter and Pentecost − the greatest feast of the Churches of the Byzantine rite. As we have already said, it is even greater than the feast of the Nativity of Christ[54]. It commemorates the baptism of our Lord by John in the waters of the Jordan and, more generally, the public manifestation of the incarnate Word to the world.

At matins for Epiphany, which are sung on the evening of January 5th or the morning of the 6th, the very short gospel already read at Sext during the great hours of the vigil (see above) is read. Here are some extracts from the chants:

'We behold an earthly event, but what we comprehend is higher than the heavens; through cleansing comes salvation; through water, the Spirit; through descent into the water, our ascent to God.'

'He who takes away the sin of the world is cleansed, that I might be made clean.'

'Christ our God, Light of Lights, God made manifest, has shone upon the world. O ye peoples, let us glorify him.'

'The true Light has appeared, illumining the world.'

'Let the whole universe rejoice, for Christ has appeared in the Jordan . . . . In flesh, God the Word has appeared to all humanity.'

At the liturgy, on January 6th[55], the following *troparion* is sung.

'When Thou, O Lord, wast baptised in the Jordan, the worship of the Trinity was made manifest. For the voice of the Father bore witness unto Thee, calling Thee the beloved Son, and the Spirit in the form of a dove confirmed His word as sure and steadfast. O Christ our God who hast appeared and enlightened the world, Glory to Thee.'

And the following *kontakion*:

'Today Thou hast appeared to the inhabited earth, and Thy light, O Lord, has shown itself to us, who with knowledge sing Thy praise: Thou hast come, Thou art made manifest, the Light that no man can approach.'

Instead of the *Trisagion*, we sing as we did on Christmas Day: 'As many of you as were baptised into Christ, have put on Christ. Alleluia'.

The epistle is the same as that read at Nones, during the 'great hours' (see above). The gospel according to St Matthew (3. 13-17) tells of the baptism of Jesus and the descent of the dove. When communion is being offered, the following is sung: 'The grace of God, that bringeth salvation unto all men hath appeared, Alleluia'. The final blessing given by the priest begins with these words: 'O Thou, who for our salvation was pleased to accept baptism from John in the Jordan . . .'.

The waters which were blessed on January 5th are blessed again on the 6th, either after matins or after the liturgy.

Meditation on Epiphany

Let us interrupt our description of the liturgical life of the Church for a little while here, as we did at Christmas, and turn our attention to the mysteries which these outward rites symbolise.

Epiphany is the first public manifestation of Christ. At the time of His birth, our Lord was revealed to a few privileged people. Today, all those who surround John, that is to say his own disciples and the crowd that has come to the banks of the Jordan, witness a more solemn manifestation of Jesus Christ. What does this manifestation consist of? It is made up of two aspects. On the one hand, there is the aspect of humility represented by the baptism to which our Lord submits: on the other hand, there is the aspect of glory represented by the human witness that the Precursor bears to Jesus, and, on an infinitely higher plane, the divine witness which the Father and the Spirit bear to the Son. We shall look at these aspects more closely. But first of all, let us bear this in mind: every manifestation of Jesus Christ, both in history and in the inner life of each man, is simultaneously a manifestation of humility and of glory. Whoever tries to separate these two aspects of Christ commits an error which falsifies the whole of spiritual life. I cannot approach the glorified Christ without, at the same time, approaching the humiliated Christ, nor the humiliated Christ without approaching the glorified Christ. If I desire Christ to be manifested in me, in my life, this cannot come about except through embracing him whom Augustine delighted to call *Christus humilis*, and, in the same upsurge, worshipping him who is also God, King, and Conqueror. This is the first lesson of Epiphany.

The aspect of humility in Epiphany consists of the fact that Our Lord submits to John's baptism of repentance. John himself refuses to begin with, but Jesus insists: 'Suffer it to be so now: for thus it becometh us to fulfil all righteousness'[56]. Obviously Jesus had no need to be purified by John, but this baptism conferred by the Precursor, this baptism for the remission of sins[57], was a preparation for the messianic kingdom; and Jesus, before proclaiming the coming of this kingdom, wished to go through all those preparatory phases which he himself was to 'consummate'. Being himself the fulness, he wished to take into himself all that was still incomplete and unfinished. But, in receiving the Johannine baptism, Jesus did more than solemnly approve and confirm a rite before transforming it — more than consummate the imperfect into the perfect. He who was without sin made himself the bearer of all our sins, of the sin of the whole world; and it is in the name of all sinners that Jesus made a public act of repentance. Moreover, Jesus wished to teach us the necessity of penitence and conversion; before we can draw near to Christian baptism itself, we must receive John's baptism, that means we have to go through a change of spirit, through an inner catastrophe. We must experience real contrition for our sinfulness. As far as we ourselves are concerned, repentance is the aspect of humility in Epiphany. And here we must go beyond the limited horizon of the Johannine baptism and remind ourselves that we have been baptised in Christ. Christian baptism has washed and purified us. It has abolished original sin in us and made a new creature of us. We were probably infants when we were baptised; baptismal grace was then a divine response, not to our personal request, but to the faith of those who brought us to baptism and also to the faith of the whole Church when it accepted us. This baptismal grace was, then, in some way provisional and conditional: it needed us, of our own free choice as we grew up and became conscious, to confirm the act of our baptism. Epiphany is, above all, the feast of baptism, not only of Jesus's baptism, but also of our own. It is a wonderful opportunity for us to renew in spirit the baptism that we received, and to revive the grace which was conferred on us. For the sacramental graces, even if interrupted and suspended by sin, can become alive in us again, if we turn sincerely to God. At this feast of Epiphany, let us ask God to wash us again – spiritually, not actually[58] – in the waters of baptism; let us drown the old, the sinful, creature in them, for baptism is a mystical death[59]; let us cross the Red Sea which separates captivity from freedom and let us immerse ourselves with Jesus in the Jordan to be washed not by the Precursor, but by Jesus himself.

The glorious aspect of Epiphany consists of the two testimonies solemnly given to Jesus. There was John's testimony, which we shall not speak of now, but when we come to the day after Epiphany. And there was the divine testimony of the Father and of the Spirit. The testimony of the Father was the voice that came from heaven and said: 'This is my beloved Son, in whom I am well pleased'[60]. The testimony of the Spirit was the descent of the dove: 'The Spirit of God descending like a dove'[61]. This is Jesus's true baptism. The word spoken by the Father and the descent of the dove[62] are more important than the baptism by water that

John conferred on Jesus. The baptism by water was but an intro-
duction to this divine manifestation. It is with good reason that,
in the early Christian liturgy, the feast of January 6th was called
not a 'theophany' but 'theophanies', in the plural, for it does not
only concern one divine manifestation: there are three manifestations. From the time of Jesus's baptism, the Father, the Son,
and the Spirit are all three revealed to the world; the Father and
the Spirit are revealed in the relationship of love which unites
them to the Son. We touch here on what is deepest and most
intimate in the mystery of Jesus. However great is the redemptive
ministry of Christ towards men, the life of intimacy of the Son
with the Father and the Spirit remains a still greater reality. Jesus
is not truly manifested to us unless we perceive something of this
divine intimacy, and unless, inwardly, we hear the voice of the
Father: 'This is my beloved Son . . .' and see the flight of the dove
lighting upon the head of the Saviour. Only on this condition will
the feast of Epiphany be a true Epiphany, the manifestation of
Christ. Our devotion must, in the Son, reach to the Father and
the Spirit. We need to be able to remember and testify, like John
the Baptist: 'I saw the Spirit descending . . .'[63]. In that lies the
glory of Epiphany. And that is why Epiphany is not only the feast
of the waters. Ancient Greek tradition calls it 'the feast of lights'.
This feast brings us, not only the grace of purification, but also
the grace of illumination (in fact baptism itself was formerly
called 'illumination'). The light of Christ at Christmas was but a
star in the dark night; at Epiphany it appears to us as the rising
sun; it will grow and, after the eclipse of Holy Friday, burst forth
yet more splendid, on the morning of Easter; and finally, at
Pentecost, it will reach its full zenith. It is not only the divine
light, manifested objectively in the person of Jesus Christ and in
the pentecostal flame that we are concerned with, it is also the inner light, for, without absolute faithfulness to this, spiritual life
would be nothing but illusion and falsehood.

God, who had sent the Precursor to baptise with water, had
said to him: 'Upon whom thou shalt see the Spirit descending,
and remaining on him, the same is he which baptiseth with the
Holy Ghost'[64]. The baptism by water is but one aspect of total
baptism. Jesus himself says to Nicodemus: 'Except a man be born
of water and of the Spirit, he cannot enter into the kingdom of
God'[65]. The baptism of the Spirit is superior to the baptism by
water. It constitutes an objective gift and a different inner experience. We shall say more about this on the occasion of Pentecost.

One could say that Epiphany — the first public manifestation of Jesus to men — corresponds in our inner life to the 'first conversion'. This must be understood as the first conscious meeting of the human soul with its Saviour, the moment when we accept Jesus as Master and as friend, and at which we take the decision to follow him. Easter (both the death and the resurrection of the Lord) corresponds to a 'second conversion' in which, confronted with the mystery of the cross, we discover what kind of death and what kind of new life this implies, and we consecrate ourselves more deeply to Jesus Christ, through a radical change in ourselves. Pentecost is the time of the 'third conversion', which is the baptism and fire of the Spirit, the entry into a life of transforming union with God. It is not given to every Christian to follow this itinerary. Nonetheless, these are the stages which the liturgical year sets out for our endeavour[66]

The Precursor

The day after Christmas is consecrated to the 'synaxis' of the Blessed Virgin Mary: all believers are invited to assemble in honour of her who made the Incarnation humanly possible. In the same way, the day after Epiphany (January 7th) is consecrated to the 'synaxis' of John the Precursor, who baptised Jesus and, in a way, was the agent in presenting him to the world. In the chants for this feast, at vespers and matins, the Church multiplies the praises of the Precursor: 'Thou who art Light in the flesh . . . filled with the Spirit . . . swallow of grace . . . who hast appeared as the last of the prophets . . . and the greatest amongst them . . .'. The very richness of these praises make it a little difficult for us, perhaps, to discern clearly what it is that we, as men, have to learn from John. During the course of the liturgical year, we shall have other opportunities to return to the person and the ministry of this man who was not only the Precursor and the Baptist, but also the Friend of the Bridegroom, the new Elijah, and the martyr who gave his life for the divine law. Today it will be enough for us to concentrate on two facets of John's ministry, and these are indicated by the gospel and the epistle which are read at the liturgy.

The epistle, already read at Nones on the eve of Epiphany (Acts 19. 1-8) tells of Paul's meeting at Ephesus with the disciples who had received only John's baptism. Paul explains to them that John conferred a baptism of repentance on the people so that they might believe in him who was to come. But Paul baptised these Ephesians 'in the name of the Lord Jesus'. Paul's words point exactly to the greatness and the limitations of John's ministry. On the one hand, we must receive John's baptism of penitence, that is to say, listen to John when he tells us what the conditions are for entry into the messianic kingdom and allow ourselves to be touched by his call to repentance. On the other hand, John's baptism is not sufficient. We must go to Jesus himself. We must be baptised in the name of our Saviour and in the Holy Spirit. This does not simply involve the sacramental rites. What matters is our constant inner attitude. I cannot go to Jesus if I have not listened to John's voice, and if I have not repented. But I cannot remain in the state of repentance that John preached: the new justice that I must move on to is that which Jesus alone procures.

The nature of this new justice is indicated in the gospel read at the liturgy (John 1. 29-34). This passage, which describes Jesus's baptism by the Precursor, begins with the following words: 'John seeth Jesus coming unto him, and saith, Behold the Lamb of God, which taketh away the sin of the world'. This is the second facet of John's ministry: not only does he preach conversion and confer a baptism of repentance, but he shows us Jesus as the Lamb of God and the propitiation for all our sins. John declares that Jesus accomplishes what the baptism of repentance cannot do: the Saviour takes upon his own shoulders the sin of the world and thus cleanses men. John's ministry, therefore, will only be effectual for us if it produces these two results: first that it rouses us to repentance, and then that it shows us the Lamb who offers himself in sacrifice as reparation for our sins. The ministry, or, as we might say, the gospel of the Precursor has a third aspect which will be revealed to us later: the relationship between the Bridegroom and the friend of the Bridegroom. But this aspect is not yet made explicit in the feast of Epiphany. What the 'synaxis' of the Precursor suggests to us today is the breaking of our hearts which repentance demands, and the act of faith by which we entrust our sins to the Lamb of God, and inwardly experience redemption.

The Sunday after Epiphany

This Sunday falls between January 7th and 13th. The gospel (Matt. 4: 12-17) is like an echo of the feast of Epiphany. It starts by mentioning the imprisonment of the Precursor, something we shall speak of later on. At this news, Jesus leaves the region of the Jordan. He comes back into Galilee and stays at Capernaum. Thus, says the gospel, the prophecy of Isaiah concerning the land of Zabulon and the land of Nephthalim is fulfilled: 'The people which sat in darkness saw great light; and to them which sat in the region and shadow of death light is sprung up'[67]. This reminds us that Epiphany is the 'feast of lights'. The light manifested on the banks of the Jordan now spreads into Galilee. Little by little, it will spread to the whole world. Jesus begins to preach. The theme of his preaching is exactly the same as John's: 'Repent, for the kingdom of heaven is at hand'. But, for John, the kingdom was 'coming', whereas for Jesus, the kingdom is already 'at hand': the kingdom is now identified with him who announces it. Jesus is the essence and the power of the kingdom. Nevertheless, this kingdom is only at its beginning. We shall see it grow, and it will not cease from growing until the end of time. This is what the epistle read at the liturgy (Eph. 4. 7-13) announces, in which St Paul declares that when the edification of Christ's body is completed we shall 'all come in the unity of the faith, and of the knowledge of the Son of God, unto a perfect man, unto the measure of the stature of the fulness of Christ'. The liturgical year, an abridgement of the history of salvation, represents this growth symbolically for us, from Christmas until the time after Pentecost. It thus outlines the development of our own inner life — the life of Christ in us.

The Three Hierarchs

The cycle of saints' feasts for this period is marked by commemorations on which we would like to dwell: for instance, there are those of Gregory of Nyssa (January 10th), of the first hermits, Paul (January 15th) and Antony (January 17th), of the patriarchs Athanasius and Cyril of Alexandria (January 18th), of Ephraim of Syria (January 28th) and of the great martyr Ignatius of Antioch, the 'theophore' (January 29th). But we must limit ourselves. We will only speak, and briefly at that, about a feast which the Church considers even greater, that of St Basil the Great, St Gregory the Theologian and St John Chrysostom, all three of them venerated on January 30th.

'Let us fittingly honour these instruments of grace, these harps of the Spirit . . . examples of true praise . . . pride of the Fathers, towers of faith and doctors of the faithful . . . rays and lamps lit by the thrice-ensunned Dawn . . . scented flowers of Paradise . . . .' It is in these terms of lyrical praise that the Church sings of the three great doctors of the Byzantine east. The gospel read at matins is that of the Good Shepherd (John 10. 9-16), which is always read at feasts for bishops who have been canonised. The epistle read at the liturgy (Heb. 13. 17-21) also speaks to us of the shepherds of the Church: 'Obey them that have the rule over you, and submit yourselves: for they watch for your souls, as they that must give account'. The gospel (Matt. 5. 14-19) reminds us that Our Lord said to the disciples: 'Ye are the light of the world . . .'.

Why has the Byzantine Church chosen Basil, Gregory of Nazianzus and Chrysostom to be the supreme representatives of both the pastoral and doctrinal ministry? All three are Fathers of the Church[68], and we know that the Orthodox Church likes to call itself the Church of the Fathers, the Church that desires to retain a devoted attachment to patristic tradition. But there are many other Fathers of the Church, amongst them many martyrs, and many doctors who are perhaps more inspired and more original than the 'three hierarchs'. Perhaps it is precisely because their doctrine and their way are so general that the Church wishes to honour Basil, Gregory and John. Their teaching and their lives constitute very sure standards of 'orthodoxy'. An Ignatius of Antioch, an Origen, a Gregory of Nyssa or an Augustine may have something which is more brilliant. But, to a much greater degree than the three hierarchs, they are outstanding 'individual cases', and they represent a rarer experience. Basil, Gregory and John express the Byzantine tradition at its most accessible; they follow to an eminent degree what might be called the 'general line'. On the other hand, each of the three hierarchs has his own distinctive features. The Church honours special gifts and different missions in each of these three fourth century Fathers.

St Basil[69], as bishop, showed himself the protector of the weak and one who organised charitable works; he drew up monastic laws, reacting against some ascetic and individualistic excesses of the 'desert', and instituted a cenobitism which was moderate, regular, and gave special place to the work of education and of mercy. Though he defended the divinity of the Son and of the Holy Spirit against heretics, he never wished to become an aggressive polemicist, and he was afraid neither of dealing tactfully with the hesitant faith of certain believers nor of showing himself conciliatory in the use of words, as long as there was no doubt about their meaning. St Gregory of Nazianzus[70] was a tender and gracious soul, ill-fitted for the struggle of practical life. He was an orator, a poet, a theologian — and such a one that the Greek Church has called him 'the Theologian'. He defended the dogma of the Trinity vigorously and earned this testimony from one of the writers of the early Church: 'It is a manifest proof of error in the faith not to be in agreement with the faith of Gregory'[71]. St John Chrysostom[72] was a master of the word and a shepherd of souls, who knew how to calm his people, and how to divert the imperial wrath vented against rebels, and who did not hesitate to shelter a brutally disgraced eunuch or to withstand a new Jezebel, a new Herodias, to her face. Unjustly condemned by the bishops, and banished by the civil authorities, he was to die of physical exhaustion suffered on the road to exile. But the teaching which above all we have received from the 'Golden Mouth', is that of a sort of 'gospel' morality, devotion to Holy Scripture — on which this faithful admirer of the apostle Paul commented with such assiduity — and the preaching of alms-giving and charity. The monastic endeavours of Basil, the high theology of Gregory, and the practical evangelism of Chrysostom: these combined are the messages which this feast of the three hierarchs brings us as a vehicle for the three great aspects of Orthodoxy. Let us remember that the Fathers of the Church are still, today, our Fathers, and that they are loving Fathers who are concerned for the salvation of their children. So let us join with the Church at matins in saying to the three hierarchs: 'O blessed Fathers, keep watch, even after your death, over us who praise you!'

The Presentation of Our Lord in the Temple

In accordance with the law of Moses[73], forty days after the birth of a male child its mother had to present it in the tabernacle and to offer as a sacrifice either a lamb or a pair of doves or pigeons for purification 'from the issue of her blood'. The presentation of a first-born son also signified redemption or buying back, for all first-born creatures, whether animal or human, were considered to belong to God[74]. Mary and Joseph obeyed this precept of the law. They brought Jesus to the Temple where he was blessed by the aged Simeon, and recognised as Saviour by the prophetess Anna. It is this event which we celebrate at the feast of February 2nd[75].

At vespers for the feast, on the evening of February 1st, three lessons from the Old Testament are read. The first (Exod. 13. 1-16) formulates the precepts relating to circumcision and purification, which are said to come from the mouth of God speaking to Moses. The second (Isaiah 6. 1-12) describes Isaiah's vision of the seraphim with six wings and the manner in which one of them, with a burning coal, purified the prophet's lips; this passage has very possibly been chosen because of some words which, symbolically, could prefigure the coming of Christ into the Temple: 'The posts of the door moved . . . and the house was filled with smoke . . . for mine eyes have seen the King, the Lord of hosts'. The third lesson (passages from the 19th chapter of Isaiah) cannot be clearly understood unless the whole chapter is read: one then sees that the coming of the Lord in Egypt, the destruction of the Egyptian idols in his presence, and the worship of him by the Egyptians can be applied to the revelation that Christ made of himself to the heathen ('the light to lighten the Gentiles', as it says in the Song of Simeon). The gospel read at matins (Luke 2. 25-32) is an abridgement of the one read at the liturgy (Luke 2. 22-40) and tells of the presentation of Jesus in the Temple. The epistle for the liturgy (Heb. 7. 7-17), speaks of Melchisedec meeting Abraham: so that Levi already paid tithes to Melchisedec 'in Abraham . . . for he was yet in the loins of his father . . .', and the priesthood of Aaron thus paid homage to the eternal priesthood. Similarly, we may infer from this text that the Temple in Jerusalem – in the person of Simeon, who welcomed and blessed Jesus – pays homage to the priesthood of Christ. We know that the Song of Simeon, 'Lord, now lettest thou thy servant depart in peace' has become part of the daily divine office in the Roman as well as in the Byzantine rite. Simeon's words [76] to Mary 'Yea, a sword shall pierce thy own soul also' throw a ray of light on the mystery of the most Holy Virgin's part in the Passion of her Son.

'Let us also go to meet Christ and let us receive him . . . . Adorn thy bridal chamber . . . and welcome Christ the King; salute Mary, the heavenly gate.' These texts from the feast of the Presentation can also be applied to our souls. Each soul ought to be a Temple of God, to which Mary brings Jesus. And each one of us should, like Simeon, take the child in his arms and say to the Father: 'My eyes have seen thy salvation'. The prayer of Simeon, 'now lettest thou thy servant depart in peace' does not simply mean that someone who has seen Jesus and has held him in his arms can now leave this life and die in peace: it also means for us that, having seen and touched the Saviour, we are released from the hold that sin has on us, and, in peace, can leave the realm of evil.

The Grateful Leper

Concern with establishing a certain link between the feasts of Christmas and Epiphany on the one hand, and the Sundays of this period on the other hand, has resulted in several Sundays (for example, the Sunday after Christmas, the Sunday before Epiphany, and the Sunday after Epiphany) becoming isolated from the other Sundays and taking on a special character. The liturgical calendar has given them a special name, and their own epistles, gospels and antiphons. We saw this when speaking of the 'specialised' Sundays, each of which was mentioned in the relevant chronological place. These 'specialised' Sundays are superimposed on some of the ordinary Sundays, that is to say, those that belong to the cycle of Sundays after Pentecost. The pentecostal cycle continues to unfold during the time of Christmas and of Epiphany without the Sundays which belong to it having any real relationship with these feasts because − as we already know − the movable cycle of Sundays and the fixed cycle of feasts remain independent of one another. Some Sundays therefore, have two epistles, and two gospels, etc., and combine those liturgical elements belonging to them as part of the movable cycle of Sundays with such other liturgical elements as are imposed by the proximity of some feast which has a fixed date. In practice, it is the proximity of the fixed feast which is the determining factor and puts what belongs to the movable cycle of Sundays into the background. Having spoken of the Sundays that have become 'specialised' by a nearby feast, we shall now say some words about the Sundays after Pentecost which may happen to fall into the time of Christmas and Epiphany. We know that the allocation of the Sundays after Pentecost − be it at Advent, Christmas or Epiphany − cannot be foretold exactly because this depends each year on the date of Easter. In dealing with the Sundays at Advent, we had reached the twenty-eighth Sunday after Pentecost. We shall now place the four following Sundays in the period of Christmas and Epiphany, and this will take us from the twenty-ninth to the thirty-second Sunday after Pentecost.

The gospel for the twenty-ninth Sunday (Luke 17. 12-19) tells how ten lepers were healed by Jesus, of whom only one − who was a Samaritan − thanked him. And Jesus is astonished that, alone, this stranger gives him thanks: 'Where are the nine?'. We can draw four main lessons from this gospel. First, there is the duty of gratitude that we have towards God, the importance of 'glorifying him' for all the goodness we receive: does thanksgiving occupy the place it ought to in our prayers? Do we not ask for more things than we give thanks for? Then there is the contrast between the ingratitude of the nine Jewish lepers and the sincere gratitude, expressed so vividly − 'with a loud voice glorified God, and fell down on his face at his feet, giving him thanks' − of the Samaritan: may it not be that people whose faith is less true than ours are sometimes more pleasing to God than we are, because their hearts are more appreciative of the divine gifts? And then, once again, there is the relationship which Jesus establishes between faith and healing: 'thy faith hath made thee whole'. Do we possess a faith strong enough to heal us? And finally, there is the analogy between leprosy and sin. The Hebrews easily associated the idea of leprosy with that of moral impurity. Are we ourselves pure and healed of all leprosy? If we are not, do we at least say, with the ten lepers: 'Jesus, Master, have mercy on us'?

The epistle (Col. 3. 4-11) contains certain phrases which − by sheer coincidence − are particularly well-suited to Christmas-time and to the episode of the lepers. Thus: 'When Christ, who is our life, shall appear . . . . Mortify therefore your members which are upon the earth; fornication, uncleanness . . .'. This theme of 'impurity' and of 'healing' reminds us of how Naaman, captain of the Syrian host, who suffered from leprosy, was healed by plunging into the waters of the Jordan, as the prophet Elisha had told him to do[77]. A spiritual interpretation of this episode leads our thoughts to Epiphany, to the manifestation of Jesus in the waters of the same river.

The Rich Ruler

The gospel for the thirtieth Sunday after Pentecost (Luke 18. 18-27) tells us of a rich and powerful man − 'a ruler' − who asked Jesus what was needed to inherit eternal life. Jesus reminds him of the commandments. 'All these have I kept from my youth up . . .'. He lacks one thing, Jesus tells him: to sell all his goods and distribute them to the poor. 'And come, follow me . . . .' But the man goes sorrowfully away, 'for he was very rich'. And Jesus says that it is easier for a camel to go through the eye of a needle than for a rich man to enter into the kingdom of God[78].

Sometimes it is material wealth which stops a man from entering the kingdom but there are possessions other than money. Beauty, intelligence, perhaps some disordered human affection or bad habit: these, just as much, can be hindrances which Jesus tells us to free ourselves of before following him. What are the earthly goods which hold and hinder me, personally, from following Jesus? How can I put these possessions to the service of the poor, and thus liberate my will? The gospel for this Sunday faces each one of us with this question. It is a good question to consider at the time of Christmas, at the time when Jesus comes to us in complete poverty, possessing nothing.

In the epistle read today (Col. 3. 12-16) St Paul enjoins us to adopt an inner attitude 'of mercies, kindness, humbleness of mind, meekness, long-suffering . . . and above all these things put on charity'. This, again, is a message which harmonises singularly well with that of the manger at Bethlehem. The apostle emphasises the calm and joyous nature of Christian life: 'Let the peace of God rule in your hearts . . . singing with grace in your hearts to the Lord'.

The Blind Man of Jericho

As Jesus was nearing Jericho, a blind man in the way called out: 'Jesus, thou son of David, have mercy on me'. Jesus asks what he wants from him, and the blind man begs that he may be given his sight. Jesus says to him: 'Thy faith hath saved thee'.

We can relate this gospel for the thirty-first Sunday after Pentecost (Luke 18. 35-43) in a special way to the feasts of Christmas and Epiphany. On these feasts, the Church gives us the same answer that the crowd gave to the blind man of Jericho: '. . . he asked what it meant, And they told him, that Jesus of Nazareth passeth by . . .'. The great light of Epiphany must not shine in vain in front of those who are blind. Let us ask the Lord Jesus to open our eyes: 'What wilt thou that I shall do unto thee? − Lord, that I may receive my sight'. Our eyes have become darkened by sin and they have lost sensitivity to the divine light. And yet, in God's intention, this vision should be mine. But is my faith strong enough for Jesus to be able to say to me: 'Thy faith hath saved thee'? The blind man of Jericho's faith was very strong, for the more they tried to silence him 'he cried out so much the more, Thou son of David . . .'. They also try to silence me – 'they' being my sins, my passions, the crowd of unbelievers. If I cry all the more strongly when sin tries to stop my voice, and if my call to Jesus rises above the voice of evil, then my faith is indeed a faith that is able to save. Is my faith really of that kind?

The epistle (1 Tim. 1. 15-17) consists of only three verses, and begins with this phrase: 'Christ Jesus came into the world to save sinners; of whom I am chief . . .'. We know these words well, for the Church repeats them to us before each communion. Today, let us give a few moments to consider two aspects of Paul's affirmation: on the one hand, to the humble avowal by which we admit the seriousness of our own sin; on the other, to the certainty that Jesus has come into the world precisely to save us from our sin. Repentance and pardon: these are the two poles of the mystery of our redemption, of which Christ's sacrifice in at the centre.

Zacchaeus

The thirty-second Sunday after Pentecost we continue to read from the first epistle to Timothy (4. 9-15). St Paul advises his disciple, who despite his youth is given high ecclesiastical responsibility, to be an example to all the believers through his faith, his charity and his purity: Paul especially exhorts Timothy to read attentively and to deepen his knowledge of doctrine. He ends: 'Meditate upon these things; give thyself wholly to them . . .'. This call to meditation, to contemplation, continues to be of great importance, even for those – especially for those – who, like Timothy, are absorbed by the duties of active or 'apostolic' life. Paul asks Timothy to give himself 'wholly' to meditating on divine things. What a difference between this 'totality of prayer' and our own meditations, which may be very rare, are often so brief, and nearly always are so far from orienting or encompassing our daily lives! 'Meditate upon these things; give thyself wholly to them . . .'. Let us listen to these words from the apostle as if they were an exhortation he addressed to each of us personally. Let us try to work out how, in practice, in the special circumstances of our own life, we can reserve this dominant place for meditation.

The gospel for this Sunday (Luke 19. 1-10) tells us about the conversion of the publican[79] Zacchaeus. As Jesus passed through Jericho, this rich publican climbed a tree, the better to see him.

Our Lord, having caught sight of Zacchaeus, says to him: 'Make haste, and come down; for today I must abide at thy house'. Jesus's words to Zacchaeus remind us of those from Revelation[80] which are so moving: 'Behold, I stand at the door, and knock: if any man hear my voice, and open the door, I will come in to him,and will sup with him, and he with me'. Jesus is saying to us what he said to Zacchaeus: he wants to come to our home, into our soul — not in a few days' time, or tomorrow — but at this very instant, 'today I must abide at thy house . . .'. Why postpone the inner change which could make Jesus our guest? Through an inner act of repentance and of consecration, I can this moment open the door to the Lord. Let me lose no time, nor allow an opportunity to slip by which might be exceptionally favourable, and which might not come again. 'Make haste, and come down'. I shall indeed hurry — and I shall come down. For Zacchaeus, to come down meant leaving his observation post in the sycamore tree and getting back to earth; for us, it also means renouncing all those poor artifices by which we try to raise ourselves above other men. 'Come down' — so, leave the sycamore into which you have climbed, and leave behind all forms of vanity and pride; it is only on the ground that you will be able to meet Jesus. Zacchaeus obeys. He hurries down. There are two points to notice in this gospel event: Zacchaeus receives Jesus 'joyfully'. Jesus is not a guest with whom we have to stand on ceremony or welcome formally. We must not think of him as one of those visitors who come seldom and are only taken into the reception rooms, the front rooms. He is to be one of those visitors one welcomes 'joyfully' and to whom one says 'make yourself at home. You are one of the household, everything here is at your disposal. Go where you please'. We will not confine him to the sitting room, we shall take him all round, even into those secret rooms — the nethermost regions of our soul — where we have let so much dust and dirt accumulate, and whose existence we conceal from strangers with such care. And then this: that Zacchaeus, who has just undergone an inner change, announces to the Lord that he is going to pay four times the value of anything he might unjustly have charged for, and that he is going to give half his goods to the poor. 'Restitution' and 'sharing', in the fullest sense of these words, in their spiritual as well as their material senses: reparation for the harm we may have done, and sharing in common the benefits we have received: these are the first fruits of all conversion[81].

Those who witnessed this gospel scene murmured that 'he was

gone to be guest with a man that is a sinner . . .'. And Jesus declares: 'The Son of man is come to seek and to save that which was lost'. It is with this saying that the gospel for this Sunday ends. 'That which was lost . . . to seek . . . to save'. Then is there also hope for me?

Here we reach a turning point in the liturgical year. For Jesus's last words in today's gospel announce a different climate from that to which the Nativity and the Baptism of Christ have introduced us. Going beyond the Gospel of the Incarnation, we enter into the Gospel of pardon and salvation. With the thirty-second Sunday after Pentecost, the time of Christmas and of Epiphany comes to an end. Now another liturgical time is coming. Already, in the distance, a procession moves towards us which is no longer that of the shepherds and the Magi, of the Precursor and of his disciples, but a procession in which praises are mixed with curses and the *Vexilla Regis prodeunt, fulget crucis mysterium*[82]. The standards of the King are coming and already, though still distant, shines the mystery of the cross.

Notes to Chapter III

1   The first signs of this celebration come from Egypt. Clement of Alexandria, around the year 200, mentions that certain Egyptians commemorated the birth of Christ on May 20th. In the first half of the fourth century, the constitutions of the Church of Alexandria laid down that January 6th was both the feast of the Nativity and the Epiphany of Christ. We know, however, from the sermons of St Gregory of Nyssa that, in 380, the faithful in Cappadocia celebrated the date of December 25th. We also know that, in 385, December 25th was not celebrated in Jerusalem. Christmas continued to be ignored by the Church in Jerusalem until the sixth century. The celebration of Christmas was introduced at Antioch around 386 by St John Chrysostom. It seems that it was also Chrysostom who introduced Christmas at Constantinople between 398 and 402. In Rome, Christmas was celebrated from 354. Meanwhile the Council of Saragossa in Spain still ignored Christmas in 380, and St Augustine, in the fifth century, omitted it from a list of feasts of the first class which he drew up. Christmas was, nevertheless, gradually recognised throughout the Christian world. Why was December 25th chosen as the feast of the Nativity of Christ? It is more than likely that the Church wished to adapt and 'Christianise' certain pagan feasts which were celebrated around that date, such as the birth of Dionysios at Delphi, the Saturnalia (December 1st — 23rd), and above all the *Natalis Invicti*, or the feast of the 'invincible' sun (the winter solstice), celebrated on December 25th itself. The Fathers of the Church, notably Cyprian, declared that this 'anniversary of the invincible' was made

actual in Jesus's birth, the only 'invincible' one and the Sun of Justice. Other considerations also influenced the choice of December 25th: the date of the Nativity has been made to depend on the date of the conception of Christ, and the Nativity was celebrated nine months after March 25th, the feast of the Annunciation. This date had been chosen for the Annunication because it was thought that Christ was conceived six months after John the Baptist; and the announcement to Zacharias was fixed for September as Zacharias had arbitrarily been made out to be a high priest, and it was remembered that the high priests entered into the sanctuary on the day of Expiation, in September. Such calculations are entirely fanciful. Historically, we know neither the month nor the year of Jesus's birth. What we call 'the Christian era', whose first year coincides with the year 754 after the foundation of Rome, is an invention of the monk Dionysius Exiguus, in the sixth century. In the same way, we have no historical certainty about the date of Jesus's death, or of his age at the time of his death, or of the duration of his public ministry. All that can be said with some degree of probability is that Jesus, at the time of his death, was about thirty years old, and that the period of his preaching could have lasted between one and three years.

2   The liturgy celebrated on December 25th is that of St John Chrysostom, except if the 25th falls on a Sunday or on a Monday, when the liturgy of St Basil is celebrated. From Christmas to Epiphany one must neither kneel during prayer nor fast.

3   Gal. 3. 27.

4   The Magi were a sacred and very influential caste in Persia. The gospel does not mention the number or the names of the Magi who came to adore Jesus. The idea of the 'three kings' belongs to the realm of legend. Various astronomical explanations have been suggested to account for the phenomenon of the star which appeared to the Magi; none of these theories can claim to be decisive. Whatever the exact historical facts were, however, the spiritual meaning of this event is in no way uncertain: the adoration of Jesus by the Magi symbolises the calling of the pagan world, and the divine answer to the longings of so many souls who do not know how to name him for whom they seek. But they do not seek in vain.

5   What is said here does not apply to the early Fathers of the Latin Church. It is in the middle ages, above all with St Bernard of Clairvaux (twelfth century) and St Francis of Assisi (thirteenth century), that western devotion became deeply attached to the humanity of our Lord. The Franciscan influence was foremost in developing the 'devotion to the crib' — which, indeed, is so moving and so spiritually rich.

6   Luke 2. 15.

7   Ps. 121. 1.

8   Luke 2. 4-5.

9   Luke 2. 1, 3.

10   Luke 2. 10, 11.

11   Matt. 2. 9.

12   John 1. 7, 9.

13   Luke 2. 7.

14   Luke 9. 58.

15   Luke 2. 12.

16   Luke 18. 17.

17   Perhaps in this there is a message which is especially well-suited to our times. We know how, in our day, St Theresa of Lisieux has become the apostle of the 'little way' or 'the way of spiritual childhood'. This way offers a remedy for pride, for complications, and also for the despair of modern man.

18   Matt. 2. 11.

19   Luke 2. 20.

20   1 Cor. 12. 27.

21   We have already spoken several times of this doctrine. Perhaps we must now give it more precision. In the phrase 'the Church is the body of Christ' can be seen a simple analogy between a human organism and a social organism. Going further, one can say that the same Holy Spirit animates both Christ and his mystical body. There is thus a communication or circulation of the same supernatural life. St Thomas Aquinas expresses something similar to this when he speaks of the grace which flows from the Head (Christ) over the members of the body (ourselves); the humanity of Christ is the instrument by means of which this 'flowing' is possible. Besides, for St Thomas, grace is a 'physical quality', that is to say it is not simply a material thing but a certain manner of being, grounded in nature. Thomistic views lead us therefore towards a 'physical' concept of the body of Christ. But the Greek Fathers have a yet more ontological, more realist, more physical, concept. For them, this has three main aspects: − (i) Christ, as the Logos or thought of God, contained within himself already, before the Incarnation, all creatures in the state of 'ideas', as objects of his will, of his intelligence and of his love; more exactly, the Logos contained the ideas or representations which corresponded to each creature. In taking human flesh, the Logos imparted this 'universality' to his humanity, so that since the Incarnation, our *ideal* presence in the Logos is mixed with the human nature and the physical body of Jesus. (ii) In addition, the Christology of the Councils and of the Fathers admits that, in the Incarnation, the Divine Person united himself not to a human *person*, but to a human *nature* which was, in a sense, human nature *itself*. The Platonists would say that the Logos assumed the 'idea' of humanity; not as a pale abstraction, but as the richest reality − the reality through participation in which men become truly men. Without necessarily professing Platonism and without going so far as to say that we are physically included in the human nature assumed by the divine person, we could say that this human nature of Christ's, which is not limited by a human person but which can carry humanity to the state of perfection, contains within itself all the potentialities which become actual in the human persons that we are, and thus does communicate with us in a certain physical manner. (iii) Finally, Christ is the new Adam. He is the archetype and supreme model of all humanity. He is what the scholastics would call the 'exemplary cause' of all men. In the same way that every model exists in the copy, and every copy in the model, by an 'intentional' presence which is very real, so the same relation of inclusion exists between Christ and us. It goes without saying that all these manners of speaking are miserably inadequate and deficient. In dealing with this great theandric mystery, we must always remember, on the one hand, that God become man remains absolutely different from man and transcends all creatures, and, on the other, that there is a very real bond of union between his humanity and our humanity, between his person and our persons. His very divinity has an influence over our humanity, for, as the Fathers say, he became man in order to make us divine. Thus, to fall back on metaphors, iron which becomes red-hot in

the fire participates in the fire without becoming identified with it, and the drop of water which is mixed with wine becomes a participant of the wine without becoming identified with the wine. It is interesting that until the end of the middle ages, the expression 'mystical body of Christ' designated the Eucharist and not the Church, which was simply called the Body of Christ. Today, we speak of these inversely. The early way of speaking brought to light clearly the gradation of realities and signs: it expressed that the total Christ, that is to say, what we today call the mystical body — the Head and the members — constitute the supreme reality, of which the historical Christ was in some way the 'sacrament'. If we meditate on this human nature 'common to all men', or, to put it better, 'in communication with all men' that the Logos assumed instead of a particular human personage, we understand better the vital value of these old christological definitions, which seem so far removed from our everyday experience. For, since the human nature of Christ includes potentially all that there is of man, except sin, there is no human situation or possibility which does not have its roots in the person of Christ, and which cannot be thought in him, or illumined and directed by him. The gospel accounts give us a fragmentary view of the human nature of our Lord; Jesus's earthly life revealed the Saviour in certain well-defined aspects: for example, that he led the life of a wandering preacher and was celibate. And yet all human life, all human experience — that of a married man, of a labourer, a financier, or of a peasant, etc. — are somehow latent in the human nature of Jesus, and, at the call and the contact of our analogous needs, graces and mysterious powers flow from these potentialities to us. This is what a Benedictine theologian called the 'reserves of Christ'. One sees what richness, not only of thought, but of practical application, lies within the doctrine of the Body of Christ.

22 The idea of Christmas as the feast of the mystical Body is wonderfully expressed in the words of St Leo, Pope of Rome, which are read on the night of Christmas by the Romans: 'Realise, O Christian, thy dignity and, now that thou art admitted as a partaker of the divine nature, do not return to thy former baseness through a degenerate way of life. Remember whose head and whose body it is of which thou art a member'. (Monastic breviary, eighth lesson of the second nocturn for the matins of the Nativity.) One can see that the Roman Church has more to offer than devotion to the crib. But the humility of the crib must not be depreciated.

23 John 1. 14.

24 The Greek word *synaxis* means assembly.

25 Following St Bernard's very apt analogy, Mary is the 'neck' of the mystical body of Christ, for she was the physical instrument of the Incarnation, and through her the Head and the members of the mystical body were linked. This is the foundation on which the doctrines of Mary's 'universal mediation' in obtaining grace rests. This relative mediation, on the plane of the Incarnation, does not go against the fact that Jesus Christ is the unique and absolute Mediator between God and men.

26 Isa. 8. 18.

27 The New Testament mentions several people with the name of James: thus, the apostle James, son of Zebedee and brother of John; another James, son of Mary the wife of Cleopas; James, brother of the apostle Jude. James, 'brother' of Jesus and head of the Church in Jerusalem, seems to have to been identified with the apostle James, the son of Alpheus. It is possible, however, that Cleopas

and Alpheus are two different transcriptions of the Aramaic name *Halpai*; following this, James son of Alpheus, James 'brother of the Lord', and James son of Cleopas and Mary, would be one and the same person. Following Semitic custom, the word 'brother' can be used of a cousin: this would be the kinship between James and Jesus. The 'legend' of the apostle we are dealing with now – called James the Minor, to distinguish him from James the Major, the son of Zebedee – is contained in numerous extra-canonical documents: it shows him as a just man of a rigorously ascetic life, who was put to death for his faith. The Acts of the Apostles emphasise several times the leading role that James played in the life of the Church in Jerusalem. The Judaising party, whose views differed from those of Paul, quoted him as an authority. There are very strong reasons for admitting that this James is the author of the epistle which bears his name. On the other hand, he cannot be connected with those apocryphal texts entitled the 'Proto-gospel of James' and 'Liturgy of St James'.

28   Those letters which are addressed by the apostles not to one or other local church, but to the faithful of all the Churches, are called 'catholic' or universal epistles.

29   Jas. 1. 13.

30   Jas. 1. 27.

31   Jas. 2. 26.

32   Jas. 3. 2.

33   Jas. 5. 1.

34   There is an abundance of apocryphal literature concerning St Joseph; but these legends, by which the Fathers of the Church have sometimes been inspired, have no historical authority. We know nothing more about Joseph than what is related in the gospels according to Matthew and Luke. We are ignorant of his life before he married Mary; we are ignorant of the place and date of his death. It is not even certain that he was a carpenter, for the Greek word *tekton* can mean a mason as well as a carpenter or a joiner (we notice, moreover, that Jesus, who several times alludes to the skills of a builder, never speaks of work with wood). The veneration of St Joseph seems to have started in the fourth century, in the Coptic Church. Joseph was not included in the Greek menology until after the eighth century. In the west, his name appears in the martyrologies of the ninth century, and his feast was fixed for the 19th March by Pope Sixtus IV, in the fifteenth century. The devotion to St Joseph made great strides in the Roman Church. Pius IX proclaimed Joseph 'patron of the universal Church' (1870). Modern Roman theology has endeavoured to plumb the mystery of the connection between Joseph and the Incarnation more deeply; without its con-clusions having any value for dogma, it attributes to Joseph a supereminent sanctity (superior even to that of John the Baptist) and a perpetual virginity; it does not base these affirmations on historical research, but on the necessities of doctrinal deduction.

35   The chronologies of Matthew and Luke do not seem, at first glance, very easy to harmonise with each other. Following Matthew (who alone mentions the flight into Egypt), the Holy Family took refuge in Egypt after the visit of the Magi, and settled in Nazareth after their return from Egypt. Following Luke, Jesus is taken from Bethlehem to Jerusalem, to be presented in the Temple; from Jerusalem, the Holy Family returns to Nazareth and lives there. This apparent divergence has led several exegetes to treat the flight into Egypt as one of the cases (the episode of Jonah in the whale would be another) when Jewish writers

set out teaching of a moral or spiritual order in the form of a historical account which does not correspond literally with the facts. This is not to say that these accounts are not true, but that their truth is of the literary type to which they belong. Their truth must be judged by the rules of the type: allegorical and poetic truth differ from actual historical truth. Thus the flight into Egypt would be, in historical guise, a poetic amplification of the text from Hosea (11. 1): 'I . . . called my son out of Egypt'. It is not for us to settle these questions. But the chronological difficulty sketched out above does not seem to us insoluble. One could allow that the return to Galilee from Jerusalem indicated by Luke (2. 39) did not take place immediately, and need not have been direct, but could have involved a long delay and long detours: after the Presentation of Jesus in the Temple, the Holy Family could first have gone back to Bethlehem, and only then would the adoration of the Magi have taken place which would have been followed by the flight into Egypt; then, when Herod had died, the Holy Family would have returned to Nazareth.

36   The Greek word *martus* means 'witness'. It is worth remarking on the fact that the first martyrs, those from the circles of the apostles, sealed with their blood a witness borne not to the truth of a doctrine, but to a person and to an event of which they had had personal experience: the person and the fact of Jesus risen from the dead. From this stems the extreme importance of the witness borne by martyrs such as, for example, Peter and James. They gave their lives as a witness of what they themselves had seen and heard. The history of martyrdom is the secret centre, the burning heart of the whole history of the Church during the first centuries. In the veneration paid to martyrs lies the origin of the veneration of the saints. The anniversary of the death of a martyr, what was so beautifully called his 'day of birth', *dies natalis*, was celebrated as a feast. Altars were consecrated by enclosing martyrs' relics within them: the passion of the martyrs was revived in the sacrifice of Jesus himself (of which it was a part) in the eucharistic offering.

37   Chapters VI and VII.

38   We do not know what the number of these children might have been. The Greek calendar speaks of 14,000, the Syrian calendar of 64,000; in the middle ages, by applying a text from Revelation (14. 3), 144,000 children were spoken of. As Bethlehem was no more than a large village, there seems room, in all likelihood, for reducing these numbers rather considerably; perhaps the number of the Holy Innocents did not, in fact, exceed a hundred. The atrocities committed by Herod were so numerous that a local crime like this could pass practically unnoticed. The feast of the Innocents was introduced into the Church during the fifth century. The Roman Church celebrates it on 28th December.

39   Gen. 4.9.

40   Luke 17. 1-2.

41   Matt. 2. 18.

42   Theologians have debated the spiritual effects of circumcision at the time of the mosaic law. The majority of the Fathers and of the Latin scholastics admitted that circumcision, the sacrament of the Old Covenant, effaced original sin: this was the opinion of St Ambrose, St Augustine, St Bernard, Peter the Lombard, and St Thomas, amongst many others. Today, this opinion seems much less common in the Roman Church. The Greek Fathers, on the whole, thought that circumcision, unlike baptism, did not justify. St John Chrysostom

insisted on the fact that Abraham was justified not by circumcision but by his faith, which was anterior to that. The adversaries of the concept of circumcision as a justifying sacrament interpret the Scriptures in a literal sense; they do not see in circumcision anything but a sign of the covenant between God and his people. The supporters of the contrary concept give a spiritual meaning to the words of Scripture: they see in circumcision a prefiguring of Christ's Passion, a sign of the redemption and the grace brought by him. St Paul's texts on the unnecessary character of circumcision in the new law are clear and decisive; since the Incarnation it is baptism (baptism of the spirit with or without baptism by water) which washes away original sin and confers grace. Nevertheless, Paul did not consider that circumcision was incompatible with baptism, as can be seen from the case of Timotheus, the offspring of a Jewish mother (Acts 16. 1-3) and, if he was against forcing the Gentiles to be circumcised, he accepted it completely for converted Jews. Circumcision was practised not only in Israel, but by the majority of the semitic peoples. Reasons of physiology and hygiene influenced this custom. But it seems that − almost universally − it also carried the sense of an initiation and of a religious consecration. On the one hand, this pact of blood indicated fitness for marriage; on the other hand, it linked the man who was circumcised with his tribe and with the god of his tribe. The flowing of blood, the wound inflicted on the human body and especially on the masculine organ of reproduction had the same fundamental meaning as sacrifice: the establishing of an exchange, or of a communion of life, between the divine and man.

43   From the first Christian centuries, the feast of the Circumcision suffered from this disadvantage, for it coincided with the Saturnalian orgies.

44   The repeated and even, in certain cases, continuous invocation of the Name of Jesus is one of the most widespread practices of Orthodox spirituality. The monks of Sinai and of Athos, and the Byzantine mystics called 'Hesychasts' have gradually worked out a method known as the 'Jesus prayer'. This, following the actual formula, consists in the phrase: 'Lord Jesus Christ, Son of God, have mercy on me, a sinner'. A shorter and earlier form of the invocation of the Name would be simply to repeat the word 'Jesus'. The Hesychasts have devised the idea of a contemplative life entirely concentrated around the Name of Jesus and absorbed by Him. But this invocation can just as well become the prayer of an active life, to which it could bring peace and be a unifying agent. If our faith were great enough, we could again become capable, as in the apostolic age, of a 'pentecostal' use of the Name of Jesus; we would know how to bring about, through the power of this Name, healings and other manifestly divine interventions.

45   Phil. 2. 9.

46   Acts 4. 29-30.

47   Luke 2. 51.

48   Luke 2. 52.

49   This problem is one that is concerned with the inner development of Jesus, with the evolution of his consciousness and of his knowledge. There is a wealth of hypotheses about the 'psychology of Jesus'. Amongst those who see in Jesus the Son of God, the God-man, but are in revolt against traditional christology, many admit that in coming into this world Jesus voluntarily 'emptied' himself of divine prerogatives (theories of 'kenosis'). His awareness of sonship and of being the Messiah would then have developed progressively. His knowledge would

have accrued as does that of all other men. In short, his former awareness and his divine knowledge would have been provisionally 'forgotten'. God would, as it were, have written bit by bit on a blank page. This theory is inadmissible for those who remain faithful to the Christological definitions of Chalcedon and who believe that in the theandric person of Christ are united two natures, the one divine, the other human, both of which remained intact. In as much as he was endowed with a divine nature, Christ, even as a child, never ceased to possess an intuitive vision and to know all things past, present, and to come, with perfect knowledge. In as much as he was endowed with a human nature, Jesus possessed an acquired or experimental knowledge, which was susceptible to progress, was formed according to the ordinary laws of intelligence, and suited to the circumstances of his life. Moreover, following the theologians of the Thomist school, Jesus would have received, in order to compensate for the limitations of his human knowledge, an 'infused' learning, that is to say a learning which was not essentially divine, but was immediately obtained from God, which, in souls that have reached the state termed 'heavenly', is substituted for acquired learning. The distinction between Jesus's human learning and his divine knowledge does not divide the soul of the God-Man into separate compartments. It is necessary to protect the integrity of each of the two natures, but these natures are united harmoniously without being confused (like water mixed with wine). Jesus, who sees all things with as perfect a vision as that of the Father, is at the same time capable of seeing, of knowing, of feeling in the same way as a man, of adapting himself to the limitations of men, and of speaking to all men in their own language: in the same way, an adult, in the company of small children, loses nothing of what is proper to him as an adult, but also sees all that the small children see, is able to feel what they feel (even though transcending their experience), and expresses himself in language which they can understand. Traditional Christology gives us a far richer concept of the person of Christ, with deeper shades of meaning, than the impoverishing 'psychology of Jesus' that belongs to 'liberal' theology. It goes without saying that for pure rationalists, these problems do not arise at all.

50   2 Cor. 10. 5.

51   In Palestine one finds certain dry fruits called 'locusts'. It seems that these fruits are what John ate, rather than the creatures we call 'locusts'.

52   This liturgy is St Basil's, except if the vigil for Epiphany falls on a Saturday or a Sunday: if it does, then the liturgy of St John Chrysostom is celebrated. If January 5th is a Saturday, the liturgy follows vespers. If it is a Sunday, the liturgy is celebrated during the morning, but vespers are carried over until the afternoon. In both these cases, the 'great hours' are said on the Friday. The blessing of the water takes place after the liturgy.

53   Paul alludes here, not to a scriptural text, but to a rabbinical legend according to which the rock which Moses struck, and from which flowed water, moved with the Israelites.

54   Epiphany is of eastern origin. To begin with, it seems to have been celebrated by heretics called the 'Basilidians'. This feast, at first, commemorated both the birth and the baptism of Christ. In the fourth century it existed in Constantinople, in so far as it was differentiated from the feast of the Nativity. It also existed in Jerusalem during the same century. Baptisms were often conferred on the day of Epiphany, at Jerusalem as well as at Constantinople. Epiphany was celebrated throughout the west only after the

fourth century; on January 6th, the Roman Church celebrated the baptism of Christ, the adoration of the Magi, and the miracle of the wedding at Cana – all on the same day. The element of 'water' is the link between the event that took place at Cana and that which took place on the banks of the Jordan. The fixing of Epiphany on January 6th has very obscure origins. Perhaps the most likely explanation is the following (although it is exceptionally confused): at first, the commemoration of the Nativity was combined with that of Christ's baptism. Now some of the eastern Churches fixed the date of the birth of Jesus on January 6th, as they assumed that he had been conceived on April 6th (a parallel calculation to the nine months which pass between 25th March and 25th December, following a different computation). Why did they decide on April 6th as the date for Christ's conception? It is by virtue of a reasoning which is as subtle as it is whimsical. In certain eastern circles which could be more or less identified with the Montanist sect, it was believed that the duration of Jesus's earthly life had to correspond with a whole number, as a fraction, being imperfect, did not satisfy the requirements of their mystical symbolism. If Jesus had lived for a whole number of years, the date of his conception and the date of his death would fall on the same day of the same month. Now these Christians commemorated the death and resurrection of Jesus on April 6th. They had adopted this date because it corresponded with the first full moon of the first month which follows March 24th, and this day, according to them, was the equinox, and also the anniversary of the creation of the world (on the assumption that the world could only have been created at the spring equinox).

55   The liturgy celebrated on January 6th is that of St John Chrysostom, except if January 6th falls on a Sunday or a Monday: in this case, the liturgy of St Basil is celebrated. We have already pointed out the same custom for Christmas day.

56   Matt. 3. 13-15.

57   Theologians have asked what, from the Christian point of view, is the significance and the value of John's baptism. This baptism, it is clear, was distinct from Christian baptism, and remained inferior to it. But there was something different and something more in John's baptism than in the Jewish baptism of proselytes or in the purifications of the mosaic law. It was, therefore, a temporary and divinely inspired rite, a rite of messianic preparation, which belonged more to the New Covenant than to the Old; this rite, by itself, had no power to bring about the remission of sins, but it gave rise to an inner state of repentance and of justice which could obtain pardon directly. It brought about a predisposition for baptism in Christ.

58   The baptismal act cannot be renewed, but baptismal grace can stay, or revive, or grow in our souls, even if the material element – in this case water – plays no part in it. However, a man who has not received the baptism of water can still receive baptismal grace (the baptism being that of blood, of a martyr, or the baptism of desire, whether explicit or even implicit). It is interesting that the evangelists are silent on this question: were the apostles baptised? Where and when? Jesus, the sovereign master of baptismal grace, did not himself confer the baptism of water. In the rites of Epiphany, the water blessed by the Church, without being the matter of a sacrament, is 'sacramental'; contact with this water can help to form inner predispositions in us by which we can revive the grace of our baptism. But we can achieve this outcome without the mediation of any material sign. Our own descent into the Jordan, at Epiphany, can take place

purely 'in spirit'.

59   Baptism is at the same time a symbol both of life and of death, which is only completely actualised in baptism by immersion. The neophyte is plunged into the water: it is the death of the sinful creature. The neophyte rises from the water: it is resurrection, birth into the new life.

60   Luke 3. 22.

61   Ibid.

62   Let us look at the symbolic meaning that, in Scripture, is attached to the dove. In the story of the flood, the dove represents faithfulness and peace; in the Song of Songs, it represents innocence and love; in the Gospels, Jesus is the model of its simplicity. Doves could, according to the mosaic law, replace a lamb as a sacrifice, and were the offering made by Jesus's parents when he was presented in the Temple: this equivalence between the dove and the lamb in Christian eyes takes on a very deep meaning. Just as the dove descended from heaven to the Jordan, so, when the world was being created, the Spirit moved upon the face of the waters.

63   John 1. 32.

64   John 1. 33.

65   John 3. 5.

66   This theme of the three conversions has been developed by several masters of the spiritual life. Although it accords as a whole with the classical theme of the three ways — the way of purification, the way of illumination, and the way of union — it cannot be superimposed on them exactly.

67   Isa. 9. 2.

68   How exactly would one define a Father of the Church? At first, the word 'Fathers' was reserved for those bishops who had sat at the Council of Nicaea and at other councils. In the fifth century, St Jerome was included, who was only a priest. The Pope Gelasius, towards the end of the fifth century, drew up a list of 'works of the holy Fathers': a dozen of the great names are mentioned, but that of a layman, Prosper, also figures amongst them. Today, we would draw up a much longer list, but no official ecclesiastical decision has ever determined who has the right to be inscribed on it. It is generally agreed, without this being a rigid limit, that the patristic age ends with St John of Damascus, who died around 749. The Fathers are the ecclesiastical writers of early Christianity, but belonging to this early period is not in itself a sufficient criterion: neither Origen nor Eusebius of Caesarea are admitted as Fathers, in the strict sense of the word, for a Father must also be a specially authorised witness of the faith. In addition, patristic and early Christian literature are not synonymous. Orthodoxy of doctrine, (relative) saintliness of life, and the approval (at least implicit) of the Church constitute the necessary marks of a Father. The Fathers, taken either in isolation or in groups, are not a decisive authority exempt from error. Only the unanimous agreement of the Fathers is, according to catholic tradition, infallible and is to be accepted as expressing the actual doctrine of the Church.

69   Basil the Great (330? — 379) was born and died at Caesarea in Cappadocia. He was the brother of St Gregory of Nyssa and of St Macrina. After studying at Constantinople and Athens, he led a monastic life in the Pontus until he became a priest, and then bishop of Caesarea. He left works on the Holy Spirit, and against Arianism, numerous homilies and monastic canons. It is certain that he played an important part in the elaboration of the Byzantine liturgy, but it would be difficult to determine this part with precision. The

'liturgy of St Basil', as it is celebrated today, acquired its form in the middle ages.

70   Gregory (329? – 389?) was born and died at, or near, Nazianzus, in Cappadocia. A fellow-student and friend of St Basil at Athens, he shared his monastic life, and with him published a selection of the works of Origen. Against his own wishes, he was made bishop of Sasima, where he did not settle, but helped his father, the bishop of Nazianzus. Then, for some time, he administered the see of Constantinople, facing there the most painful difficulties. He ended his life in retreat. His works consist of poems, letters and speeches.

71   Rufinus of Aquilia, Migne P. G., vol. XXXVI, col. 736.

72   John (345 – 407) was born at Antioch. He spent ten years in the desert. After twelve years of priesthood at Antioch, he became bishop of Constantinople. His preaching and his charity earned for him the affection of the people, but his reforming zeal brought him many enemies. Two councils of bishops, one after the other, deposed him. The Empress Eudoxia and the Emperor Arcadius persecuted him. He died at Comana, while being taken to a distant place of exile. He left numerous homilies, letters, and biblical commentaries. The liturgy called that of St John Chrysostom is an abbreviated version of that of St Basil; it is impossible to say precisely what part Chrysostom may have played in the composition of this text.

73   Lev. 12. 2-8.

74   Num. 18. 14-18.

75   This feast existed in Jerusalem from the first half of the fourth century. The Emperor Justinian I introduced it throughout the Byzantine empire in 542. We find it celebrated in Rome in the seventh century. In the east, the Presentation (or, according to the Greek term, the 'meeting') is considered to be one of the feasts of Our Lord. In the west, it is thought of more as a feast of the Holy Virgin; there, it is generally known as the 'Purification of the Blessed Virgin Mary'. The Roman custom of blessing the candles on 2nd February dates from the eleventh century.

76   We do not know who Simeon was, any more than we know who Anna was. It is possible that Simeon was a son of the famous rabbi, Hillel, and the father of the pharisee Gamaliel, who is mentioned sympathetically in the Book of Acts (5. 34). Certain rabbinical texts could be interpreted in this way. It is also possible that Simeon had two sons, Gharinus and Leucius, who are spoken of in the apocryphal gospel of Nicodemus. But we have no vestige of historical certainty about this.

77   2 Kings 5. 8-14.

78   There are various interpretations of this comparison. It has been suggested that the Greek word translated here by 'camel' can also mean 'thick cord', or 'cable'. It has also been suggested that the term 'needle' was the name of a very narrow gate in Jerusalem, reserved for pedestrians. But the Koran uses exactly the same comparison of a camel going through the eye of a needle, and the Talmud speaks of an elephant.

79   The publicans of Palestine were Jews employed in the Roman fiscal service. Other Jews thought of them with hostility, as agents of the occupying authorities, and also because they had a reputation for venality.

80   Rev. 3. 20.

81   Roman theology assigns an important place in morals to the treatise 'On Restitution'. But how can one make good either material damage or moral hurt,

when this is no longer physically possible (because of distance in time or space)? There must at least be a desire for reparation. Then, when, like Zacchaeus, we receive our Lord at our table, we can bring those with whom we have sinned and those against whom we have sinned with us to meet Jesus — in the secret of our soul, through remembrance and prayer.

82   The start of a Latin hymn, sung at the time of the Passion.

Chapter IV
THE TIME OF LENT

SUMMARY

Great Lent. The Gates of Repentance (Sunday of the Publican and the Pharisee). The Return to the Father (Sunday of the Prodigal Son). When the Son of Man Cometh (Meat-fare Sunday). Forgiveness (Cheese-fare Sunday). The Start of Lent. The First Sunday of Lent (Sunday of Orthodoxy). Second Sunday of Lent (St Gregory Palamas). Third Sunday of Lent (Adoration of the Holy Cross). Fourth Sunday of Lent (St John Climacus). Fifth Sunday of Lent (St Mary of Egypt). Certain Saints' Days and the Feast of the Annunciation.

Great Lent

Easter — which is both the Passion of our Lord and his Resurrection — is the climax of the Orthodox liturgical year. The Church gives us a lengthy preparation for this painful and luminous period. The time of the Passion and of the Resurrection is preceded by the time of Lent. This Lent, also called Great Lent (to distinguish it from that of the Most Holy Virgin Mary, preceding the Feast of the Dormition in August, and of the Apostles, preceding the Feast of St Peter and St Paul in June, as well as that of Christmas), is a time of special prayers and fasting. If we set on one side Holy Week, or Passion Week, which immediately precedes Easter Sunday, and we add to Lent itself — that is, to the weeks of strict fast — the weeks which precede and prepare us for it, we have a total period of ten weeks, starting with the Sunday called the Sunday of the Pharisee and the Publican, and ending with the Saturday called Lazarus Saturday, on the eve of Palm Sunday[1].

The significance of Great Lent is fairly complex. It is the result of a long historical development[2] during which very diverse elements have become mixed. Let us take a look at what these are.

Lent is a time of penitence. In the first centuries of the Church, the 'penitents', or sinners who repented publicly, were solemnly reconciled with the community of the faithful during this period[3]. Public penitence has more or less — one could say, generally — fallen into disuse in the Orthodox Church, but the idea of penitence has remained. Are we not all, in different degrees, sinners and penitents? And this period which leads us towards Easter is surely a time which is very propitious for repentance and expiation. Lent will therefore be an opportunity for us to examine our conscience and seek reconciliation with the Lord.

Lent is also a time of spiritual growth and of illumination. In the early Church, 'catechumens', that is to say those who were being prepared for baptism, were the subject of special solicitude during Lent[4]. They were instructed with redoubled zeal, and were baptised during Easter night. The catechumenate, or the state of adults who were being prepared for baptism is now no longer usual in the Orthodox Church; all the same, during the course of each liturgy we are invited to pray for the catechumens. In the liturgy of the presanctified gifts, of which we shall speak further on, they are prayed for with special fervour. This prayer has not lost its meaning, for still, in missionary countries, there are catechumens preparing for baptism. In Africa, India, Japan and the countries of eastern Europe, and still other places, the Orthodox Church has catechumens. We will be praying for them during Lent. We shall also pray for the catechumens of Christian missionary Churches that are non-Orthodox. And we shall pray for the millions of men who belong to non-Christian religions, to Judaism, to Islam, to Hinduism and Buddhism, and to so many other groups. In a certain sense they, too, are catechumens. All that there is of truth in their beliefs and of good in their actions is taught to them by the inner Master of whom they are unaware or whose name they do not know, by the divine Word, the 'true Light, which lighteth every man that cometh into the world' (John 1. 9). And we ourselves, after all, never stop being catechumens. The Word of God made flesh never ceases to educate us. The Holy Spirit never ceases to educate us. The Holy Spirit never stops knocking at the door of our hearts. Lent is a time which is particularly well suited to hearing, to listening to, the voice of God.

Lent — according to the liturgy of the presanctified — commemorates Israel's forty years of wandering in the wilderness, those forty years during which the chosen people, having left the captivity of Egypt and crossed the Red Sea, went forward with faith towards the far-off promised land, receiving their earthly food from God in the form of manna and their spiritual food in the form of the Ten Commandments: sometimes they rebelled and fell into sin, but still they reached their goal. Lent also speaks to us of liberation, of pilgrimage, of crossing an arid desert, of the divine manna, of a meeting with God on Sinai, and also, of fall and reconciliation.

Lent recalls the forty days that the Lord Jesus spent in the desert during which he contended with Satan, the tempter. Our Lent must also be a period of fighting against temptation, and especially against the temptation of our most habitual sin. 'Thou shalt worship the Lord thy God, and him only shalt thou serve' (Luke 4. 8). May it be granted to us, during Lent, to learn and understand these words with which the Lord opposed Satan, and which summarise the whole of the spiritual battle.

One can see that Lent is a very rich, very deep agglomeration of different elements. They serve to purify and to enlighten us. During the time of Lent, the Church leads us, as if by the hand, towards the radiant paschal feast. The more serious our Lenten preparation has been, the deeper we shall enter into the mystery of Easter and gather its fruits.

The Gates of Repentance
Sunday of the Publican and the Pharisee

'Open unto me, O Giver of Life, the gates of repentance . . .' sings the Church at matins for the first of the four Sundays which prepare us for Lent. Indeed, this Sunday could be thought of as a gate: a gate through which we enter the sacred period which leads us on to Easter; a gate which opens into that atmosphere of repentance, to that life of repentance which Lent should bring to each one of us. But we must remember that the word "penitence" or "repentance" is a translation of the Greek gospel term *metanoia*: and that this means "change of spirit". Much more is involved than the observance of some kind of outward repentance. What is asked of us is radical change, renewal, conversion.

This Sunday, in the liturgical calendar, is called the 'Sunday of the Pharisee and the Publican'. The Church, in order to exhort us to true repentance, sets before us the scene of two men who go to the Temple to pray, and of whom one is justified on account of his humility and his sincere contrition. The parable of the

Pharisee and the Publican (Luke 18. 10-14) that is read at the liturgy is, if one may dare to say so, the most dangerous of all the parables. For we are so accustomed to condemn Phariseeism that here we seem to say: 'At least, despite all my sins, I am no Pharisee. I am not a hypocrite'. We forget that the prayer of the Pharisee is not wholly bad. The Pharisee states that he fasts, that he gives tithes, that he is free of the grosser sins; and that is all true. Moreover, the Pharisee does not take the credit for his good actions; he recognises that they come from God, and he gives thanks to God. There are two ways in which the prayer of the Pharisee errs: it lacks repentance and humility. He does not seem aware of the shortcomings — perhaps excusable ones — of which he, like all men, is guilty; and, what is more, he compares himself to the publican with a certain pride, a certain disdain. Do we have the right to condemn the Pharisee, and to consider ourselves more righteous than him if, first of all, we break the commandments that the Pharisee observes? Have we the right to place ourselves — in contrast to the Pharisee — on the same level as the justified publican? We cannot do that unless our attitude is exactly the same as that of the publican. Would we dare to say that we have the publican's humility and repentance? If we ostentatiously condemn the Pharisee without truly becoming like the publican ourselves, we fall into Phariseeism itself.

Let us now look more closely at the publican. He does not dare to lift up his eyes; he smites his breast; he implores God to have mercy upon him, for he realises that he is a sinner. His whole bodily attitude is one of humility. (Jesus Himself, as a saint once said, has taken the last place so completely that no one has ever been able to take it from him.) This is why the Saviour said: 'This man went down to his house justified rather than the other'. We notice that Jesus says 'rather than the other', in some way leaving the Pharisee's case open to our thought. And Jesus adds: 'Everyone that exalteth himself shall be abased; and he that humbleth himself shall be exalted'.

Let us try to explore this episode more deeply. Is the publican justified simply because he confesses his sin and stands humbly before God? In his case, there is something more. The heart of the publican's prayer is an appeal, filled with trust, to the goodness and the tenderness of god. 'God be merciful to me a sinner', he says. These first words, 'God be merciful' echo the opening words of Psalm 51, which is essentially the psalm of penitence: 'Have mercy upon me, O God, according to thy lovingkindness:

according to the multitude of thy tender mercies blot out my transgressions'. The fact that Jesus chooses to place these words in the mouth of the publican and so to make them the model of our prayers of repentance, throws a great light on the soul of the Saviour, and on what he intends. What Jesus asks of a penitent sinner (and so, of each one of us), is above all this abandon, this absolute trust in the tender mercy and the favour of God.

At matins, the Church sums up the gospel parable and formulates the central thought for this Sunday thus: 'Lord, who didst reproach the Pharisee with justifying himself and taking pride in his actions; Thou who didst justify the publican when he approached thee humbly, seeking with groans pardon for his sins — for Thou dost not come nigh to arrogant thoughts nor turn Thyself away from a contrite heart. Because of this, we also humbly kneel before Thee, O Thou who hast suffered for us. Grant us Thy pardon and Thy great mercy'.

The epistle for this Sunday is taken from the second letter of St Paul to his disciple Timothy (3. 10-15). The apostle reminds Timothy briefly of all that he, Paul, has had to suffer: persecutions and afflictions of all sorts. He exhorts Timothy, who from childhood has been raised believing in Christ and in the Scriptures, not to be discouraged, and to persevere with charity and patience. On the eve of Lent, this epistle warns us that trials and difficulties will not be lacking during the holy preparation for Easter. As much to us as to Timothy, Paul says: 'But continue thou in the things which thou hast learned and hast been assured of, knowing of whom thou hast learned them'.

The Return to the Father
Sunday of the Prodigal Son

This Sunday, the theme of repentance and forgiveness, already dealt with on the Sunday of the Pharisee and the Publican, continues to be developed. But the epistle (1 Cor. 6. 12-20) opens up what is a sort of digression and touches on a special subject, that of mortification of the flesh. This is explained by the fact that, eight days after this Sunday, we will be entering the period of the fast; and, already, the Church gives us a warning from St Paul to listen to. The apostle first of all says to the Corinthians that not all lawful things are profitable. We must not allow ourselves to be dominated by anything, even if it is permitted. Foods are for the stomach; the stomach is for food. But neither the stomach nor foods are of importance in spiritual life, for God will destroy both foods and the stomach. Enlarging on this theme, the apostle then speaks of impurity. Although foods are for the stomach, our body is not for fornication. Our body is for the Lord; the Lord is for our body. Here we have an argument which is very characteristic of Paul, who judges all things 'in terms of Christ'. One could expect the apostle to condemn impurity by adopting a moral standpoint, that of the law, of vices and virtues. But Paul sees things from a different perspective. 'Know ye not that your bodies are the members of Christ? Shall I then take the members of Christ, and make them the members of an harlot?'. Not only are we members of Christ, but we are the temple of the Spirit 'Know ye not that your body is the temple of the Holy Ghost . .?'[5]. Therefore, 'Flee fornication . . .'. Fasting from food is neither the only nor the highest form of fasting. Sexual purity, of heart and thought, as well as of the body itself, is imperatively required of us, each according to our condition, whether in marriage or in celibacy.

We now come to the theme which is central to this Sunday. It is set out in the gospel read during the liturgy, and is the parable of the prodigal son.

Of all the gospel parables, that of the prodigal son (Luke 15. 11-31) is perhaps the best known and the most familiar. It is certainly one of the most touching. Possibly we do not always realise where the centre of the parable lies. Is it in the change of heart experienced by the young man who has left his father, squandered his inheritance in a life of debauchery, suffered such hunger that he envied the pigs who had husks to eat, and then decided to leave and return to his father? Certainly the young man's words: 'I will arise and go to my father, and will say unto him, Father, I have sinned against heaven, and before thee, And am no more worthy to be called thy son' – indeed, these words are a deeply moving expression of repentance. The prodigal son's decision, 'I will arise and go to my father', throws a clear light on the importance of vigorous action, of an act of will (one cannot go to the Father without first getting up and setting off). All the same, the repentant young man is not the most attractive figure in the parable. His repentance is neither the result of a totally disinterested change of heart, nor is it free from all self-interest: the prodigal son wants to escape from misery, and he chooses the only way open to him. The central figure in the parable is, rather, the person of the father. Here we are in the presence of a completely unselfish and freely given expression of tenderness. A tenderness which has waited and kept watch, which is on the look-out for the return of the prodigal, and which, when seeing him still far off, can no longer wait or restrain itself. The father, overwhelmed with compassion, runs out to meet his child, falls on his neck and kisses him warmly. (In the east, such behaviour would be considered most unsuitable to the dignity of an old man.) And then the father, without voicing any reproach to the prodigal, gives orders that a ring be put on his finger (the sign of an heir), and shoes on his feet (the sign of a free man as distinct from a slave), and for the fatted calf to be killed, and a feast prepared. He has the 'best robe' brought and put on his son: we notice that it is not the best from among the robes that the prodigal might have possessed before his departure, but the best robe to be found in the house. God does not simply restore a repentant sinner to the grace he might have possessed before sinning: he bestows on him the greatest grace he could receive, a maximum of grace.

The story of the prodigal is our own story. The self-willed departure, the blameworthy life, the misery, then repentance, return and forgiveness: we have lived all that − and how many times! We can also look at the role played by a third person: the elder brother of the prodigal. In the parable, the elder son shows that he is jealous of his brother. He is annoyed that forgiveness should be granted so generously, and refuses, despite the entreaties of his father, to take part in the rejoicing. But this is just the opposite of what actually takes place when a sinner returns. Every prodigal son who returns does so at the prompting of the elder son, the son to whom the father says: 'Thou art ever with me, and all that I have is thine' − the Lord Jesus − who takes the sinner by the hand and leads him to the Father with ardent affection.

Vespers and matins for this Sunday contain passages which are eloquent comments on the teachings of this parable. Here are some:

'I have wasted the wealth which the Father gave to me, and in my wretchedness I have fed with the dumb beasts and being hungry, desired their food . . . That is why I shall go back to my father, crying and saying to him: receive me as a hired servant, who kneels before Thy love for men . . . . Compassionate Saviour, take pity on me, cleanse me . . . and give me once more the finest robe in Thy Kingdom . . . .'

'Our desire, brethren, is to understand the power of this mystery. For, when the prodigal son departed from sin and returned to his father's home, his loving father received him, embraced him and restored to him all the signs of glory.'

When the Son of Man Shall Come in His Glory
Meat-fare Sunday

The Saturday before this Sunday is specially consecrated to the commemoration of the faithful departed. There is an obvious link between this commemoration and the recalling of the last judgement, which is the principal theme for this Sunday.

In the same way as on the previous Sunday, fasting figures as a secondary theme in the liturgy of the day. This Sunday is called 'Meat-fare Sunday', because it is the last day on which the consumption of meat is authorised. From the next day, Monday, one should, if one can, abstain from meat until Easter. On the other hand, the use of milk, butter and cheese is allowed during all the days of this week, including Wednesday and Friday. During the liturgy a portion of the first epistle of St Paul to the Corinthians (8. 8-13 and 9. 1-2) is read in which the apostle, in substance, says the following: Eating or not eating meat in itself is not a matter of importance, but this liberty which we have must not scandalise or be a stumbling-block to the weak. A man who believes in the only God and does not believe in the reality of idols may, with a clear conscience, eat the flesh of beasts sacrificed to idols; but, if one of his brothers is less enlightened and thinks that this means some sort of association with the worship of idols, then he should abstain from doing this, and respect the conscience of those brothers for whom too, Christ died[6]. And so, if we are inspired by St Paul's idea, someone who feels he has valid reasons for not fasting, or for modified fasting during Lent, will all the same be careful to avoid anything that might scandalise or offend the conscience of those who are less strong.

The gospel for the liturgy (Matt. 25. 31-46) describes the last judgement. 'When the Son of man shall come in his glory', with all the holy angels, all the nations will be gathered before his throne. He will separate the sheep from the goats, setting the righteous on his right and the sinners on his left. He will invite those who have fed, clothed and visited him in his human guise of the poor, the prisoners and the sick, to enter the kingdom of the Father. He will exclude from the kingdom those who have acted otherwise. This description of the judgement obviously is partly symbolic. We pass judgement on ourselves when, voluntarily, we adhere to God or reject him. It is our love or our lack of love which will place us amongst the 'blessed' or amongst those who are dismissed (or perhaps deferred). Even if we do not have to interpret the details of the judgement literally, exactly as the evangelist describes them, we must listen very carefully to what the Saviour says about his presence in those who suffer, for it is in them alone that we are in any way able to help the Lord Jesus.

The prayers at vespers this Saturday evening and at matins for the Sunday give a general impression of terror in the face God's judgement. There is mention of open books, of fearful angels, of rivers of fire and of trembling before the altar. All this is very sound, and many sayings in the Gospels urge us to be converted before it is too late. But this shadowed side, the darkness into which a stubborn sinner can choose to throw himself, must not make us forget the side of light and hope. Here is a phrase from one of the chants at vespers in which these two aspects find themselves well united:

'O my soul, the time is near at hand; make haste before it is too late, and cry aloud in faith: I have sinned, O Lord, I have sinned against Thee; but I know Thy love for man and Thy compassion. O good Shepherd . . . .'

Forgiveness
Cheese-fare Sunday

This Sunday is the fourth of the Sundays which prepare us for Lent. It ends, and is the last day of this period of preparation. From the following day, Monday, we shall be in Lent itself. This Sunday itself is called 'Cheese-fare Sunday' because, beginning with the next day, the tradition of the Church is that we should abstain from eggs, milk, butter and cheese.

The Saturday preceding this Sunday is dedicated to the memory of those saints, men and women, who have given themselves to the ascetic life. At the threshold of Lent, we honour them as inspirers and intercessors in this difficult way of penitence.

The epistle of St Paul to the Romans (13. 11-14. 4), read at the Sunday liturgy, exhorts us to cast off the works of darkness and to put on the armour of light, to walk honestly as in the day, fleeing drunkenness, debauchery and the lusts of the flesh. Paul links this theme of the flesh to the theme of fasting. One person believes that he may eat all things; another eats only herbs. Let not him that eats despise him who does not, and let not him who does not eat judge him who does. Who are you to judge another? Both you and he are dependent on the same Master.

The gospel for the liturgy, taken from St Matthew (6. 14-21), opens with the precept of forgiveness: 'If ye forgive men their trespasses, your heavenly Father will also forgive you: But if ye forgive not men their trespasses, neither will your Father forgive your trespasses'. The fact that the Church has chosen this saying to introduce the gospel for the day shows that she intends to make forgiveness the dominant theme for this Sunday[7]. It is true that the rest of the gospel for this day speaks of fasting; but the Greek particle which joins the verses about fasting to the verses about forgiveness seem to assign to the former a position of dependence on the latter. The Lord Jesus advises those who fast not to look gloomy or to be of a sad countenance like those hypocrites who want to be noticed when they fast. 'Thou, when thou fastest, anoint thy head, and wash thy face.' The Father, who sees in secret, shall reward thee openly. Let thy treasure and thy heart be not on earth, but in heaven.

The chants for vespers and matins contrast the blessedness of paradise with the wretched state of man after the fall. But Moses, through fasting, so purified his eyes that they were able to see the divine vision. In the same way, may our fasting, which will last forty days as did that of Moses, help us to repress the passions of the flesh and free us so that we may 'with light step . . . set out upon the path to heaven'. Let us pay attention to the words 'with light step'. Our penitence must not be something heavy and burdensome. We must go through Lent lightly and airily, in a way which somehow makes us kin to the angels.

The Entry into Lent

The Monday that follows Cheese-fare Sunday is the first day of Great Lent itself. We have now begun on this succession of forty days[8] which prepare us for the time of the Passion and for the time of Easter. But before going into the details of these weeks of Lent, let us give a little time to the consideration of some of its general characteristics.

The first of these characteristics is, of course, the fast. One cannot ignore or treat the question of fasting from food lightly, and we have devoted a special note to this[9]. The Fathers of the Church and the collective conscience of the faithful have discerned clearly the spiritual value — a value which is both penitential and purifying — of abstention from certain foods. It would, however, be a serious mistake to think that this abstention constituted the only observance necessary to Lent. Bodily fasting must be accompanied by another fast. In the first centuries the discipline of the Church prescribed conjugal abstinence during Lent; it forbade participation in feasts and attendance at public festivals. This discipline has perhaps become weakened, and is not presented to believers quite as forcefully as in the times of the Fathers. All the same, it remains as a precious indication of the spirit, the intention of the Church. But most surely, this intention is that during Lent we exercise a much stricter control over our thoughts, our words and actions, and concentrate our attention on the person of the Saviour and what he requires of us[10]. Almsgiving is also one of the forms of lenten observance that the Fathers recommended most highly. A fast that is pleasing to God is therefore a 'whole' which cannot be separated into inner and outward aspects; of the two the former are certainly the most important[11].

A second feature of Great Lent lies in certain characteristics of ritual, and we will now say a few words about these.

First of all there is the reciting of 'Great Compline'. We know that the office of Compline (in Latin *completorium*, that which completes; in Greek *apodeipnon*, that which comes after supper), is the last of the daily offices. Ordinary compline, or 'little compline', is a fairly short office. But on Mondays, Tuesdays, Wednesdays and Thursdays of Great Lent, it is replaced by 'great compline', with a fairly long reading of psalms and *troparia*, amongst which will be noticed a long biblical prayer: Manasseh, king of Judah's, prayer of penitence.

Furthermore, the liturgy which is celebrated on Sundays during Great Lent is not the usual liturgy attributed to St John Chrysostom. It is the liturgy attributed to St Basil, Archbishop of Caesarea, in the fourth century[12]. This liturgy is longer than that of St John Chrysostom and the text is sometimes slightly different. In certain passages, it has an archaic and moving quality, for example when prayers are offered for those of our brothers who are in the house of Casear and for those who are condemned to hard labour in the mines (here we can think of the concentration camps of our own days).

On Wednesday and Friday during Great Lent, the liturgy called the 'presanctified' is celebrated, that is to say the liturgy for which the holy gifts have been consecrated in advance. It is not a eucharistic liturgy in the full sense, as there is no consecration. It is a communion service in which the priests and congregation take communion with the elements which were consecrated during the previous liturgy of St Basil or St John Chrysostom, and which have been reserved since then. The liturgy of the presanctified is added on to vespers. That is why, in principle, it should be celebrated in the evening. It includes certain psalms, certain special biblical readings, and certain prayers borrowed from the liturgy of St John Chrysostom [13]. The latter is celebrated every Saturday morning.

On Friday afternoon during Great Lent the hymn called the 'akathist' [14] is recited or sung. It is a long poem of praise to the most holy Virgin and Mother of God. It comprises twenty-four stanzas set out in alphabetical order and broken up into four portions. These portions are read one after another − one each Friday − during the first four Fridays of Lent. On the fifth Friday, the akathist is read in its entirety.

The 'great canon' of St Andrew of Crete is read in its entirety during the evenings of the first week in Lent [15]. It is an enormous composition of two hundred and fifty stanzas. These are divided up into nine series of odes that express the longings of a guilty and penitent soul; they contrast human frailty with the goodness and mercy of God.

Finally — and perhaps above all — the admirable prayer attributed to St Ephraim [16] must be mentioned. In this, neither poetry nor rhetoric (which are not lacking in the compositions we have just spoken of) play any part. We are here faced with a pure upsurge of the soul − short, sober and full of ardour. This prayer, accompanied by prostrations, is said for the first time on the evening of the Sunday which immediately precedes Lent (the evening service being counted as already belonging to Monday, the first day of Lent). It is repeated during most of the lenten services, especially in the liturgy of the presanctified. The prayer of

St Ephraim is widely known by Orthodox believers; this is its text:
'O Lord and Master of my life, give me not a spirit of sloth,
vain curiosity, lust for power, and idle talk. But give to me,
Thy servant, a spirit of chastity, humility, patience and love.
O Lord and King, grant me to see my own faults and not to
judge my brother; for blessed art Thou unto the ages of ages,
Amen.'

This prayer sums up all that is essential in spiritual life. A
Christian who used it constantly, who nourished himself from it
during Lent, would be at the simplest and best school. Even
someone who restricted himself to repeating and meditating on
these words, 'Lord and Master of my life', would enter deeply into
the reality of the relationship between God and the soul, the soul
and its God.

The First Sunday of Lent
Sunday of Orthodoxy

The word 'Orthodoxy' was first used in connection with this
Sunday in a fairly restricted sense. When it was first instituted, in
842, it marked the defeat of iconoclasm and proclaimed the
legitimacy of the veneration of icons[17]. Later, the scope of the
word was extended. By 'Orthodoxy' was understood the whole
body of dogma upheld by the Churches in communion with Constantinople. An official document, the *Synodikon*, which
anathematised by name all the leaders of heresy, was read in the
churches on this Sunday. It seems that Byzantine Christianity
thought it a necessary duty to confess its faith at the beginning of
Lent. Nowadays, we would probably be more concerned than was
then the case to express ourselves with charity towards those who
erred, and to separate the true from the erroneous in their thinking. But it was right and useful that the 'Orthodox' Church
should affirm its own attitude unambiguously. The 'ecumenical'
concerns which it shares nowadays with other Churches should
not be a sign of any abandonment or watering down of its fundamental beliefs. And it is also necessary to weed out parasitic
growths, and not to profane the adjective 'orthodox' by allowing
it to cover what might be either superstition or superfluity.

The texts which are read or sung at vespers and matins for this
Sunday insist on the reality of the Incarnation. In fact, the coming of Christ in the flesh is the foundation of the veneration of
icons. Christ Incarnate is the essential Icon, the prototype of all

icons. Some phrases from the *Triodion*[18] express very well the deep meaning of the veneration given to icons.

'In truth, the Church of Christ is adorned with the finest ornament by the holy icons of Christ our Saviour, of the Holy Mother of God and of all the glorified saints . . . . In keeping the icon of Christ which we praise and venerate, we do not risk being led astray. May those who do not believe this be put to confusion. For it is our kneeling before the incarnate Son and not the adoration of His icon that is a glory for us.'

The glorified saints were living, even though imperfect, images of God. They were weaker reproductions of the true divine Image, which is Christ. During the liturgy this Sunday, in the reading from the Epistle to the Hebrews (11. 24-26, 32-40), we will hear their inspired author[19] describe the sufferings of Moses and of David, of the patriarchs and martyrs of Israel, of those 'of whom the world was not worthy', who were scourged, slain with the sword, and beheaded, and whose faith yet overcame the world. These were images drawn not on wood, but in the flesh. They already prefigured and announced the coming of the definitive Icon, the Person of Christ.

The gospel for the day has no direct bearing on either images or Orthodoxy. In the gospel reading (John 1. 43-51) we see the apostle Philip bringing Nathanael, who will also become a disciple, to Jesus. Jesus says to Nathanael: 'Before that Philip called thee, when thou wast under the fig tree, I saw thee'. Nathanael, overwhelmed by this revelation, declares: 'Rabbi, thou art the Son of God'. Jesus replies that Nathanael will see 'greater things' than these powers of long-distance sight. 'Ye shall see heaven open, and the angels of God ascending and descending upon the Son of man.'

These words open a vast field for meditation. We do not know what Nathanael was doing or thinking under the fig tree. Was it a moment of temptation, or of perplexity or grace — or simply one of rest. But it seems as if the Lord would not have mentioned this if it had not been a decisive moment, a turning point in Nathanael's life. In the life of each one of us, there has been a moment, or perhaps moments, when we were 'under the fig tree', critical moments, in which Jesus, himself invisible, saw us and intervened. Did we accept or repel the intervention? Let us remember these moments . . . . Let us adore these divine interventions. But let us not rest in them, or try to live in a vision that is gone. 'Thou shalt see greater things than these.' Let us always be prepared for new grace, new vision. For the life of a disciple, if it is authentic, rises from light to greater light. We may see 'the heaven open and the angels ascending' towards the Saviour or descending to us. This is indeed a precious indication that familiarity with the angels should be habitual with us. The world of the angels is neither less close to us nor less loving than the world of men.

The Second Sunday of Lent
Sunday of St Gregory Palamas

The gospel for the first Sunday of Lent ended with an allusion to the ministry of angels. And angels are also called to mind by the epistle for this day (Heb. 1. 10-2. 3). The sacred text compares the ministry of angels with that, which is so much greater, of the Saviour himself. If disobedience to the messages transmitted to us by the angels is justly punished, how much greater will be the punishment of the man who neglects the salvation that is announced and brought by Christ. For 'to which of the angels said he at any time, Sit on my right hand, until I make thine enemies thy footstool'?

The gospel for this day (Mark 2. 1-12) tells of the healing of the man sick of the palsy at Capernaum. Jesus forgives him his sins, and, as the scribes are astonished that anyone other than God can forgive sins, he answers: 'Whether it is easier to say to the sick of the palsy, Thy sins be forgiven thee; or to say, Arise, and take up thy bed, and walk? But that ye may know that the Son of man hath power on earth to forgive sins . . . I say unto thee, Arise, and take up thy bed, and go thy way into thine house'. The central theme of this episode is the power of both pardon and healing that the Lord Jesus possesses. Then there is the affirmation — even more, the demonstration — that healing and the forgiveness of sins cannot be separated. The man sick of the palsy, lying on his bed, has been put down at the feet of Christ. Now Jesus's first words are not: 'Be healed', but: 'Thy sins be forgiven thee'. In our physical illnesses, before imploring actual release, we must ask for inner purification and to be absolved from our offences. Finally, Jesus tells the man who was sick of the palsy to take up his bed and to go to his house. On the one hand, the crowd will be more fully convinced of the reality of the miracle if this man is now seen to be strong enough to carry his litter; and, on the other, he who has been forgiven, and inwardly changed by Jesus, must show those of his house, by some unmistakable sign (not only by carrying his litter, but by words, actions, behaviour), that he is a new man resuming life in his own surroundings.

One notices that neither the epistle nor the gospel for this day have any bearing on St Gregory Palamas, with whose name the calendar none the less associates the second Sunday in Lent. This is because the commemoration of Palamas was only introduced in the fourteenth century, when the liturgical structure for this Sunday had already become established along different lines. The memory of Gregory Palamas is, however, evoked in the services for vespers and matins. St Gregory[20] expounded and defended, in the course of heated controversy, the theological doctrine relating to divine 'light'. The texts of the services do not go into detail or give explanations of the concepts attributed to Palamas, but speak in a general way of light and of him who said: 'I am the Light of the world'. In a considerably abridged form, one of the texts for matins brings together three ideas: that of Christ who illumines sinners, that of lenten abstinence, and that of the word 'arise', which the Saviour spoke to the man sick of the palsy, and which we now address to him: 'To those who live in the darkness of sin, Thou has brought light, O Christ, at this time of abstinence. Show us therefore the glorious day of Thy Passion, so that we may cry to Thee: Arise, O God and have pity on us'.

The Third Sunday in Lent
Sunday of Adoration of the Holy Cross

In the middle of Lent, the Church sets before us the Cross of Christ. On two other occasions during the year, September 14th and August 1st, the Cross is presented for our remembrance and veneration. Both these feasts link the adoration of the Cross to historic events[21]. However, the remembrance of the Cross on the third Sunday of Lent speaks only to our faith and reverence. It is to proclaim the part played by the Cross in the history of salvation and to prepare us for the vision, still far-off, of the Cross which, on Holy Friday, will be erected on Golgotha.

During matins, towards the end of the great doxology, the priest places a cross on a tray covered with flowers and, carrying the cross above his own head, he leaves the sanctuary and the iconostasion. He is preceded by lighted candles and censers. Having reached the middle of the church, he places the cross on a table. He censes it. The choir sings: 'We venerate Thy Cross, O Master, and we glorify Thy holy Resurrection'. The congregation comes to kiss the cross, which remains thus exposed in the middle of the church during the whole of the feast. The meaning of the feast is well expressed by this chant for matins:

'When, on this day, we look at the precious Cross of Christ, in faith let us adore it, let us rejoice, and embrace it ardently, beseeching our Lord, who of His own choice gave Himself to be crucified on it, to make us worthy of adoring His most precious Cross so that, free from all defilement, we may attain the day of Resurrection.'

The epistle for the liturgy (Heb. 4. 14 – 5. 6) exhorts us, as we have Jesus for our great high priest, to approach the throne of grace boldly, so that we may obtain pardon for our sins: 'We have not an high priest which cannot be touched with the feeling of our infirmities; but was in all points tempted like as we are, yet without sin.'

The gospel (Mark 8. 34 – 9.1) brings us the very serious and urgent words of the Master: 'Whosoever will come after me, let him deny himself, and take up his cross, and follow me. For whosoever will save his life shall lose it; but whosoever shall lose his life for my sake and the gospel's, the same shall find it'. Am I ready to follow Jesus, bearing my cross? (Not the cross that I may choose, but the one he himself places on my shoulders.) Am I ready to accept all the trials or sufferings which may come to me, as sharing in the Cross of the Saviour? When, in due course, it is my turn to come and place a kiss on the cross which is displayed in the middle of the church, will my kiss be that of an unrepentant sinner, the kiss of Judas, or will it be a gesture which is respectful and superficial but changes nothing in my life, or will it be a sign of adoration, of faith, and of tenderness which will be binding on my whole life?

The gospel for the day ends with this phrase: 'Verily I say unto you, That there be some of them that stand here, which shall not taste of death, till they have seen the kingdom of God come with power'. This does not imply the second and glorious coming of Christ at the end of the world. It means the coming of Christ with the power inaugurated by Pentecost, which the first generation of Christians was about to witness. But it also means an invisible, unspectacular, coming of the Kingdom in fervent and believing hearts. Oh, that this may be my own destiny, and that before I die, the Kingdom of Jesus will have taken possession of my soul.

The Fourth Sunday of Lent
Sunday of St John Climacus

This day, the Church calls our attention to St John Climacus[22] because this Father, who lived in the seventh century, realised in his own life the ideal of penitence on which we should fix our eyes during Lent. 'Let us honour John . . . glory of ascetics . . .', we sing at vespers. At matins, we address the saint thus: 'As thy body became thin through abstinence, so didst thou renew the power of thy soul, enriching it with heavenly glory'. However, the Church gives a correct interpretation to the doctrine of St John Climacus when it proclaims that asceticism has neither sense nor value if it is not an expression of love, and, again at vespers, it addresses these words to the saint: 'This is why thou dost entreat us: Love God so that ye may live in his eternal goodwill, and let nothing be set higher than this Love'.

During the liturgy we continue reading from the epistle to the Hebrews (6. 13-20). This tells of the patience and endurance of the patriarch Abraham, and of the final realisation of the promises that God had made to him. It is impossible for God to lie: that is why, like Abraham, we have 'strong consolation, who have fled for refuge to lay hold upon the hope set before us'. Do we really live in this great hope?

The gospel (Mark 9. 16-30) describes the healing of the boy with the dumb spirit, whose father brings him to Jesus. The Lord says to the father: 'If thou canst believe, all things are possible to him that believeth'. The father cries out with tears: 'Lord, I believe; help thou mine unbelief'. We could find no better way to express both the fact of our faith's existence, and of its weakness. But do the same burning tears fall from our eyes when we say to our Saviour: 'I believe; help thou mine unbelief'? Jesus takes pity on the father, He accepts such a faith, and heals the son. Later, speaking to the Master privately, the disciples ask him why they were not able to cast out such a spirit. Jesus answers: 'This kind can come forth by nothing but by prayer and fasting'. We must not imagine that prolonged fasting and repetitive prayer will suffice to give us a power which the disciples did not yet possess. Prayer and fasting, in the deepest sense, mean a radical renunciation of self, a concentration of one's soul in an attitude of trust and humility which leaves *all* to the mercy of God, the submission of our will to the will of the Lord, placing our whole being in the hands of the Father. He who − by the grace of God − reaches this state is able to cast out demons. Could we not take at least the first steps along this path. If we tried, we should be astonished by the successes that follow.

The Fifth Sunday of Lent
Sunday of St Mary of Egypt

It is not possible to establish with any certainty what part history and what part legend play in the traditions that relate to 'St Mary of Egypt'[23]. One may as well simply admit the fact that the Church wished to make her, as we sing during matins, 'a pattern of repentance'. She is a symbol of conversion, of contrition, and of austerity. On this last Sunday of Lent, she expresses the last and most urgent call that the Church addresses to us before the sacred days of the Passion and the Resurrection.

The epistle read at the liturgy (Heb. 9. 11-14) compares the ministry of Christ to that of the High Priest of the Jews. Once, each year, he entered into the Tabernacle, but Christ 'entered in once into the holy place, having obtained eternal redemption for us'. The High Priest purified and sanctified the faithful by sprinkling them with the blood and ashes of sacrificed animals. 'How much more shall the blood of Christ, who through the eternal Spirit offered himself without spot to God, purge your conscience from dead works to serve the living God?'

The gospel (Mark 10. 32-45) describes Jesus's ascent to Jerusalem before His Passion. Jesus takes the twelve apostles aside and starts to tell them that he will be betrayed, condemned and put to death, and that he will rise again from the dead. At the threshold of Holy Week could we be 'taken aside' by the Saviour for a talk in which he explains to us, personally, the mystery of Redemption? Do we ask the Master to help us understand at greater depth what is taking place for our sakes on Golgotha? Do we make it possible for Jesus to meet us in secret? Do we seize opportunities to be alone and quiet with the Lord? Then the sons of Zebedee come to Jesus and ask him to let them sit with him in his glory, one on his right and the other on his left. Jesus asks them − and puts the same question to us: 'Can ye drink of the cup that I drink of?' The Master then explains to the disciples that true glory lies in serving others. For 'the Son of man came not to be ministered unto but to minister, and to give his life a ransom for many'.

Already the evening of this last Sunday of Lent allows a glimmer of the light of Holy Week, the following Sunday, to shine in it. Next Saturday will be the Saturday of Lazarus, whom Jesus will raise from the dead; and vespers which are celebrated on the evening of the fifth Sunday of Lent, by alluding to Lazarus, the beggar in the gospel parable, announce Lazarus who was raised from the dead. 'Grant me to be with the poor man, Lazarus, and deliver me from the punishment of the rich man . . . . Allow us to rival his endurance and long-suffering.' The Church, as if somehow impatient to enter the very holy days which begin the following week, urges us, on this last Sunday of Lent, to anticipate the feast which we will celebrate in seven days: 'Let us sing a hymn in preparation for the Feast of Palms, to the Lord who comes with glory to Jerusalem in the power of the Godhead, that He may slay death . . . . Let us prepare the branches of victory, crying: "Hosannah to the Creator of all!" '

Some Saints' Feast Days and the Feast of the Annunciation

Before starting on the commentary for the holy days of the Passion, let us say a few words about some of the saints whose feasts generally fall during the time of Lent.

On February 24th, the calendar records: 'First and second discoveries of the honourable head of St John the Forerunner'. No historical certainty can be attached to the incident thus mentioned in the calendar[24]. But this title carries a deep spiritual significance. It was for upholding justice that John the Baptist was beheaded. We 'discover' his head each time that in remembering him we remember that it is better to die than to transgress the law of God. That is why the *kontakion* for this feast, referring to John's head, says: 'Through it, at all times, we seek healing, for, as in the past, thou art always in the world, preaching repentance'.

On March 9th, the Church keeps the memory of the 'forty martyrs of the city of Sebaste'. This refers to soldiers who suffered for the Christian faith in the fourth century, at Sebaste in Armenia, during the persecution of the Emperor Licinius[25].

On April 23rd, the feast of St George is celebrated. The 'great martyr' St George is one of the most popular saints. He is especially honoured in Orthodox countries of the Middle East, and in England. Despite the wealth of hagiographical legend that surrounds him, historically, all that we can say is that he was martyred near Lydda, in Palestine, probably before the reign of the

Emperor Constantine[26]. In the prayers for matins, the Church entreats him, through his intercession, to save 'those who are in diverse tribulations' and to deliver them 'from all oppression'.

But assuredly the greatest feast which falls during this period of the year is the feast that celebrates the Annunciation of her divine motherhood made by the Angel Gabriel to the Mother of God, the most holy Virgin Mary[27]. One sentence from the chant at matins sums up the whole significance of this feast: 'Today is revealed the mystery that is from all eternity. The Son of God becomes the Son of man . . . .' The epistle to the Hebrews, read at the liturgy (2. 11-18), stresses that, because of the Incarnation, 'he that sanctifieth and they who are sanctified are all of one: for which cause he is not ashamed to call them brethren'. The gospel (Luke 1. 26-38) tells of Gabriel's revelation to Mary at Nazareth. Mary's reaction 'How shall this be?' is not an expression of doubt, and in this it differs from the reaction of Zacharias, when the birth of John was foretold to him. Mary simply poses a respectful question: and, when the angel explains that the Holy Spirit shall come upon her and shall overshadow her, Mary answers, with the humility and obedience which characterise her whole nature: 'Behold the handmaid of the Lord; be it unto me according to thy word'.

There are really two sides to the feast of the Annunciation. One of them turns towards the most holy Mother of God and concerns her glory and our devotion to Mary. The declaration of this glory and the expression of this devotion find their perfect form in the first words of the angel's message: 'Hail, thou that art highly favoured, the Lord is with thee'. We cannot address the holy Virgin better than by repeating these words, with veneration and tenderness. The other side of the mystery turns towards men. In the life of every Christian there will be divine annunciations, moments when God lets us know his will and his intention concerning us. But all these annunciations must unite to become the one essential Annunciation: the Annunciation that Jesus can be born in us, can be born through us -- not in the same way that he was conceived and brought into the world by the Virgin Mary, for that is a unique miracle that cannot be equalled, — but in the sense that the Saviour takes spiritual and, at the same time, very real possession of our being. And then let us remember that every authentic Annunciation is immediately followed by a Visitation: the divine favour that has been granted to us must straightaway release an impulse in us to let it flow out to our brothers, which is expressed through some loving word or act. This is why the gospel reading at matins for the Annunciation is the account of Mary's visit to Elisabeth. Immediately after her meeting with Gabriel, the Mother of God goes to her cousin, to share with Elisabeth and John the radiance of its grace.

Notes for Chapter IV

1   To put this perhaps slightly more clearly: the period we are about to consider consists of four weeks preparation for Lent, five weeks of Lent itself, and then Holy Week.

2   It was in the fourth century that Lent, with its chief characteristics, came to be more or less what it is today. During the second and third centuries, only what was called the 'ante-paschal' fast was observed, which lasted from Holy Friday till Easter Sunday. But by the fourth century, the Council of Nicaea already speaks of 'the forty days'. By the seventh century, Lent was established nearly everywhere in its present form.

3   Until the third century, the idea that the Church could grant pardon for serious sins was not generally accepted. If a baptised Christian committed a crime, the Church abandoned him to divine justice and mercy, but did not acknowledge that it had the power to keep him in the communion of the faithful. During the third century, despite opposition from Africa, the 'indulgent' opinions which prevailed in Rome carried the day. Repentant heretics and sinners were granted the possibility of reconciliation. But this presupposed public penitence, and in the churches special, inferior, places were assigned to penitents. The bishop 'reconciled' penitents at the end of Lent. Public penitence was considered necessary for the three categories: of idolatory (or apostasy), homicide and adultery; and heresy was more or less assimilated to apostasy. Lesser sins were not subject to public penitence. Private penitence, or confession, began to appear in Constantinople during the fourth century, due to St John Chrysostom. No ecumenical council has ever drawn up rules on this practice. The example and influence of the monasteries, where monks confessed their secret faults to their superiors or 'spiritual fathers', greatly forwarded the spread of confession. In the Latin Church, it is obligatory; in the eastern Churches, the discipline of private confession has varied, and still varies greatly, depending on the place and the period. There are Orthodox countries where it is generally practised, and other Orthodox areas where it is practically ignored. It is worth mentioning that right up to the first centuries of the middle ages, in the West as in the East, absolutions could be granted by laymen, superiors of monasteries or renowned ascetics, who were not of the priesthood; the women superiors of monasteries themselves absolved the nuns in their charge. Later, absolution came to be concentrated in the hands of the priests.

4   It was in the second half of the second century that the discipline of the catechumenate was instituted. This became general during the fourth century, and disappeared during the sixth century. Baptism was then conferred most frequently at the time of Easter. The catechumens were submitted to a preliminary laying-on of hands, to exorcisms, to examinations or 'scrutinies', and special prayers were said over them; shortly before baptism, the creed was 'given' to them. They were sent out of the church before the reciting of the Creed — this is why the first part of the liturgy is called the 'liturgy of the catechumens' in con-

trast to the part which follows and which is called the 'liturgy of the faithful'.

5   We are the temple of the Holy Spirit. We are also members of the Body of Christ. What relationship is there between these two mysterious realities? The Holy Spirit is *in us*, and we are *in Christ*. Because the Holy Spirit, which is the Spirit of Christ as it is the Spirit of the Father, lives in us, this Spirit incorporates us in the person of Christ. And in this there is something very far from metaphorical.

6   The question of meats consecrated to idols, in Greek the *idolothyta*, faced the first Christians with a very real problem. These meats were either consumed in the pagan temples during the course of ritual meals, or sold in the market place. The letter sent by the Apostles in Jerusalem to the Gentiles at Antioch, whom Paul had converted, ordered them to abstain from 'meats offered to idols' (Acts 15. 29). However, St Paul's exact thought seems to have been this: obviously there can be no question of a Christian eating the *idolothyta* during the ritual meals in the temples of pagans; but if these meats are sold in the market or are offered at a meal in a private house, the Christian can rely on his own judgement, his own conscience, and eat the *idolothyta* if he feels there is nothing wrong in doing so; but, should he risk scandalising another brother, he will abstain. The *Didache*, Irenaeus, Cyril of Jerusalem, John Chrysostom and Augustine are far stricter than the Apostle, and forbid the consumption of *idolothyta* absolutely.

7   In Orthodox Russia, this Sunday was called 'Forgiveness Sunday'. The Russian custom is that each person, on that day, asks forgiveness of anyone he might have offended.

8   The exact number of forty is reached in this way: there are seven days between the Monday, first day of Lent, and the following Sunday, first Sunday of Lent; seven days between the Monday which follows and the second Sunday, between the following Monday and the third Sunday – and so on until the fifth Sunday of Lent; then there are five days starting on the Monday following the fifth Sunday of Lent till the Friday evening when, with vespers, Lazarus Saturday begins. From Lazarus Saturday, we are no longer in the forty days of Lent, but in Holy Week.

9   The Lenten fast originates in the total fast observed during the second and third centuries on Holy Friday and Holy Saturday. This two-day fast indicated the absence of Christ, from the time of his death to his resurrection. It was seen as conforming to the situation described by Jesus in these words: 'Can the children of the bridegroom mourn, as long as the bridegroom is with them? but the days will come, when the bridegroom shall be taken from them, and then shall they fast' (Matt. 9. 15). This interpretation of the fast, as mourning for the absence of Christ, is perhaps not very familiar to modern Christians, and in it lies the most intimate, the deepest and most moving reason we have for fasting. Towards the end of the third century, the *Didascalia* mentions a fast of six days during Holy Week. In the fourth century, we find that a fast of forty days is an established custom in Jerusalem, in memory of the fast that Jesus underwent in the wilderness. The pilgrim Etheria and St Cyril of Jerusalem both mention this forty-day period. Roundabout the year 400, the *Apostolic Constitutions* prescribe a forty-day fast to be observed from the morning until Nones (three o'clock in the afternoon) or until evening. This meant abstention from all nourishment during the day. The consumption of meat and *tyrophagia* (dairy products and eggs) was forbidden; at meals the consumption of *xerophagia* (dry

foodstuffs) alone was authorised. The use of fish and of wine gave rise to rather vaguer interpretations. The *Constitutions*, speaking about fasting in general, say: 'if your health permits . . .'. This is the form under which Basil, Chrysostom and Augustine understood Lent, and it seems, moreover, that they gave advice rather than rigorous precepts about it. The Council *in Trullo*, in 692, speaks of the seven weeks of Lent as being observed generally in the East. By the eighth and ninth centuries, the observance of Lent was well established in the Greek Church. In the tradition that relates to the Lenten fast, it is difficult to distinguish what is of monastic origin and inspiration and what the laity was meant to follow. In fact, many lay people follow a fairly strict fast throughout the whole of Lent; most of them observe Lent in a less severe form; some fast during the first week and during Holy Week. What exact weight do these regulations relating to Lent carry? They are worth what the documents that contain them are worth. It is evident that an apocryphal text, such as the so-called *Apostolic Constitutions* composed around the fifth century, has nothing like the authority of texts that derive genuinely from the Apostles or from a decision taken by an ecumenical council. In general, the Orthodox Church prefers to give directives rather than literal instructions: it indicates the goals, puts forward models, states what is to be aimed at; but as (contrary to the Roman Church) the Orthodox Church has no human authorities who can accord dispensations, when faced with a tradition that has become a rule, it leaves it to the conscience of each individual to judge what adaptations their personal circumstances dictate or permit. Where fasting is concerned, this means distinguishing between the spirit and the letter. Someone who abstains from meat, but eats very special fish, or who follows a refined and expensive vegetarian diet, may be faithful to the letter, yet would not be faithful to the spirit of the fast. Someone who eats the cheapest forms of meat, and who refrains from all elaborate cooking, may violate the letter, yet keep within the spirit of the fast. Furthermore, by itself, a fast from foods will be worthless unless it is accompanied by more important observances.

10   Is it possible to keep one's attention concentrated on Jesus, to look towards him, if one turns to dancing, the radio, television, films, the theatre or novels for one's pleasure? And I am not speaking only of erotic novels or entertainments; even things which, in themselves, are not bad — for example some detective novel or other — distract our attention from the Saviour, and make us insensitive to His presence. A saint can find Jesus everywhere, but this is difficult for the ordinary Christian.

11   Let us remember the words of the Prophet Isaiah (58. 5-8): 'Is it such a fast that I have chosen? a day for a man to afflict his soul? is it to bow down his head as a bulrush, and to spread sackcloth and ashes under him? wilt thou call this a fast, and an acceptable day to the Lord? Is not this the fast that I have chosen? to loose the bands of wickedness, to undo the heavy burdens, and to let the oppressed go free, and that ye break every yoke? Is it not to deal thy bread to the hungry, and that thou bring the poor that are cast out to thy house? when thou seest the naked, that thou cover him; and that thou hide not thyself from thine own flesh? Then shall thy light break forth as the morning, and thine health shall spring forth speedily'.

12   We must remember that none of the three Byzantine liturgies now in use (those of St Basil, St John Chrysostom and St Gregory) represents exactly, in its present form, the original work of its author. It is moreover possible that St Basil

(329-379) abbreviated the liturgy called that of St James of Jerusalem, or took over, modifying it more or less, a liturgy which existed in Neo-Caesarea. Chrysostom abbreviated the liturgy of Basil, and, in Lent, his own liturgy is celebrated on Saturdays and on Palm Sunday. At least in substance, our liturgies were established in their present form in manuscripts dating from the eighth century.

13   Three elements can be distinguished in the liturgy of the presanctified. First, vespers, with their biblical readings. Then the 'great entrance' which is made in silence (the priest carrying the sacred gifts, which have already been consecrated, from the prothesis to the altar), followed by the prayer of St Ephraim. Finally, there is the litany which precedes the Lord's prayer and the remainder of the eucharistic liturgy of St John Chrysostom, with a few variants. As well as on Wednesdays and Fridays, the liturgy of the presanctified is celebrated on the Thursday on which the canon of St Andrew of Crete is read, on the day of the feast of St Charalampias, the day of the feast of the Head of the Forerunner, and the day of the feast of the Forty Martyrs — as long as these feasts do not fall on a Saturday or Sunday. The composition of the liturgy of the presanctified has been attributed to St Gregory the Great, pope of Rome in the sixth century. Gregory did in fact stay in Constantinople, where he was the representative of the See of Rome, but there is no evidence which would allow him to be considered the actual author of the liturgy which bears his name. In fact, this is very similar to the work of Epiphanios of Salerno (+ 403). The Greek liturgical texts give St Gregory the name of *Dialogos*, for he wrote four books of dialogues.

14   The Greek word *akathistos* means that one does not sit down during the singing of this office. We do not know who wrote the akathist hymn, but it was sung for the first time in Constantinople in 626, to commemorate a victory won by the Emperor Heraclius.

15   St Andrew, archbishop of Crete, was born in Damascus and died around 720.

16   St Ephraim the Syrian died in 373; we do not know the date of his birth. He lived at Edessa, and is remembered especially as a writer of hymns. These have a very substantial theological content, and, as a result, are of considerable importance in the history of dogma.

17   Here, we will touch on some of the fundamental ideas that concern icons. First of all, an icon is neither a representation nor a resemblance. The many modern icons which are akin to the likenesses or pictures that belong to the religious imagery of the West and, moreover, which are quite without artistic merit, constitute to the Orthodox church a real misinterpretation. The traditional icon does not copy and does not portray. It suggests, it expresses. In an icon, the essentials are not the features of a face, but the attitudes, the movements, a rhythm, the colours. Each of these elements possesses a symbolic meaning and expresses an invisible spiritual reality. In this respect, iconography is an abstract art. This art, which was once codified on Mount Athos, implies submission to strict rules, and, on the part of the painter, a life of asceticism and prayer. The icon is not 'adored' as are the three divine Persons; it is venerated and honoured. Its value lies in its capacity to teach, in the sense that it offers examples and models for us to meditate on and which can inspire our actions. But an icon has more than pedagogical value. Once blessed, an icon becomes a sacred object, a meeting place between God and man. For whatever its theme,

be it the Person of Christ, the Mother of God, an angel, a saint, or a biblical episode, every icon is a ray emanating from the unique and indivisible light of God; it is a particular aspect of the divine presence. God himself is the final objective for every icon, though sometimes the reference is indirect. Finally, the role of the icon in Christian worship ought not to be exaggerated. Some people are helped by icons, others are not attracted to them. The Church has never made it obligatory for believers to have icons in their homes or to reserve for them a special place in their prayers or personal devotions, but an Orthodox believer who denied the legitimacy of the private or public veneration of icons would fall into the heresy of iconoclasm.

18 The *Triodion* is a special liturgical book which contains the prayers proper to Lent and Easter. The *Pentekostarion*, which contains the prayers for the time of Pentecost, is often thought of as a second part of the *Triodion*.

19 It is generally agreed that the 'epistle of Paul the apostle to the Hebrews' was not written by St Paul himself, but by someone close to him, who was familiar with his dominant trains of thought.

20 Gregory Palamas (1269-1359) was canonised by the Patriarch Philotheus and the synod held in Constantinople in 1368. The main point of 'Palamism' is the distinction between the divine essence, inaccessible to men, and the divine 'energies', which are uncreated but are accessible to human vision. The vision of 'uncreated light' − a divine energy − held a great place in the doctrines of the Byzantine mystics called 'hesychasts'.

21 The feast of September 14th − the 'Exaltation' or 'discovery' of the Cross − commemorates the dedication in 335 of the basilicas erected in Jerusalem after the 'discovery' of the Cross by St Helena, the mother of the Emperor Constantine. This episode, however, does not rest on any sound historical foundation. The feast of August 1st commemorates the *hypsosis*, a solemn procession (*proodos*) with the Cross which took place in Constantinople in 641.

22 The Greek word *Klimakos* means 'ladder'. This title was given to John, a higumen of Sinai, who died around 670, because he wrote a famous book on asceticism entitled *The Ladder to Paradise*. It is possible that the fourth Sunday in Lent was dedicated to St John because, in monasteries, the book was read at table around the middle of Lent.

23 In the sixth century, near the monastery of Sauca in Egypt, pilgrims venerated the tomb of a holy woman called Mary, who had lived in the desert as a solitary and a penitent. This is all that we can say with historical certainty. During the seventh century, the Patriarch-Sophronios of Jerusalem wrote a life of Mary the Egyptian which cannot be traced back to any reliable historical source, but which has served as the basis for all the subsequent literature about her. According to this tradition, Mary, after years of a life of sin, was converted and spent forty-seven years in the desert in the company of angels and of wild beasts, and was helped by some holy monks.

24 The Byzantine writer, Sozomenes, writing during the second half of the 5th century, tells that a certain higumen, Marcel, discovered the skull of St John the Baptist hidden in the ground.

25 The forty martyrs are said to have been buried together at Zela, in Asia Minor. St Basil speaks of them, which seems to confer a guarantee of historical authenticity on this tradition, for Basil and they lived in the same century. The case of these soldier-martyrs raises the more general question of the relationship between Christianity and bearing arms. If a certain number of soldiers, like

those of Sebaste, were put to death for their refusal to take part in the official pagan cult, obligatory in the Roman legions, and if many other Christian soldiers of this era do not seem to have had any scruples about military service, we do come across other cases of soldiers who were put to death as 'conscientious objectors'. Their objection was directed against the fact of carrying arms rather than against official idolatry. Violence and the shedding of blood seemed to them incompatible with the Gospel. Tests that contain the judicial proceedings directed against them, the interrogations and their sentences, have survived to our day. Amongst these conscientious objectors, we can name the soldiers Tipasius, Julius, Fabius, Maximilian of Carthage, and, much later, when Christianity had become the religion of the Roman Empire, Martin of Tours and Victrice of Rouen. The Church of the first four centuries canonised as authentic martyr saints those soldiers who suffered death for refusing military service. Their stand was the same as the stand of the Church, as can be seen from ecclesiastical texts such as the *Canons of Hippolytus*, which forbade the military profession to Christians. Many Christian writers, amongst them Origen and Tertullian, considered there was something irreconcilable between Christ and the bearing of arms. Later on, when the Empire was somehow baptised in the person of Constantine, this attitude changed. The Church made military service and war legitimate. Even so, however, this approval was not general. St Basil, who lived in the empire after it had become Christian, deprived all soldiers who had taken part in a war – even a 'just' one – of the sacraments for nine years. But one of the results of the Church being granted official status was that, gradually, the bearing of arms, 'holy wars' (the Crusades, etc.), and national wars received its blessing. At the same time, the Church began to approve or provoke violent measures against heretics. It has not been from the bosom of the Church that protests against violence and war have emanated; it has been from the fringes, from the Anabaptists, the Mennonites, the Quakers, Tolstoy, Gandhi. In our day, the collapse of the 'Constantinian' Church in its various forms, the invention of atomic weapons, and the growing numbers of conscientious objectors, have sharpened the conflict in the Churches between those who, in defiance of the Sermon on the Mount, decide for Caesar, and those who, in defiance of Caesar, decide for the Sermon on the Mount.

26   From the sixth to the eighth centuries, pilgrims went to Lydda to venerate the memory of St George. The hagiographical accounts that concern this saint (amongst others, the legend of the dragon) emerged much later, during the twelfth and thirteenth centuries.

27   The first time that mention was made of the feast of the Annunciation was at the Council of Toledo, in 656. The Council *in Trullo*, in 692, mentions the Annunciation as being a feast celebrated during Lent. It seems probable that, if March 25th was already established as a great occasion by the seventh century, its origins go back even earlier. In the notes for Chapter III, we have spoken of the manner in which the feasts of Christmas and the Annunciation became historically bound to each other. If the feast of March 25th falls on Holy Friday or Holy Saturday, the observance of the feast of the Annunciation is transferred to Easter Sunday itself.

Chapter V
THE TIME OF THE PASSION

SUMMARY

Lazarus Saturday. Holy Week — 'Behold thy King Cometh' (Palm Sunday). 'As Lightning Cometh out of the East' (Holy Monday). 'Be Ye Therefore Ready' (Holy Tuesday). 'To What Purpose this Waste?' (Holy Wednesday). The Upper Chamber (Holy Thursday). Golgotha (Holy Friday). The Tomb of the Lord (Holy Saturday).

Lazarus Saturday

Strictly speaking, Lent ends on the Friday which follows the fifth Sunday of Lent: the period of forty days is then over. The time of the Passion lasts from the end of Lent until the feast of the Resurrection, anticipated on Holy Saturday. It therefore comprises the Saturday which follows the fifth Sunday of Lent, called 'Lazarus Saturday', and the first six days of Holy Week.

Lazarus Saturday has a very special place in the liturgical calendar. It is not included in the forty days of Lenten penitence; it is not included in the harrowing days of Holy Week — which are counted from the Monday to the Friday. Together with Palm Sunday, it forms a short and joyous prelude to the days of grief which follow. A topographical link unites it to Palm Sunday: Bethany is the place of Lazarus's resurrection, and is also the point of departure for Jesus's entry into Jerusalem[1] Lazarus's resurrection, which this Saturday commemorates, is an event that, as we shall see, carries a very deep meaning. It is mysteriously linked to the resurrection of Christ himself; in relation to that event, it is like prophecy in action. One could say that Lazarus raised from the dead is shown to us, at the threshold of the Easter feasts, as the precursor of Jesus Christ triumphant over death, in the same way that, on the threshold of Epiphany, John when he baptised was the precursor of the Messiah who was about to be revealed. But, as well as its principal significance in relation to the resurrection of Christ, the raising of Lazarus has secondary aspects which will be useful to stop and meditate on.

The epistle read at the liturgy (Heb. 12. 28-13. 8) has no direct bearing on the raising of Lazarus. All the same, one of the verses — 'Remember them that are in bonds, as bound with them; and

135

them which suffer adversity, as being yourselves also in the body'
– could, by a spiritual exegesis, be applied to the compassion
shown to Lazarus by Jesus. The epistle contains various moral
precepts: to continue in brotherly love, to practise hospitality, to
honour marriage, and to obey our superiors. Those who may be
tempted to pass fleetingly over these ethical recommendations,
judging them to be important, of course, but really rather
elementary, should read with attention the three verses in which
they are set, one at the beginning, another in the middle, and the
third at the end: 'Our God is a consuming fire . . . . For he hath
said, I will never leave thee, nor forsake thee . . . . Jesus Christ the
same yesterday, and today, and forever'. For the highest spiritual
truths cannot be isolated from those very simple practical
imperatives which form their daily currency.

The gospel (John 11. 1-45) gives an account of the raising of
Lazarus[2]. The interpretation of this event given to us by the
Church is contained in the chants for matins. Let us listen to
them.

'When Thou didst wish . . . O my Saviour, to establish the
truth of Thy glorious Resurrection, Thou didst deliver Lazarus
from Hades . . . .' Here we find expressed the principal meaning
of the raising of Lazarus. It was, as the sacred poem says in
language that is a little strange, but striking: anticipation,
'establishing the truth' of the resurrection of Christ, a preliminary
proof of Jesus's power over death. 'Through Lazarus, O Death,
Christ has released thy captives . . . . Before Thy death, Thou
hast shaken the power of death.' The Church establishes a certain
link between this victory of Christ's over death, and the triumphal
entry into Jerusalem which will be celebrated the next day. 'O
Death, where is thy victory? . . . We offer Him the palms of
triumphant victory . . . . Like the children, we carry tokens of victory and acclaim Thee, who art the conqueror of death.'

In the second place, the raising of Lazarus announces the
resurrection of the dead which is a consequence of Jesus's resurrection: 'O Christ, when Thou didst bring Lazarus back to life
from amongst the dead, Thou didst establish the principle of
universal resurrection . . . . Thou didst raise him, Thou the giver
of life, thus confirming the resurrection of the world . . . .
Through Thy friend as intermediary Thou didst predict that
humanity was released from corruption'. Lazarus Saturday is, in
a way, the feast of all the dead. It gives us the opportunity to
confirm and give precision to our faith in the resurrection. Our

Lord, in correcting Martha's state of mind, gives us precious teaching about our own dead, for when he had said to her: 'Thy brother shall rise again', she had replied, 'I know that he shall rise again in the resurrection at the last day', and Jesus said, 'I am the resurrection'. Martha's faith was insufficient in two ways: she thought of her brother's resurrection in terms of the future, and only of the future, and then she could not conceive of this resurrection except in relation to some sort of general law. But Jesus indicates that the resurrection is a fact which is already actual, because he himself *is* (and does not *bring about*) resurrection and life. Our dead live through and in Christ. Their life is bound up with the personal presence of Jesus, and is manifested in it. If we seek to unite ourselves in spirit with someone who is dead that we love, let us not try to revive him in our imagination, but enter into contact with Jesus, and in Jesus we shall find him.

Thirdly, the resurrection of Lazarus is a wonderful illustration of christological dogma. It shows us how, in the person of Jesus, human and divine nature are united — without confusion: 'O Christ, by Thy presence at the tomb of Lazarus Thou hast confirmed our faith in Thy two natures . . .'. For, on the one hand, in Jesus, man can give way to emotion and grieve for the loss of a friend: 'Jesus wept. Then said the Jews, Behold how he loved him!' On the other hand, God, in Jesus, can command death with authority: 'He cried with a loud voice, Lazarus, come forth. And he that was dead came forth . . .'.

Finally, the resurrection of Lazarus allows a sinner to hope that, even though he seems spiritually dead, he could come alive again: 'So I pray to Thee, O Thou lover of mankind, to raise me to life, I, who through my passions am dead . . .'. Sometimes this spiritual resurrection seems as impossible as that of Lazarus: 'Lord, by this time he stinketh: for he hath been dead four days . . .'. For all things are possible to Jesus — the conversion of the most hardened sinner as much as the raising of the dead: 'Jesus said, Take ye away the stone . . .'.

This is what we shall learn if, on this Saturday, we go to Bethany, to Lazarus's tomb. We want to meet Jesus at Bethany and to start Holy Week with him, close to him. Jesus invites us to be there, and waits for us. Martha goes to say, in secret, to her sister: 'The Master is come, and calleth for thee'. And Mary 'as soon as she heard that, she arose quickly, and came unto him'. The Master calls me. He wants me to stay with him, not to leave him throughout the days of his Passion. During these days he wants to reveal himself to me – who perhaps 'already stink' – newly and overwhelmingly. Master, I come.

Holy Week

We now enter the most sacred week of the year[3]. It starts with the feast of Jesus's entry into Jerusalem, which, as we have already said, taken with the raising of Lazarus, forms a prelude of joy and glory to the harrowing humiliations which are to follow. The Monday, Tuesday and Wednesday of Holy Week are a preparation for the Passion. They already have a strongly accented character of mourning and repentance. The Thursday, Friday and Saturday of Holy Week belong to the paschal solemnities – each one of these days reveals to us a special aspect of the mystery of Easter. One could even say that this mystery has three aspects, each of which corresponds to a day: Holy Thursday, Holy Friday and Holy Saturday. One could also say that each of these three aspects corresponds to a place: the Upper Room, Golgotha, the Holy Sepulchre. Holy Thursday commemorates the mystery of the upper room, Holy Friday the mystery of Golgotha, Holy Saturday the mystery of the tomb of Christ. On the Thursday, in the upper room, Jesus, through a sacramental action, both announces and represents, consecrates and offers what is to take place during the following days. On the Friday, at Golgotha, Jesus, by his death on the Cross, accomplishes our redemption. On the Saturday, Jesus rests in the tomb; but the Church, already looking ahead to the feast of Easter Sunday, speaks to us of the victory over death that our Saviour has won. This anticipation of the Resurrection on Holy Saturday allows us to say that the mystery of Christ's Resurrection, triumphantly celebrated on Easter Sunday, already belongs, although incompletely, to Holy Week. And so this week constitutes a summary of the whole economy of our salvation.

It would be a great mistake to want to concentrate on one of the aspects of the paschal mystery by separating it from the others. The word 'Passover', in the traditional language of the Church, does not only designate the Sunday of the Resurrection, it also covers the mystery of the eucharist, the mystery of the Cross, and the mystery of the empty tomb. Holy Thursday, Holy Friday, Holy Saturday, and, finally, the Sunday of Easter altogether make up one and the same unique paschal mystery. This whole unity is the Christian transposition of what the Jews call 'the Passover'[4], that is to say, the passage. The elements of the Jewish mystery of the passover correspond to those of our paschal mystery. For them, there is the feast in which the lamb is eaten. There is the blood of the lamb — the sign of salvation for those houses whose door was painted with it and whom the angel of death would spare. There is the crossing of the Red Sea — the departure from the land of Egypt and from slavery — the miraculously divided waters and the passage across on dry ground and, at last, the arrival on the other side, the side of freedom and hope. Holy Week will only have its true meaning for us when we see it as a 'passover', a passage from death to life.

We have said that the time of Christmas and Epiphany in a way express the 'first conversion' of the soul, the first manifestation of Jesus, his first meeting with us, and the beginning of the shared life of Master and disciple. The time of the Passion, or rather of the whole paschal mystery, expresses the 'second conversion', the confrontation of the disciple with the cross and the tomb of his Master. Now, no longer is it enough to follow Jesus along the roads of Galilee, along the paths of his earthly pilgrimage, and to abandon oneself to that very gentle intimacy of his friendship (an intimacy which our unfaithfulness has so often ruptured and which Jesus, nevertheless, is always ready to renew). Holy Week confronts us with the redemptive ministry or office of the Christ, rather than with his person. It offers us the objective grace and inner experience of salvation through the Christ. It sets before us and invites us to participate in the great realities: awareness of sin, repentance, the substitution of the Lamb of God for the sinner so that sin may be redeemed, the sacrifice of the Cross, and God's acceptance of this sacrifice as it is revealed by the Resurrection. We are called to let the blood of Christ flow over our spiritual wounds, to unite ourselves to the sacrificial death of the Saviour so that we may be united to his new life. *Mors et Vita*, death in Christ and life in Christ: such is the 'second conversion'; this is the ordeal to which Holy Week invites us. We should not draw near to the mysteries of this week — which are the mysteries of the Christ, but are also the mysteries of our own selves — without trembling, yet also with infinite trust. 'God so loved the world that he gave his only begotten Son[5] . . . . Greater love hath no man than this, that a man lay down his life[6] . . . .' O my Saviour, grant that during this week I may come to know the profound significance of the Father's gift of his only Son, of the gift of his own life made by the Son, and of that 'greater love' which the paschal mystery reveals. Grant me to know, too, what to 'lay down his life', and 'greater love' implies for me.

Behold thy King Cometh

From the first day of Holy Week, we must 'receive' Jesus Christ, and accept that his will is sovereign over us. The meaning of Palm Sunday[7] lies in this welcome given to the Christ who comes to us.

At vespers for Sunday, which are celebrated on the Saturday evening, three lessons from the Old Testament are read. The first, taken from Genesis (49. 1-2, 8-12), contains the last things that Jacob told his sons; this passage was chosen because, in a few words, it alludes to the 'sceptre', the 'ass's colt', and to the 'blood of grapes' that washes garments — all of them things to which the entry of Jesus into Jerusalem before his Passion gives a new meaning: 'The sceptre shall not depart from Judah . . . until Shiloh come; and unto him shall the gathering of the people be. Binding his foal unto the vine, and his ass's colt unto the choice vine; he washed his garments in wine, and his clothes in the blood of grapes'. The second lesson, drawn from the prophet Zephaniah (3. 14-19), also announces the consolation that the presence of the king brings: 'Shout, O Israel; be glad and rejoice . . . the king of Israel, even the Lord, is in the midst of thee: thou shalt not see evil any more'. The third lesson is the prophecy of Zechariah (9. 9-15) which finds its fulfilment on Palm Sunday: 'Rejoice greatly, O daughter of Zion . . . behold, thy King cometh unto thee: he is just, and having salvation; lowly, and riding upon an ass, and upon a colt the foal of an ass'[8].

The chants at matins invite us, too, to go and meet the King who comes: 'Come, and with great rejoicing let us magnify Christ with palms and branches . . . . The Lord is God and has appeared to us; let us keep the feast together. Come, and with great rejoicing let us magnify Christ with palms and branches, and let us cry aloud . . . . We also, bearing palms and olive branches, cry aloud to Thee in thanksgiving: "Hosanna in the highest, blessed is He that comes in the name of the Lord"'. The gospel read at matins (Matt. 21. 1-11, 15-17) describes the triumphal entry of Jesus into Jerusalem[9]. Towards the end of matins, the bishop or priest recites a prayer and blesses the palms or branches, and these are then distributed to the congregation.

At the liturgy[10], the epistle of St Paul to the Philippians (4. 4-9) announces the nearness of the Lord: 'Rejoice in the Lord alway: and again I say, Rejoice . . . . The Lord is at hand'. The gospel (John 12. 1-18) tells of the last anointing, when Mary poured ointment on Jesus's feet at Bethany — the Church calls our attention to this episode again on the morning of Holy Saturday — and then of the entry into Jerusalem. The final blessing begins thus: 'May he who consented to ride on the foal of an ass for our salvation . . .' etc.

Let us now try to recollect some of the teachings brought by this Sunday.

'Behold thy King cometh unto thee . . . .' Jesus comes to us today as our King. He is more than the Master who teaches his disciples. He requires that in all things we acknowledge his will, setting aside our own desires. He comes to take solemn possession of our soul, and to be enthroned in our heart.

'Unto thee . . . .' It is not simply to humanity in general that Jesus comes, it is to each single one of us: 'thy King'. Jesus desires to be *my king*. To each one of us he is king in a way which is unique, entirely personal and exceptional. He demands inner and intimate loyalty and obedience.

This king is 'humble'. He comes to us seated on a lowly animal, the symbol of humility and meekness. One day he will come again in his glory to judge the world. But today he lays aside all the trappings of majesty and power. He seeks no visible kingdom. He desires only to reign in our hearts: 'My son, give me thine heart'[11].

And yet the crowd was instinctively right when it acclaimed Jesus as the visible king of Israel. Jesus is not only the King of individuals, but of human society. His royalty is of a social nature. It extends over political and economic spheres just as much as over the moral and spiritual sphere. Nothing lies outside its dominion[12].

The crowd which acclaimed Jesus carried palms and branches. These branches were probably olive branches — the most common tree around Jerusalem. Palms and olives both have their symbolic meaning. The palm stands for victory and the olive for peace and anointing. So let us go before Jesus and pay homage both to his power and to his tenderness, in offering our victories (which are in fact his victories) both over ourselves and over sin, and our inner peace (which is his peace).

'A very great multitude spread their garments in the way . . . .'

Let us throw at Jesus's feet our garments, our possessions, our security, all our worldly goods, and also our false appearances and, above all, our ideas, desires, and our feelings. Let the King in his triumph trample underfoot everything that is ours. Let everything that we hold precious be submitted and offered to him.

The crowd shouted: 'Hosanna![13] Blessed is he that cometh in the name of the Lord'. If I can say these words with complete sincerity and submission, if they mean that the impulse of my whole being goes towards the King whom, from henceforth, I acknowledge, then, in that instant, I have turned away from my sins and have received Jesus Christ. May He be welcomed and blessed, He who comes to me.

'As the Lightning cometh out of the East'

There is a striking contrast between the 'spirit' of Palm Sunday and that of Holy Monday. Palm Sunday spoke to us of the coming of the King. Holy Monday announces the coming again of the Son of Man, at the end of time. But, whereas the entry of our King into Jerusalem — and his entry into our soul now, if we will but allow it — reveals humility and tenderness, the second coming, which the Church contemplates on Holy Monday, will be more like a sudden and violent catastrophe. Before his death, Jesus gives men a serious warning.

At vespers on Holy Monday, which are celebrated in the evening on Palm Sunday, the Church marks the transition: 'Let us, the faithful, hasten to pass from one divine feast to the next. From the branches and the palms, let us turn to the fulfilment of the saving sufferings of Christ'. Vespers are immediately followed by a special matins service, called 'the service of the Bridegroom'. After the matins psalms and the *alleluia*[14], a *troparion* is sung slowly which begins thus: 'Behold the Bridegroom cometh in the middle of the night. Blessed is the servant He shall find awake. But he who is found negligent shall be judged unworthy. Be careful, my soul, and fall not into a deep sleep . . .'. The *Kathismata*[15] announce Christ's Passion: 'Verily, on this day, the Passion shall be revealed to the world as the light of salvation . . . . Verily, this day marks and announces fully the Passion of the Lord'. Then a passage from the gospel according to St Matthew (21. 18-43) is read. This passage falls into three parts. The first tells how our Lord curses a fig tree, which immediately withers. The spiritual implication is obvious: the fig tree was in leaf, but bore no fruit; so will a man be cursed whose soul gives the appearance of fertility yet is, in fact, barren. The second tells of a confrontation in the temple between Jesus and the priests: 'By what authority doest thou these things?' Jesus's answer is that he will reveal to them the source of his authority when they have answered his question: 'The baptism of John, whence was it? from heaven, or of men?' The priests, who fear to compromise themselves by accepting either alternative, remain silent. The third part contains two parables. First that of the two sons whose father sends them to work in his vineyard; the one refuses, but repents and goes; the other agrees, but does not go: thus 'the publicans and the harlots go into the kingdom of God before you'. Then follows the parable of the vineyard whose husbandmen kill the servants sent by the master and, finally, the master's son himself; their punishment will be terrible[16], but the stone that the builders had rejected will become the head of the corner. The verses of the canon allude several times to the patriarch Joseph who, hated and sold by his brothers and imprisoned, is seen as a figure of the suffering Christ.

During the offices which precede the liturgy of the presanctified (Sext and vespers), three prophecies are read. They start with the first twenty verses from the Book of Ezekiel: the vision of the four winged creatures, each having four faces, which were driven by the breath of the spirit. An allegorical interpretation, albeit a very late one, has seen in these four beings the four evangelists. It seems that this passage is read today not because it relates specially to Holy Monday, or to Holy Week, but simply because it is the start of the Book of Ezekiel, from which more will be read during the week. The next reading is the first chapter of the Book of Exodus, which speaks of the sufferings of the Jews, captive in Egypt. The choice of this passage is very natural, for the Book of Exodus is the account of Israel's deliverance, of which Easter is the Christian transposition. Lastly, the beginning of the Book of Job is read (1. 1-12): he, too, in his afflictions is a figure of Jesus Christ. At the liturgy[17], the gospel according to St Matthew (24. 3-35) again takes up the theme of the second and dreadful coming of Christ, which will be accompanied by disasters, darkness, by wars and tribulations 'such as was not since the beginning of the world to this time . . . nor shall ever be'. One of the verses of this portion of the gospel summarises the whole teaching of Holy Monday well: 'As the lightning cometh out of the east, and shineth even unto the west; so shall the coming of the Son of man be'.

Be Ye Therefore Ready

Holy Tuesday continues to develop the theme of the coming of Christ and of the judgement he will exercise over men. There is, however, a shade of difference between Holy Monday and Holy Tuesday in the way this theme is treated. Yesterday, the accent was placed on the objective conditions of suddenness and terror that accompany the second coming. Today, the divine Revelation concentrates especially on the vigilance that the prospect of this judgement calls for from us, and on the inner preparation which is necessary.

The services for Holy Tuesday begin on the eve, on the Monday evening. After great compline, the 'Service of the Bridegroom' is celebrated as it was on the Sunday evening: it constitutes matins for the Tuesday. Today, we sing: 'Brethren, let us love the Bridegroom who comes. Let us prepare our lamps as did the wise virgins of the Lord'. A long extract from the gospels is read (Matt. 22. 15-23. 39): Jesus anathematises the priests, the Pharisees and the scribes who put specious questions to him and who, incapable of entering the kingdom themselves, shut it to others. 'Woe unto you, scribes and Pharisees, Hypocrites . . . . Woe unto you, ye blind guides'[18]. He grieves over Jerusalem: 'O Jerusalem, Jerusalem, thou that killest the prophets, and stonest them which are sent unto thee . . . . Your house is left unto you desolate'.

At the liturgy of the presanctified, the readings from the prophets which were begun yesterday are continued, starting with Ezekiel's vision (1. 21-2. 1); this culminates in the revelation of the glory of the Lord and in the sound of a voice saying: 'Son of man, stand upon thy feet, and I will speak unto thee'. God addresses these same words to us, at every moment; but do we really want to hear what he wants to communicate? Are we listening? How much time do we spend each day talking to him spontaneously? Will this Holy Week be a time when we shall hear him? The reading from the Book of Exodus (2. 5-10) is also continued: today we hear how Moses, after his birth, was exposed to the waters and saved by the daughter of Pharaoh[19]; similarly, the whole people of Israel, later, were saved from the great waters of the Red Sea – and we are saved from the waters of sin and death. In the continuation of the Book of Job (1. 12-22), we hear of the misfortunes that are heaped upon him, and also of his resignation: 'The Lord gave, and the Lord hath taken away; blessed be the name of the Lord'. The gospel for the liturgy (Matt. 24. 36 – 26. 2), which is very long, begins with a reminder that the coming of the Son of man will be sudden and unexpected; Jesus then develops this theme in three parables: first, that of the unworthy servant whom the master surprises by returning 'in a day when he looketh not for him, and in an hour that he is not aware of'; then that of the wise and the foolish virgins; and, lastly, that of the servants whom the master calls to account for the talents he had entrusted to them during his absence. After these parables, Jesus describes the judgement in which he will reward those who have served him and punish those who have ignored him in ignoring the sick, the poor, the prisoners or strangers. We have already had an opportunity to meditate on this astonishing statement of Jesus — that he is present in the members of his mystical body[20]. We have also already meditated on the parable of the talents[21]. We will now, therefore, only pause to consider the parable of the ten virgins. In this parable, there are two principal points. The lamp which is needed in order to go out and meet the Bridegroom cannot be lighted unless it is filled with oil. Oil symbolises charity. Without the oil of charity, it is impossible to have that fire, that warmth, that light, which the Bridegroom requires of those whom he will acknowledge as his. Moreover, the oil of charity which alone makes the inner flame possible, is not something that can be 'borrowed' from others; it is something that can only be acquired strictly personally; it must be 'bought', that is, obtained through some costly effort. The intercession of the saints and of the whole Church is very powerful, but neither the saints nor the Church can substitute their oil for that which we have to buy from the Holy Spirit, the source of all unction and all charity. 'We shall be judged on love'[22]; now, one cannot lend love or borrow love: each, at his own cost, or at his own risk, loves or does not love; and, if he does not love, he will not be able to go out to meet the Bridegroom, for he will have no oil for his lamp and will be too late to buy any for himself.

The conclusion which our Lord gives to the parable of the ten virgins can also serve as a conclusion to the whole prayer of Holy Tuesday: 'Be ye therefore ready also: for the Son of man cometh at an hour when ye think not' (Luke 12. 40).

The gospel for the liturgy ends with our Lord's prediction to his disciples: 'Ye know that after two days is the feast of the passover, and the Son of man is betrayed to be crucified'.

To What Purpose This Waste?

Holy Wednesday faces us with the contrast between two figures, two states of soul. It is devoted to the remembrance of two actions: the action of the woman who, at Bethany, came to pour a jar of precious ointment on Jesus's head, and the action of the disciple who betrayed his Master. These two actions are not without a certain link, for the same disciple had protested against the apparent prodigality of the woman.

After great compline on Tuesday evening, as on the two preceding days, the 'Service of the Bridegroom' is celebrated. The chants make several allusions to the 'ungrateful disciple' and the 'adulterous woman'. However, the gospel at matins (John 12. 17-50) does not touch on this episode at Bethany. It tells us how, during one of his last meetings with the crowd, Jesus asks of the Father: 'Glorify thy name'. (What a model of filial prayer this brief phrase is for us — disinterested, adoring and loving!) A voice comes from heaven and says: 'I have both glorified it, and will glorify it again'. Jesus's Passion and the Resurrection will be this glorification. Some sentences from this gospel announce the Passion directly: 'I say unto you, except a corn of wheat fall into the ground and die, it abideth alone: but if it die, it bringeth forth much fruit . . . . Now is the judgement of this world: now shall the prince of this world be cast out; And I, if I be lifted up, will draw all men unto me'.

At the presanctified liturgy on Wednesday we continue reading from Ezekiel (2. 3 – 3. 3): God commands the prophet to go amongst men fearlessly and to tell them the divinely spoken words he has heard. We also go on with the reading from Exodus (2. 11-22): Moses, having killed the Egyptian who struck an Israelite, flees into the country of Midian, and there he marries. The last of these readings, again, is from the Book of Job (2. 1-10): Satan asks God's permission to test Job in his flesh itself, but Job, even though covered with sores and despite his wife's provocation, still refuses to curse God. The gospel (Matt. 26. 6-16) tells of the anointing at Bethany. A woman bearing precious ointment in an alabaster box, pours it on Jesus's head[23]. The disciples[24] are indignant: 'To what purpose this waste? For this ointment might have been sold for much, and given to the poor'. Jesus answers with praise for the woman's deed: 'For ye have the poor always with you; but me ye have not always. For in that she hath poured this ointment on my body, she did it for my burial'. Judas Iscariot, one of the twelve, then goes to find the priests: 'What will ye give me, and I will deliver him unto you?' The priests covenant to give him thirty pieces of silver[25].

Jesus approved of the woman's action, first because it was homage, rendered to him in anticipation of his death and burial, and then because it was an expression of great love which could, for the short time of life he still had left, legitimately be shown him, whereas the poor would always be there. But can we find in these words of Jesus's a clear directive for our own actions? It seems that we can. For one thing, Jesus blesses the woman's prodigality because of certain very special circumstances: the fact of Jesus's visible presence among men and of the near approach of his burial. But, now that these circumstances no longer exist, the duty is different. While we need not condemn offering riches and beauty to the service of God, it is above all through those members of the mystical body who suffer that we are able to honour its Head. For it would be offensive to God if sumptuous churches were built while the poor were allowed to die of hunger[26]. The episode at Bethany, however, has a significance that goes further than the offering of a jar of ointment. It is not only through material goods that we can still give generously to Jesus, but also by consecrating to him our intangible wealth: for example, a life of prayer, an ascetic or contemplative life, or some costly sacrifice which seems useless. The world will protest, as did the disciples at Bethany: to what purpose this prodigality, this waste? Would not a normal life, devoted to the service of men, be much more use? And yet assessment of the 'value of loss' remains the nerve of all religion that is truly alive. If we have the duty to do what we can in cases of real and obvious distress before concerning ourselves with cultural luxury, we have the right, in what concerns only ourselves, to pour *invisible* ointment on Jesus's head — that is to say to 'lose' for his sake (but in reality to gain) the best of our life. Our heart is the first jar of ointment that we must break before him, for him.

The case of Judas is so terrible and obscure that we do not dare to try and explain it or enter into it. But let us keep in mind a sentence from the 'Service of the Bridegroom' for Holy Wednesday: 'The ungrateful disciple, whom Thou hadst filled with Thy grace, has rejected it'. It is indeed possible to reject grace, even when one has been filled with it. And how many Christians are there who, during the course of their lives, have not said to their ruling passion — the flesh, money, or pride: 'I am ready to sell Jesus to you. Tell me what pleasures you will give me, and I will deliver him to you'?

In many churches, the sacrament of unction is conferred during the afternoon or evening of Holy Wednesday to all those believers who desire to receive spiritual or bodily relief.

The Upper Room

Holy Thursday takes us into the mystery of the passover [27]. It both commemorates and makes present to us the first part of this mystery, the part that was unfolded in the Upper Room.

Matins for Holy Thursday are sung on the Wednesday evening. There is no 'Service of the Bridegroom'. After the psalms for matins and a *troparion*, the account of events, from the secret meeting of Judas with the priests until the moment when Jesus left the upper room to go to the Mount of Olives, is read from the gospel according to St Luke (22. 1-39). Then, a canon is sung. At the office of Prime, there is a reading from the Book of Jeremiah (11. 18 — 12. 15) in which we notice the following verses: 'I was like a lamb . . . that is brought to the slaughter . . . . I have given the dearly beloved of my soul into the hand of her enemies . . . . Many pastors have destroyed my vineyard . . . . After that I have plucked them out I will return, and have compassion on them, and will bring them again, every man to his heritage, and every man to his land'.

Vespers are sung before the liturgy. We continue with the reading from Exodus (19. 10-19): God descends upon Sinai in fire and smoke, but does not yet promulgate the commandments. Moses warns the people, 'Be ready against the third day', and they wash their clothes and purify themselves. These are figures of the resurrection of Christ on the third day and of his revealing himself to men after Easter, and also of the purity with which we must approach the paschal mystery. We continue with the reading from the Book of Job (38. 1-23, 42. 1-5). In it, God speaks to Job, questioning him; He says: 'I will demand of thee, and answer thou me'. Then Job in his turn speaks to God, using very much the same words: 'Hear, I beseech thee, and I will speak: I will demand of thee, and declare thou unto me'. This is a model of marvellous exchange, of the intimate dialogue which could, and which should take place between God and man. Moreover, Job has come to the end of his trials, and has remained faithful. He says to the Lord what all souls must aspire to say one day (and what many loving and prayerful souls can already say): 'I have heard thee by the hearing of the ear: but now mine eye seeth thee'. To end with, we read some verses from the beginning of the Book of the prophet Isaiah (1. 4-11). God reproaches Israel, 'Ah sinful nation, a people laden with iniquity' and declares himself tired of the sacrifices offered up to him: 'I am full of the burnt offerings of rams, and the fat of fed beasts; and I delight not in the blood of bullocks'. A better sacrifice is going to be offered to him.

At the liturgy, we read the passage from the first epistle to the Corinthians (11. 23-32) in which St Paul expounds the institution of the Eucharist: 'The Lord Jesus the same night in which he was betrayed took bread . . .'. The gospel for the liturgy is a long juxtaposition of texts (Matt. 26. 2-20; John 13. 3-17; Matt. 26. 21-39; Luke 22. 43-44; Matt. 26. 40-27. 2). It tells of the priests holding counsel, of the anointing at Bethany, the preparation for the passover, the washing of the feet, the institution of the Eucharist, the agony at Gethsemane, Judas's kiss, the arrest of Jesus, the interrogation at the high priest's, of Peter's denial, and ends with Jesus being handed over to the Roman procurator. The final blessing begins thus: 'O Thou, who through thine infinite goodness hast revealed to us humility as the most excellent way when Thou didst wash the feet of Thy disciples . . .'. And, in cathedral churches, after the liturgy, the bishop proceeds to the ceremony of washing the feet — the twelve apostles being rep-represented by twelve priests.

The service of the twelve gospels, which one usually thinks of as characteristic of Holy Thursday, really belongs to the services of Holy Friday. We shall therefore speak of it together with tomorrow's services.

One of the chants for matins, called the *Ikos*, sums up very exactly the meaning of the rites for Holy Thursday: 'Let us draw near with fear to the mystery of the table and, with souls that are pure, may we receive the Bread. Let us stay with the Master to see how He washes the feet of His disciples and dries them with a towel. Let us learn to imitate what we gaze upon and so let us give ourselves each to the other, washing each other's feet, for Christ Himself called His disciples to do as He has done. But Judas, the ungrateful servant, paid no heed and remained in his wickedness'. Three aspects of Holy Thursday are focused on here: the washing of the feet, the Lord's supper, and Judas's betrayal. Let us concentrate on each of these three aspects for a while.

However, before we consider what takes place in the upper room, let us think about the room itself. Jesus sends word to the master of the house: 'I will keep the passover at thy house with my disciples [28] . . . . Where is the guestchamber, where I shall eat the passover with my disciples' [29]. These words are addressed to each one of us. At every Easter feast, Jesus desires specially to come into us and to celebrate, spiritually, the passover in our soul. And even when it is not Eastertime, each time that, at his own table, the Lord Jesus shares out the bread which is the communion of his body and the wine which is the communion of his blood, he celebrates this meal in the upper room of our own selves at the same time as the celebration of the sacrament takes place outwardly. But there is more. Not only at the feast of Easter, not only at the visible eucharist, but every day, at every moment, we have the possibility of celebrating an invisible and silent passover in the upper room of our soul. Every time we desire it, this possibility of receiving the Lord Jesus in us through faith and love, and of letting him be our spiritual nourishment, is ours. And at this meal, too, which is purely inward and spiritual, Jesus says to us: 'With desire I have desired to eat this passover with you . . .' [30]. But where is the room in which we shall receive him? Is everything ready? No room in my soul is cleaned and adorned for such a visit. Besides, it is not enough to prepare a corner of my soul, hiding away the disorder which exists in the other parts of myself [31]. It is my whole soul that has to be washed, to be clean. I have not the strength to do it. So, Lord, I must ask thee to prepare for thyself an upper room in me. Stay in me for longer than a passing visit. Become the permanent guest of my soul, become its master; here are the keys which open all the doors; it is I who am now the guest, in thy house.

And if thou dost wish to come to me with thy disciples, Lord, that means I must receive thee into myself 'catholicly'. I cannot claim to separate thee from the members of thy mystical body. In receiving thee, therefore, I receive spiritually the whole community of thy disciples, thy whole Church. My soul must open itself lovingly and join in the same prayer with all those who believe in thee, all those who love thee, and all those who call upon thee. May I, therefore, become one with them all — those

who live in thee and those who have died in thee — with thy most
blessed Mother, thy apostles, thy martyrs, thy saints of yesterday,
today and tomorrow. Come into me, Lord, with thy disciples.

Thou dost come near me, Lord, to wash my feet, and dost not
allow me to protest against the exceeding humility which makes
thee kneel before me to wash me. Thou dost say to me: 'If I wash
thee not, thou hast no part with me'[32]. Through these words,
Jesus indicates two things. First, that we must allow ourselves to
be purified from our sins by him, from the dust of the daily road
as well as from the greater impurities: 'Lord, not my feet only,
but also my hands and my head', as Peter said[33]. And then, that
to have a part with the Lord truly, one must partake in his
humility and his abasement. To have a part with Christ is to have
part with the God-Man who washes the feet of men. I shall have
part with the Christ who washes feet if I allow my feet to be
washed by him and if I, myself, through his example, wash the
feet of others: 'If I then, your Lord and Master, have washed your
feet; ye also ought to wash one another's feet'[34]. What is meant by
washing the feet of other men? Before we can pour water on their
feet, we have first of all to get into the only position from which it
is possible to do this, in an attitude of complete humility: we have
to be at their level and to kneel before them. Briefly, we have to
abase ourselves. This points to something of great value for our
whole spiritual life. We can go towards God either by raising
ourselves up or by lowering ourselves: by an ascent or by a
descent. At certain times, it is as if we had no wings; dryness
invades us; it is impossible for us to rise towards God. At these
times, when we cannot find God above us, or perhaps we may no
longer find him within us at all, we can find him lower than
ourselves. We can stoop to the suffering caused by a moral misery
or a sin — let us not say 'worse' than our own (for if we see clearly,
we know that our own sins have also reached the depths of the
abyss) — but one that appears to be in more 'crying' need, that is
more conspicuous, or towards a physical distress which we
ourselves have been spared: in the desire to alleviate this pain, in
this movement of descent, we shall find God. To wash men's feet
is to bring refreshment or relief to those who suffer. But it is also
to try and separate the sinner from his sin. The method of
'washing the feet' which can be used with a sinner is both very
special and very delicate. It has nothing to do with reproach, or
the formulation of moral precepts. The voice of authority that
sometimes is legitimate has no place here. In relation to the

sinner, one's attitude can only be that of service and humility. This humility and this love must give rise to such a *pressure* on the sinner that they incontrovertibly impel him, without discussion of any kind, away from his sin. Such are the deep and difficult perspectives opened to us by the gospel episode of the washing of the feet[35].

The central mystery of the upper room, however, lies in the Last Supper. The Lord Jesus, really present both as he who distributes and as he who is distributed, gives himself to us in the Eucharist[36]. That we receive in the sacrament the bread of life, the body and the blood of the Saviour, all faithful Orthodox who approach the altar believe: this point does not need enlarging on here. But some other aspects of the Eucharist are perhaps less familiar to their thought, and these we will touch on briefly. The Eucharist, before it becomes the presence of Christ in us, is the sacrifice of Christ for us[37]. At this feast of Holy Thursday, it is particularly important to remember the link which our Lord wanted to establish between the meal in the upper room and the Jewish Passover[38], and between this same meal and the Passion[39]. Every eucharist is a sacrificial meal. Each time that we make our communion with the body of Christ that has been broken and with his blood that has been shed, we are in communion with his Passion, and take part in his sacrifice. We ought to break and offer our own selves, our selfish desires, our will: we should plunge the knife of the sacrificer into our own hearts. Communion is a spiritual breaking. But we must not forget that the actual sacrifice does not exhaust the whole concept of sacrifice: God's acceptance of the victim is an integral part of it; the supper in the upper room and our eucharistic liturgies are the sacrament not only of the Lord's suffering, but also of His glorification and of the Father's answer, as it is revealed by the Resurrection and the Ascension[40]. There is an eternal and heavenly eucharist, with which our earthly eucharists keep us in contact[41]. Another aspect of the Supper which Christians are not, perhaps, sufficiently aware of is communion with the total Christ, that is to say not only with the Head, but with all the members of the mystical Body: being in communion with Jesus Christ, we are brought into communion with all men, in as much as they participate − through nature and through grace − in the God become Man[42]. The Eucharist, because it means incorporation into the person of Jesus, is incorporation into the Church with all our brothers and sisters. And lastly, what we said before on the subject of the upper room of our soul must be remembered. As well as the visible Passover, as well as the sacrifice and sacramental communion, there is an invisible Passover, a purely spiritual sacrifice and communion that we can always offer and receive in the secret of our soul, and this inner eucharist, of which we are both the ministers and recipients, can bear much fruit. It is possible to be nourished by the living bread come down from heaven, and to consume the body and blood of the Lord in spirit. At every moment, Jesus Christ, our eternal Priest, says to us − as does the priest at our earthly liturgies: 'With fear of God, with faith and love draw near'[43].

Holy Thursday also makes us contemplate the betrayal by Judas. This had already taken place before Judas made his compact with the Jewish priests to hand over his Master to them. But the betrayal was shown up during the last supper in the upper room in a particularly painful way. 'He that eateth bread with me hath lifted up his heel against me . . . . Verily, verily, I say unto you, that one of you shall betray me . . . . He it is, to whom I shall give a sop, when I have dipped it. And when he had dipped the sop, he gave it to Judas Iscariot . . . . And after the sop Satan entered into him . . . .'[44] Judas, with betrayal in his heart, accepts the sop that Jesus offers him, and we find his gesture odious. He has profaned the table of the Lord. But, how many times have we taken a place at this table without having purified our hearts sufficiently? How many times, having shared the Lord's supper, have we given way to sin, in serious matters and through our own free will? Judas betrayed his Master once and, if one may use the expression 'en bloc'. We constantly betray Jesus − in details. But it is no less a betrayal. Jesus says to Judas: 'That thou doest, do quickly'[45]. Judas goes out, in order to consummate his work of death: 'and it was night' − it was the hour of darkness outside the upper room as well as in the heart of the traitor. Jesus's words, in sending Judas out to fulfil his crime, are deeper and more merciful than they seem. The disciples, as the fourth evangelist tells us, believed that Jesus had sent Judas out in order to buy certain things, or to give money to the poor in view of the feast. And that was true, but not in the sense that the disciples imagined. Jesus sent Judas out to buy, for thirty pieces of silver[46], the true Lamb of the Passover, for Judas in handing over his Master, procured for the world the victim of the Passover who was to atone for all sin. The generosity revealed by Jesus in the Redemption dominates the horror of all betrayals.

We can summarise, in a prayer, the meaning of this day of Holy Thursday. This prayer is the *troparion* which is sung at today's liturgy with particular solemnity, and is said each time that a believer takes communion:

'Of Thy mysterious supper, Son of God, today admit me a partaker: for I will not tell the secret to Thine enemies, nor give Thee a kiss like Judas, but like the thief I will acknowledge Thee: Remember me, Lord, in Thy kingdom.'

Golgotha

On Holy Thursday we followed Jesus to the upper room. Today, Holy Friday[47], we follow him up to Golgotha. We will follow him, not as Peter followed him, from 'afar off . . . to see the end'[48], but as his mother, as John and the holy women, who did not abandon him.

The liturgical day of Holy Friday begins on Thursday evening with the service of 'the twelve gospels'. This service constitutes matins for Holy Friday. After the matins psalms, a juxtaposition of gospel texts is read, which is divided into twelve parts[49], so that an account of the Passion is formed from which virtually no detail is omitted. This account begins with Jesus's words after the Supper, and with the priestly prayer[50]. It continues with his arrest in the Garden of Olives – strangely, the agony in the garden[51] is passed over in silence – then the Jewish proceedings against Jesus, followed by the Roman proceedings (but his appearance before Herod is not mentioned), the scourging, the crowning with thorns, his bearing of the Cross, the Crucifixtion, his death and, finally, the burial of the Lord. After each gospel, the response is: 'Glory to Thy longsuffering, O Lord, glory to Thee', and various hymns and antiphons are sung. One of the most beautiful is the fifteenth antiphon, which is sung between the fifth and the sixth gospel and which begins: 'Today hangs from the Cross He who hung the earth over the waters. He who is King of the angels is crowned with thorns. Vain purple is thrown over Him who casts the sky over the clouds . . .'. While this is being sung, a cross is solemnly placed in the middle of the church; the people come to adore and kiss it[52]. When the reading of the twelve gospels is over, the service ends with a litany and a blessing, which begins with these words: 'May He who suffered spittings, scourgings, blows, humiliations, the Cross and death for the salvation of the world, Christ, our true God . . .'.

The structure of the canonical hours for Holy Friday is similar to that of Christmas and Epiphany. Each one includes three (at Terce, two) psalms, and readings from the Old Testament, an epistle and a gospel. At Prime, one of the psalms is Psalm 21 (in English versions, 22), the first verse of which is spoken by Jesus on the Cross[53]. The reading from the prophet Zechariah (11. 10-13) alludes to the thirty pieces of silver thrown, as were those of Judas, into the sanctuary[54]. The epistle of Paul to the Galatians (6. 14-18) was chosen because of the first verse: 'But God forbid that I should glory, save in the cross of our Lord Jesus Christ, by whom the world is crucified unto me, and I unto the world'. The gospel according to St Matthew (27. 1-56) recounts the Passion, from Jesus's appearance before Pilate to the earthquake which follows his death; the episode of Judas's remorse and the buying of Hakeldama, the 'field of blood', connects this gospel with the prophecy that has just been read[55]. At Terce, the reading from the prophet Isaiah (50. 4-11) evokes the Passion, especially in the following verse: 'I gave my back to the smiters, and my cheeks to them that plucked off the hair: I hid not my face from shame and spitting. For the Lord God will help me; therefore shall I not be confounded . . . .'. The epistle of Paul to the Romans (5. 6-10) speaks to us of the Redemption: 'Christ died for us . . . . When we were enemies, we were reconciled to God by the death of his Son'. The gospel reading (Mark 15. 16-41) takes us from the crowning with thorns to Jesus's death and the conversion of the centurion. At Sext, we hear Isaiah's famous prophecy (52. 13-54. 1) which has been called the 'fifth gospel', and which describes the lot of the 'Suffering Servant'[56]: ' . . . despised and rejected of men; a man of sorrows, and acquainted with grief . . . . Surely he hath borne our griefs, and carried our sorrows . . . . But he was wounded for our transgressions, he was bruised for our iniquities . . . and with his stripes we are healed . . . he is brought as a lamb to the slaughter, and as a sheep before her shearers is dumb so he openeth not his mouth . . . he bare the sin of many, and made intercession for the transgressors'. The epistle (Heb. 2. 11-18) was read at Nones, on the eve of Christmas; it is read again today because of the last two verses, which speak of Jesus, who 'it behoved . . . to be made like unto his brethren, that he might be a merciful and faithful high priest in things pertaining to God, to make reconciliation for the sins of the people. For in that he himself hath suffered being tempted, he is able to succour them that are tempted'. The gospel (Luke 23.

32-49) takes us from the crucifixion to Jesus's death. At Nones, the first psalm (68; in English versions, 69) opens with words that are well-suited to the Passion: 'Save me, O God: for the waters are come in unto my soul . . .'. In the reading from the prophet Jeremiah (11. 18-12. 5, 9-10, 14-15), the second verse is of central importance: 'But I was like a lamb . . . that is brought to the slaughter; and I knew not that they had devices against me . . .'. The epistle to the Hebrews (10. 19-31) exhorts us to have 'boldness to enter into the holiest by the blood of Jesus, by a new and living way, which he hath consecrated for us, through the veil, that is to say, his flesh . . .'. The gospel (John 19. 23-37) takes us from the sharing out of Jesus's clothes to the piercing of his side.

Holy Friday is the only day of the year when no eucharistic liturgy is celebrated.

Vespers for Holy Friday are celebrated during Friday afternoon. They are called the 'Burial Service'. After the evening psalms and several chants, three portions of the Old Testament are read. First, a passage from Exodus (33. 11-23); God says to Moses: 'While my glory passeth by . . . I will put thee in a clift of the rock, and will cover thee with my hand while I pass by'. The Church applies these words to the entombment of Christ. The reading from the Book of Job comes to an end today: we hear the account of the final prosperity of Job and of his death, and his resurrection is announced: 'He will be raised with those whom our Lord raises'[57]. We remember that Job's afflictions and his subsequent consolation prefigure those of Christ. Finally, the 'Passion according to Isaiah' which was read in the morning is read at Sext. After the Old Testament reading, we hear a portion of the first epistle of St Paul to the Corinthians (1. 18-2. 2): 'We preach Christ crucified, unto the Jews a stumblingblock, and unto the Greeks foolishness . . . . For I determined not to know any thing among you, save Jesus Christ, and him crucified'. There follows a gospel reading which, once again, is a mosaic of texts[58]. It goes from the handing over of Jesus to Pilate to the entombment. After this, the rite of the 'burial' takes place. A procession goes round the church. The *epitaphion*, a rectangle of material on which is painted or printed an image of the dead Christ, is carried up to the 'tomb' which has been prepared in the middle of the church and is decked with flowers. The *epitaphion* is placed on the tomb, and the book of the Gospels is placed on the *epitaphion*. The congregation come and kiss them. The choir sings. After the Song of Simeon, 'Lord, now lettest thou thy servant depart in peace', the service comes to an end with the *troparion*: 'The noble Joseph takes Thy immaculate Body down from the Cross, he wraps it in white linen with spices . . . and places it in a new tomb'.

The burial rite in fact belongs to Holy Saturday, for, in one of the chants, the choir sings: 'On this Saturday Thou didst prepare for Thy Glory'. But the vespers service which precedes it clearly belongs to the Passion and to Holy Friday, because at it is sung: 'On this day, the Lord of creation stood before Pilate, and the Creator of the universe is handed over to be crucified'. This service in the afternoon of Holy Friday marks a transition between the Friday and the Saturday. It comes to an end at about the hour when the body of Jesus would have been brought down from the Cross and placed in the tomb[59].

After these long and rich Church services, it is not useless to recollect ourselves, individually and in silence, at the foot of the Cross, and try to sift out the general meaning of Holy Friday. Of course, each episode of the Passion offers us very rich material for reflection, but, in order to give greater precision and awareness to our devotion, it is helpful to group these impressions around some main themes.

Holy Friday confronts us with Jesus Christ crucified[60] for our salvation. In our encounter with the Cross of Jesus on Holy Friday, we can distinguish several essential moments or elements.

There is first of all the objective mystery of the Redemption. The Cross is the instrument of our salvation, the instrument of Christ's sacrifice. But in what way are we saved by the Cross? In what sense do we speak of Christ's sacrifice? We say that Jesus Christ died for us. But have we any kind of clear idea what these words 'died for us' mean? We repeat the formula — but does it have living content, does it correspond to a reality that we experience deeply? It is to be feared that, not only for many 'Orthodox' Christians, but even for many 'Orthodox' theologians, the meaning of the Passion of Christ is very vague. Thinking about the Passion does not come naturally to them; perhaps they even feel, although very mistakenly, that this is a characteristically 'Orthodox' attitude (but, by such a standard, St Paul was not orthodox). Without going into the subtleties of dogma, we need to see at least this clearly. Jesus Christ wanted, by means of his voluntary death, to 'make satisfaction' superabundantly for all sins[61] and to substitute a new life — his — for our irremediably corrupted life. He has become in reality and to the highest degree what the paschal Lamb showed figuratively. The 'satisfaction' that Jesus makes for my own sins is the most important event of my life.

It is only through contrition or repentance[62] that we can assimilate the mystery of this Redemption. Jesus, nailed to the Cross, represents the objective aspect of the mystery. Peter, crying bitterly after denying his Master, and after Jesus's look fell on him, and the thief who implored Jesus while he was crucified, represent the subjective aspect. Holy Friday will bear no fruit for us unless a violent upsurge of contrition throws us to Jesus's feet. Is this Holy Friday to be a day of holy sorrow in my life?

Forgiveness is declared from the height of the Cross. Jesus says to the thief: 'Today shalt thou be with me in paradise'[63]. It is not enough that on this Holy Friday I should embrace the Cross and the mystery of my salvation through my faith, or in contrition. I must try to obtain from the lips of the Saviour himself a word of forgiveness. Perhaps I shall hear a word, which is totally personal, spoken by Jesus in the secret depths of my soul. But such a word of forgiveness spoken by the Church or through Scripture has the same value as this intimate declaration, if I know how to welcome it as the word of the Saviour himself[64]. On this Holy Friday, have I sought a word of forgiveness?

Finally, Jesus's Cross must be placed at the centre of my life. The Cross of Jesus: not only an instrument of suffering, but an instrument of victory. To make Jesus's sacrifice the centre of my life − of my thought, my will, and my feelings − to look at men and things from the perspective of the Cross, to be convinced that nothing is of greater importance to the world than Christ's sacrifice, eternally present and offered; in this lies the 'second conversion' of which we have already spoken, the new and dazzling vision which reduces to insignificance what fascinated us before. This vision demands a radical change of our whole life. Jesus crucified becomes the filter through which, from now on, we shall make everything pass. The day when a man understands the 'centrality' of the Cross − of the radiant Cross as well as of the blood-stained Cross − is the great day of his life. May this Holy Friday be a birthday in my life. *O crux, ave!*

The Tomb of the Lord

On Holy Saturday, the Church directs and concentrates our attention on our Lord's tomb.

In the whole liturgical year, there is no day with a more complex character than Holy Saturday[65], for this day shares both in the sorrow of the Passion and in the joy of the Resurrection. The celebration of Easter, which has been more and more advanced, has ended by annexing the greater part of the day of Holy Saturday. It is possible to distinguish in Holy Saturday two consecutive parts, one of which still belongs to the time of the Passion, and the other already to the time of Easter. In this chapter, we shall only consider the part of Holy Saturday which brings to an end the time of the Passion. The other part of Holy Saturday, in which the celebration of the Resurrection is anticipated, will find its place naturally in the following chapter.

As we have indicated, Holy Saturday already 'pierces' into the rite of Christ's burial which is celebrated on the Friday afternoon. But it begins properly with matins for Saturday, sung either in the evening on the Friday, or on the morning of Saturday itself. After the matins psalms and some other prayers, a 'canon' of nine canticles is sung. After the ninth canticle, a procession forms in the middle of the church, near the tomb which is covered (as we saw yesterday) by the *epitaphion*. Then the *"encomia"*, which are a series of stanzas divided into three parts separated by litanies, are sung. Here are some of them:

'Thou who didst establish the measure of the earth, Jesus, King of the Universe, today art held by a narrow grave . . . . Jesus, my Christ, King of all creation, what dost Thou seek in entering hell[66]? Dost Thou wish to set free the race of mortal men? The Lord of all creation lies beneath our eyes; He is dead, He who empties the tombs is placed in a new grave . . . . He who amongst all mortals is beautiful is seen as dead; He who made the natural universe beautiful . . . . All creation, O Word, is overwhelmed by Thy Passion, for with Thee all creatures suffer . . . . Like the grain of wheat buried in the womb of the earth, Thou hast brought forth a heavy ear in raising mortal men to life . . . . Thy side was opened, Thou, who didst take a rib from Adam to fashion Eve . . . . Stretched on the wood[67], O Jesus, Thou dost gather all men, from the wound in Thy side whence flows life, Thou dost pour out forgiveness to all[68]. I adore Thy Passion, I hymn Thy burial . . . O my joy . . . how shall I bear the three days of Thy burial? . . . My entrails suffer as do those of mothers[69] . . . . The earth trembles to see Thee resting in its bosom . . . . With the myrrh-bearing women, let us hasten to anoint, as one would a corpse, Him who lives . . . .'

The congregation is then sprinkled with rose water. The *encomia* are followed by several other canticles. After the 'Great Doxology' (which is a mixture of the *Gloria in excelsis* and the *Te Deum*), a new procession takes the *epitaphion* and the book of the Gospels back into the sanctuary. The *epitaphion* is placed on the altar, where it will remain throughout the whole of Easter week. A prophecy from Ezekiel (37. 1-14) is read: it is the vision of the dried bones that the Spirit covers again with flesh and breathes life into; these bones, which live again, designate the people of Israel, the risen Christ (although his body did not know corruption), and the sinner who is pardoned. Then two passages from St Paul (1 Cor. 5. 6-18; Gal. 3. 13-14) form one reading; the main text is: 'Christ our passover is sacrificed for us: Therefore let us keep the feast, not with old leaven, neither with the leaven of malice and wickedness; but with the unleavened bread of sincerity and truth'[70]. This epistle is followed by the last of the twelve gospels read on Holy Thursday (Matt. 27. 62-66); the priests persuade Pilate to have Jesus's tomb sealed and guarded. Matins come to an end with a litany and the normal prayers of dismissal.

Here that part of Holy Saturday which belongs to the Passion of Christ ends. The rest of this day belongs to the time of Easter.

Before ending this chapter, which has been devoted to the time of the Passion, let us stop for a while near the tomb of our Lord. Two passages from Holy Scripture will help us to take in the message of Holy Saturday. The first, a text from the gospel according to St Luke: 'And the women also, which came with him from Galilee, followed after, and beheld the sepulchre, and how his body was laid. And they returned, and prepared spices and ointments; and rested the sabbath day according to the commandment'[71]. In the life of every disciple of Jesus, there come times when the Master seems to withdraw himself and to remain absent — as if in some way he is buried. These Galilean women show us what our attitude should be at such moments. They have observed the grave; they know where Jesus is. And we, too, must not doubt that Jesus is there, even if he does not seem to answer, even if he has become invisible: we must keep our eyes fixed, if not on him, at least in his direction. The women are not idle, they do not say: 'Now nothing can be done'. They prepare spices with which to anoint Jesus's body. They continue to honour him, although life has withdrawn from his human body. In the same way, during the times when Jesus veils himself and is silent, let us not cease to keep him at the centre of our adoration. Let us prepare spices − the spices of our affections and works − to offer from now on to the Friend whom we do not see, and also to offer to him when once again we shall feel his presence − for we know he will come back to us. But there is no agitation in the women's preparations; they keep the sabbath, they rest. While Jesus is in the tomb is a time of waiting and of silence: a time for secret life, hidden and contemplative, near him, with him. Holy Saturday is the feast of those mystics whom the world is unaware of, and who wish to be known only by Jesus. The peace of Holy Saturday is entirely oriented towards the great event of Sunday morning, towards the power and the joy of the Resurrection. But we have to safeguard this peace 'which waits': Oh! that invasion of external preparations for Easter, which prevents so many Orthodox from keeping this feast as a retreat and in silence. On this day, let us read again the words of Paul to the Romans: 'We are buried with him by baptism into death . . . . Likewise reckon ye also your-selves to be dead indeed unto sin, but alive unto God through Jesus Christ our Lord'[72]. If I were able to persuade myself sufficiently that I was dead with Jesus, buried with Jesus, my spiritual life would become so much simpler and easier. To every temptation, to everything that distracted me from the one thing necessary, I should answer only: 'What is the point? I am dead. I am in the tomb of my Master'. Instead of arguing and fighting with life, I should place myself straight away on the other side, outside life (naturally, this means the desires of worldly life), and then, dead to the world and to sin, I should be more than ever alive 'in God'. One could even say that in this there is a spiritual tactic, a singularly efficacious tactic, open to those in all walks of life, of 'entombment' with our Lord. We have sung today: 'I praise Thy entombment'. We might now add: 'Grant that I may be entombed with Thee'.

Notes for Chapter V

1   In the fourth century, the celebration of Holy Week in Jerusalem began on Saturday, the eve of Palm Sunday, with a service in the sanctuary called the Lazarium, at Bethany.

2   We know nothing more about Lazarus himself than what the gospel tells us: that Lazarus was the brother of Martha and Mary of Bethany, the friend of Jesus, and that he was raised from the dead by our Lord. A cycle of legends grew up around Lazarus later on: that he and his sisters, put onto a boat without sails, oars or rudder by the Jews, were miraculously landed on the shores of Provence. Lazarus, it is said, then evangelized the South of France and became the first

bishop of Marseilles. These legends seem to have their root in the fact that a certain Lazarus, consecrated Bishop of Aix at Marseilles during the fifth century, had visited Palestine.

3   The week that precedes the Sunday of the Resurrection is called 'Holy and Great Week' by the Greeks, and 'Great Week' (*hebdomada maior*) or 'Holy Week' (*hebdomada sancta*) by the Romans. The Russians call it 'Passion week'; but this name tends to create confusion, for the Romans call the week which precedes Palm Sunday — which by the Greeks is called 'Palm Week' — 'Passion week'. It emerges from historical documents that Holy Week was celebrated with special services and particularly strict fasts throughout nearly all the Christian world by the end of the fourth century. We have numerous details and much precious information about the celebration of Holy Week in Jerusalem at this time, thanks to an account that has come down to us from an eye-witness, the pilgrim Etheria, around 388.

4   The Greeks made the word *'Paskha'* derive from the Greek verb *paskhein*, 'to suffer', but, in fact, it comes from the Hebrew term *pessah*, 'passage'.

5   John 3. 16.

6   John 15. 13.

7   Both the Greeks and the Romans give this name to the Sunday which precedes Easter. We know that in Mesopotamia, from 397, palms were blessed in churches on this Sunday. In Jerusalem, at around the same date, Palm Sunday was celebrated as follows: believers gathered together at the break of day in the Anastasis (the Church of the Holy Sepulchre); from there, they went to the Martyrium (the Church of Golgotha) where the ordinary Sunday service was celebrated. At the beginning of the afternoon, a procession went to the Mount of Olives, where there was a service. Around three o'clock, the procession went on to the Imbomon, the place where, according to one tradition, the Ascension of our Lord took place. Another service was celebrated there. At about five o'clock, the procession came down to Jerusalem, the children bearing palms and olive branches, and vespers were sung in the Anastasis. Prayers at the Martyrium completed the day.

8   The prophet wants to replace the classic image of kings riding in chariots or mounted on horses by a new image: a king whose entry into his own rightful capital is an act of humility — for an ass is the opposite of a horse, which suggests war and conquest.

9   Matthew's account reproduces, with light retouching, the account in Mark (11. 1-11). Matthew makes Bethphage the place of departure for the entry into Jerusalem, whereas Mark mentions both Bethphage and Bethany. Bethphage means 'house of the green figs'. Might there be a connection here between this name and the cursing of the sterile fig-tree at the start of Jesus's last week of teaching?

10   The liturgy for this Sunday is that of St John Chrysostom.

11   Prov. 23. 26.

12   Certain Churches — particularly those which receive support from the State (and especially the Orthodox and Lutheran Churches) — have too often accepted the authority of the State as supreme and unarguable in matters of social, national and international ethics. One even sees one or other of these Churches prepared to acclaim and bless a State which now combats and oppresses Christianity. The Roman Church preaches the Kingdom of Christ and has instituted a feast for the royalty of Christ; however, its silences in certain

recent cases have troubled the souls of some who expected clear speaking from her. At Byzantium, caesaro-papism was spreading at the very moment when those who were decorating the churches delighted to represent Christ with all the attributes of sovereignty. Herod also crowned Jesus, and dressed him in purple, in his own way . . . .

13   At the time of Christ, with a population who no longer spoke Hebrew, the Hebrew word *Hosannah* had lost its original vigour and meaning. It had become simply an acclamation, a cry of joy or welcome. It is in this sense that it was used on the seventh day of the feast of the Tabernacles, called 'the day of Hosannah' or 'the Great Hosannah'. Originally, however, the word *Hosannah* had a very strong meaning: 'save now, we pray'. The implications of the term were precisely messianic. It is in this deep sense that, at the entry of Jesus into Jerusalem, the Holy Spirit placed this word on the lips of the people – without their being conscious of it.

14   The Greek Church multiplies the *alleluias* during Lent and Holy Week, while the Roman Church suppresses them during the same periods. On the night of the Passover, the Jews sang the 'hallel from Egypt', that is to say six psalms in which *alleluia* is repeated. It is very possible that Jesus and his disciples would have sung these psalms before leaving the upper room to go to Gethsemane. The word *alleluia* means: 'Praise be to thee, Yahveh'.

15   'Kathisma' is the name given to certain parts of the service during which sitting is permitted.

16   This portion of the gospel was read on the 13th Sunday after Pentecost. See Chap. 1.

17   Normally, the liturgy of the presanctified does not include a reading from either an epistle or a gospel. Their presence is characteristic of Holy Week.

18   To a certain extent, the gospel readings for Holy Week correspond to the historical and chronological order of events. The discussions with the priests and the scribes, and the parables of the Second Coming belong to Jesus's teaching in the Temple, during the first days of the last week of his earthly life. It was then that the irreconcilable opposition between his message and the religion of the official doctors of Judaism made itself clear.

19   Something analogous is said to have happened to Sargon I, King of Babylon, but one must not rush to the conclusion that the account in Exodus derives from an Assyrio-Babylonian myth. The abandonment of children – either voluntarily or from necessity – by placing them in floating baskets was a very ancient custom, practised just as frequently in the region of the Nile as of the Euphrates.

20   See the gospel for the 3rd Sunday of preparation for Lent in Chap. IV.

21   See the gospel for the 16th Sunday after Pentecost in Chap. I.

22   A saying of St John of the Cross.

23   This episode raises several questions. First of all, was Jesus anointed once or more than once by a woman during his last days on earth? Matthew and Mark speak of one anointing, which took place 'two days before the Passover'. But John (12. 1) seems to indicate that the anointing took place 'six days before the Passover'. However, if one rereads John's account carefully, one sees that the words 'six days' apply to the arrival of Jesus at Bethany, and not necessarily to the supper during the course of which Jesus was anointed. One could then admit – without excluding the possibility of two distinct anointings – that probably one and the same anointing are involved, and that this would have taken place

four days after Jesus's arrival at Bethany and two days before the Passover. Secondly, who was the woman who anointed Jesus? Matthew and Mark give no name. John specifies that it was Mary of Bethany, sister of Martha and Lazarus. Thirdly, is Mary of Bethany to be identified with Mary of Magdala, 'out of whom went seven devils' (Luke 8. 2), and, in her turn, is she to be identified with the woman who was a sinner and who anointed the feet of Jesus during the meal with Simon the Pharisee (Luke 7)? This question of identification has been discussed for centuries. What is said in the gospels does not allow of any certain answer. One could say that, on the whole, the fourth gospel favours the theory of identity between Mary of Bethany, Mary of Magdala, and the woman who was a sinner: it would be the same woman seen at different moments. But, again, this cannot be affirmed with any certainty. Contrary to the legend (surely false) according to which Mary of Bethany went to Gaul with Martha and Lazarus, a Greek tradition relates that she retired to Ephesus with the Virgin Mary, that she died there, and that her relics were transferred to Constantinople in the fourth century.

24   Matthew does not name any particular disciple, but John (12. 4-6) attributes the words of protest to Judas Iscariot, son of Simon, 'which should betray him' and adds: 'This he said, not that he cared for the poor; but because he was a thief, and had the bag, and bare what was put therein'.

25   These thirty pieces of silver correspond to a prophecy. We will come back to this at the time of the reading from the prophet Zechariah during the service of Prime on Holy Friday.

26   St John Chrysostom returns to this theme several times, with moving eloquence. He reproaches certain believers with adorning the altars of the churches whilst they neglected those living altars – the poor – standing at the corners of every street. 'This needed to be done, and that should not be neglected'. And, insisting on the presence of Christ in the poor, he said to the rich: 'Admit Christ at least into your stables'.

27   Holy Thursday, Holy Friday and Holy Saturday form what the old Latin liturgy called the *triduum sacrum*, 'the three sacred days'. In the fourth century in Jerusalem, the liturgy was celebrated towards the end of the afternoon on Holy Thursday. All believers took communion. Then they went to the Mount of Olives where a special service, made up of hymns and readings, commemorated Jesus's agony in the garden and his arrest. The procession returned to the city at the break of day on the Friday. In Rome, however, all services on Holy Thursday took place during the day time. In the African Churches, the Eucharist on Holy Thursday was celebrated after the evening meal; which is why the 29th canon of the Council of Carthage dispensed believers from the eucharistic fast on that day. The centre of liturgical thought for the day was the institution of the Eucharist. At the same time, some other special rites also became characteristic of Holy Thursday. First, the washing of the feet. Then, at least in Rome, the 'rendering of the Creed', that is to say, the recitation of the Creed by the catechumens, and the baptism of neophytes (although, on the whole, Holy Saturday was the baptismal day). Then, the *exomologesis* or reconciliation of penitents, which took place in Rome as well. Finally, there was the consecration of the chrism. This last rite still takes place both in the Byzantine and the Roman Churches; but whereas each Roman bishop consecrates the chrism for his diocese, in the Byzantine Churches this consecration is carried out only by patriarchs or the premier hierarch of a national Church.

28 Matt. 26. 18.
29 Mark 14. 14.
30 Luke 22. 15.
31 In some way or another, each soul has its secret rooms where dust and dirt accumulate, and which we would prefer not to open to anyone. There is danger in thinking of our communions as 'ceremonial visits', when we are careful to receive Christ 'in the drawing room', in the front rooms. But, on the contrary, it is into the lowest places of our soul, into our 'chamber of horrors', that we must allow Christ to enter.
32 John 13. 8.
33 John 13. 9.
34 John 13. 14.
35 The Church attaches great importance to the rite of the washing of the feet, which is still observed in cathedral churches, both Orthodox and Roman, in the East and the West. From 694, the 17th Council of Toledo made it obligatory for all the churches in Spain and Gaul, on Holy Thursday. We know that the English name *Maundy Thursday* comes from the Latin word *Mandatum*, which designates the service of the washing of the feet (the service text begins with the word). The account in the fourth gospel of the washing of the feet raises two questions on which we would like to touch briefly. John is the only one of the four evangelists to describe the washing of the feet; he is also the only one of the four evangelists to say nothing about the institution of the Eucharist. How should one interpret this? John was not unaware of the breaking of the bread any more than the other evangelists of the washing of the feet. But John (who, moreover, had announced the Eucharist in the sixth chapter of his gospel) seems to have substituted the washing of the feet for the breaking of the bread deliberately and systematically to show clearly that the two actions, all things considered, express one and the same thing, although in a different manner and degree: Christ's humble and sacrificial love. ('Having loved his own . . . he loved them to the end'). And this is the second question. Jesus says to Peter, 'He that is washed needeth not save to wash his feet, but is clean every whit: and ye are clean . . . .' It seems here that the words 'He that is washed' prefigure baptism, and that the washing of the feet refers rather to a partial cleansing, the removal of such dust as has accumulated during the journey of life. But in what sense could the apostles who had not received Christian baptism (which did not, in fact, exist before the redemptive death of Christ) be said to have been washed? One could assume that they had received the baptism of John and that their inner dispositions would have earned them sanctifying grace. But one could also admit that, in their case, daily contact and intimate union with Jesus had constituted this complete washing which purifies from sin. The washing of the feet was an accessory and special act through which Jesus washed from them stains of lesser importance which did not affect the general character of the cleansing. This type of washing did not constitute an essential change, but was meant to perfect the total change that had already taken place. The same distinction applies, in a way, to the spiritual life of a baptised Christian. As long as we, who are baptised or penitents who have been forgiven, are in a state of grace, our permanent love for Christ, our adherence to him and our intimacy with him keep us clean; but perhaps an additional washing might be useful, to take away the dust that, day after day, gets on our feet.

36   The Orthodox Church believes that there is a real presence in the Eucharist of our Lord (something other than a symbolic or dynamic presence), and that this presence is conditioned by a certain change brought about by the working of the Holy Spirit in the sacramental elements. But the Orthodox Church has never tied itself to any more precise theological theory concerning this presence and this change than that. It goes no further than what is said in the words of the epiclesis: 'And make this Bread the precious Body of Thy Christ, amen. And that which is in this Cup, the precious Blood of Thy Christ, amen. Changing them by Thy Holy Spirit, amen, amen, amen'.

37   The Byzantine liturgy often speaks of the Eucharist as of an 'unbloody sacrifice', of a 'sacrifice in spirit'. Theologians have discussed at great length the exact nature of the 'eucharistic sacrifice', and it will continue to cause much discussion. The Orthodox Church has never pronounced on this subject by means of a dogmatic definition; but it might be useful to inquire what the Church understands by the term 'sacrifice' in relation to the Eucharist. Without wishing to go into very technical developments, we think that the following reflections are not unfaithful to the spirit of the liturgy and of the Fathers and, also, are in harmony with the western eucharistic tradition. First of all, the Eucharist possesses all the essential features of a sacrifice. In it, there is a certain offering that we make to God, and this bringing of bread and wine to the altar expresses symbolically the consecration of the creation, of our earthly goods, and of our very selves. There is a certain alteration or loss, or, in a way, destruction, of this bread and wine which we offer to God, because in making them his, we take them out of ordinary usage and make them unusable for ordinary and purely human ends. At this point, gloriously, and somehow like a flash, the acceptance of our offering by God intervenes. This acceptance consists of the fact that the Holy Spirit, as a fire falling from heaven, changes the bread and the wine into the body and blood of Jesus Christ; from now on Christ himself is substituted for the elements which we offered, his own sacrifice is substituted for their loss, the perfect Priest and the perfect victim substitute for men and their poor presents, and, if this sacrifice remains in any way our sacrifice, it is only in as much as we are the members of Christ. Then there is communion. The faithful share in the offered victim, who is sacrificed and accepted; and, because this victim belongs to God, they are thus united to divinity. All that the Jewish and pagan sacrifices contained in symbolic outline finds itself realised in the Eucharist. But what is the connection between the eucharistic sacrifice and the sacrifice of the Cross? It seems that here we must watch out for two errors, one of which is committed through excess and the other through default. The error of excess is to see in the Eucharist a sort of second sacrifice, new in its relation to Golgotha. The error of default (without mentioning the only too obvious one which seeks to reduce the Eucharist to a simple commemoration of the sacrifice of the Cross), ignores the existence of a present sacrifice and makes the Eucharist only an offering for the sacrifice of Holy Friday. We are saved from both these errors by the idea of the 'efficacy of the sign'. (The fact that St Thomas Aquinas developed this idea is not enough to disqualify it from the Orthodox point of view). The Eucharist 'signifies efficaciously' the sacrifice of the Cross. On the one hand, it makes it present by certain symbolic actions. On the other, it renews it mystically and makes it actual, for, without Christ having to relive his sufferings, the relationship of reciprocal causality that exists between the sign (the Eucharist) and the thing signified (the sacrifice of the Cross) allows us to speak of

a present sacrifice. Finally, the Eucharist brings to us the fruits of the sacrifice of the Cross. The perfect immolation, offered once and for all on the Cross, is not multiplied quantitatively by our eucharists, but these make it capable of being shared and assimilated at this or that point in space and moment in time. Our eucharists are thus projections onto human becoming of the unique sacrifice of the Cross. God, whom no institution can bind, is able, moreoever, to communicate the grace of the Cross to us in ways that are different from the form of sacrifice offered by the Church. It remains to be seen in what sense the death of Jesus on the Cross is itself a sacrifice. We will come back to this question on the occasion of Holy Friday.

38   Was the Jewish passover Jesus's last meal? From the historical point of view, the question remains obscure. There is an apparent divergence here between the synoptic gospels and the fourth gospel. We will not go into technical details, but it is certain that Jesus considered the meal in the upper room as a passover meal. It is probable that he anticipated the Jewish passover meal, so that his death took place at about the same time as the passover lamb was sacrificed in the Temple, on the afternoon of Friday. The fourth evangelist highlights particularly the correspondences between the immolation of Jesus and the Jewish passover. He calls Jesus the Lamb of God 'which taketh away the sin of the world'. After the sacrifice of this Lamb, no other passover lamb would ever be needed again. John observes that Jesus's bones have not been broken: and it was laid down that the bones of the passover lamb must not be broken. Finally, according to John, when Jesus was on the Cross, a sponge dipped in vinegar was offered to him on a branch of hyssop. It is impossible not to see in this an allusion to the branch of hyssop with which, at the time of the first passover in Egypt, the blood of the passover lamb was sprinkled on the door posts (all the more because John is the only evangelist to mention Jesus's words: 'I am the door'). A striking allusion to salvation through the blood of the Lamb can also be found in the episode of the prostitute Rahab who, because she had given hospitality to the spies sent by Joshua, was spared from the general massacre in the city, thanks to a sign agreed in advance: a piece of scarlet thread in the window. Thus, even despite innumerable prostitutions, every soul can be saved if it binds 'the scarlet line in the window' (Josh. 2. 21) – that is to say if it seeks salvation in the blood of Christ, the wellspring of justification and of renewal.

39   The Last Supper and the Passion have become indissolubly united, although they are quite distinct. Whereas our eucharists are the 'efficacious sign' of the sacrifice of Christ which has already been accomplished, the Eucharist in the upper room was the 'efficacious sign' of the sacrifice of Christ before it was accomplished. In both these cases, a relationship of reciprocal causality, in accordance with the term we have already used, connects the sign and the thing signified: on Holy Thursday, the sign is antecedent to the thing signified; after Holy Friday, it is subsequent to it. The Last Supper was the pledge of the Passion. Not only did it constitute a frame that the sacrifice of the Cross came to fill with historical and bloody reality, but the Passover in the upper room called for the immolation of the Lamb on the Cross, and made it inevitable. That Thursday evening, Jesus, having offered himself sacrificially, found himself 'pledged'. He had already, morally, entered the Passion. The consideration of this fact throws a penetrating light on the meaning of our own eucharistic communion. Each time that we take part in the Lord's Supper, we 'pledge' ourselves to his Passion.

40   The Byzantine *anaphora* and the canon of the Roman mass each express this remembering, *anamnesis*, of the victory and glorification of the Saviour. The liturgy of St John Chrysostom says: 'Remembering this saving precept, therefore, with all that for our sakes was brought to pass, the Cross and tomb, the Resurrection the third day, the Ascension into heaven, the sitting on the right hand, the coming again the second time in glory'. The eucharistic liturgy is thus a synthesis of Christ's work.

41   In heaven Jesus Christ continues to offer himself to his Father, as a sacrificed victim, who is accepted and glorified. The very presence of his body which has been nailed to the Cross is a continual intercession for the world. The fulness of the divine acceptance of the sacrifice of the Son is manifested by the supreme honour of the victim. This is why in Revelation the Lamb is represented as both sacrificed and glorified in heaven. This 'heavenly sacrifice' is the continuation, the glorious prolonging in eternity of the sacrifice of the Cross, of which the supper in the upper room was the first fruit and the foretaste (in technical language, the 'prelibation'). Already, our earthly eucharists open this heavenly Eucharist to us; they have an 'eschatological' significance and are turned towards the 'day without evening' of the messianic kingdom. 'For as often as ye eat this bread, and drink this cup, ye do shew the Lord's death till he come' (1 Cor. 11. 26). The sacrifice of the upper room, the sacrifice of the Cross, the heavenly sacrifice, and the eucharistic sacrifice of the Church are one and the same sacrifice. There is only one liturgy.

42   St Augustine, in his sermons to the people, liked to insist on this aspect of the Eucharist: 'It is your own mystery which is placed on the altar'.

43   We do not at all wish to diminish the value of the sacrament, of the objective mystery celebrated by the Church. It may not diminish it in any way, however, to remind ourselves that eucharistic grace – that is to say union with our Lord as the sacrificial victim who has become our food and drink – is not indispensably linked to an external action and to visible elements. As firm a 'sacramentalist' as St Thomas Aquinas admits the reality and efficacy of 'spiritual communion' in the order of grace. One of the first French members of the Society of Friends, Etienne de Grellet, said that he never sat down at table without making an inner remembrance of the Lord's supper. It is impossible not to see in this a state of soul that one would call 'eucharistic', although it is not connected with any sacramental rite of the Church.

44   John 13. 18, 21, 26, 27.

45   John 13. 27.

46   On the subject of the thirty pieces of silver, see the reading from the prophet Zechariah at Prime, on Holy Friday, and the note attached to that.

47   Before the fourth century, in St Irenaeus and Tertullian, we find the word 'passover' used to designate Holy Friday: Later on, a distinction is made between the 'Passover of the Cross', or the passing over to death, which is celebrated on Holy Friday, and the 'Passover of the Resurrection', or passing over to life, celebrated on the following Sunday. In Jerusalem during the fourth century, the celebration of Holy Friday included three distinct services. On the Friday morning, relics of the Cross were venerated. At three o'clock in the afternoon, the Passion and death of the Lord were commemorated; weeping and the lamentations of the congregation accompanied this commemoration. In the evening, there was a vigil. In our era, those Christians of the Byzantine rite who fast strictly abstain from all food on Holy Friday until the middle of the afternoon.

48   Matt. 26. 58.

49   The twelve readings are as follows: (i) John 13. 31-18. 1: (ii) John 18. 1-28; (iii) Matt. 26. 57-75; (iv) John 18. 28-19. 16; (v) Matt. 27. 3-32; (vi) Mark 15. 16-32; (vii) Matt. 27. 33-54; (viii) Luke 23. 32-49; (ix) John 19. 25-37; (x) Mark 15. 43-47; (xi) John 19. 38-42; (xii) Matt. 27. 62-66.

50   The 'priestly prayer' (ch. 17 of John) could, even better than the 'Our Father' be called 'The Lord's Prayer'. For, in the 'Our Father . . .' Jesus speaks for men, whereas, in John 17, he speaks in his own personal name. The prayer after the Last Supper nevertheless offers a model and a frame for our own prayers, and we ought to think about the order in which the thoughts contained in it are developed and the proportion which is kept in their development. Jesus begins by asking for the manifestation of the Father's glory, then he prays for his disciples, then he prays for the 'world'. Such should be the hierarchy of our requests when we address our prayers to God.

51   This scene is of the highest importance. In this sorrow 'unto death' (which is why we speak of the 'agony') when Jesus feels his human nature being shaken, and he sweats drops of blood, all the sufferings of the Passion are presented to him (the 'cup'); it is as if they are rehearsed before him. Not only do they involve the physical tortures and death − which, because of the infinite sensitivity and perfection of his human nature, meant physical suffering immeasurably greater than that of other men − but, above all, they involve the intimate and unutterable contact that Jesus then experiences with all the sins of the world. They invade him like a hideous leprosy, like a corruption which consumes and burns him − yet without defiling him. Our pride, our unbelief, our impurity, our cruelty, the hatred and betrayal, the sleep and desertion by his own friends − all sins are there. They are on him. In a certain way, they are in him, instead of the ineffable peace in which he was established. Doubtless, nothing alters the beatific vision and essential union with the Father which his divine nature enjoys, but his human nature experiences with infinite intensity the contact with sin and guilt. Jesus himself is not guilty, but he 'lives' all the guilt of the world. And because he undergoes this experience of guilt, he has to experience separation from the Father. The absolute holiness of God cannot be touched by any stain; all sin is rejected by it into outer darkness, and, because Jesus has taken upon himself the weight of sin, he himself now knows the ocean of darkness. He who is none other than the Son, none other than the Word and image of the Father, feels for the first time − for the only time − that his human nature is becoming estranged from the Father, even contrary to the Father, to the extent that he identifies with sinners. There is in this a sort of tearing away and destruction which is more painful than physical death. And, in this agony, each one of us, every person who is born, has his share. 'Jesus is in agony until the end of the world . . . . This drop of blood I have shed for thee', wrote Pascal.

52   This rite is of Syrian origin. It does not appear in the ancient rituals of the Byzantine Church and was not introduced even to Constantinople until the nineteenth century.

53   The fact that Jesus, dying, quotes the beginning of the psalm − 'My God, my God, why hast thou forsaken me?' − does not in any way imply that he has given in to feelings of abandonment and of despair. The psalm applies strikingly to the sufferings of the Crucified One. 'I am poured out like water, and all my bones are out of joint: my heart is like wax . . . they pierced my hands and my

feet'. But it ends on words of trust and thanksgiving: 'I will declare thy name . . . . For he hath not despised nor abhorred the affliction of the afflicted; neither hath he hid his face from him . . . . My praise shall be of thee . . .'. Jesus had the whole of the psalm in his spirit.

54   ' . . . They weighed for my price thirty pieces of silver. And the Lord said unto me, Cast it unto the potter . . . . And I took the thirty pieces of silver, and cast them to the potter in the house of the Lord'. The man who speaks thus is a shepherd who has failed to carry out his responsibilities to the flock; historically, it is possible that this may be a sarcastic allusion to the king of Egypt, Ptolemy III, represented prophetically by this shepherd. One can also see the person of Judas in the unsatisfactory shepherd. The allusion to the treasure of the Temple has no historical explanation. The thirty pieces of silver constituted the price of a Hebrew slave (Exod. 21. 32). The gospel according to St Matthew (27. 9) sees this passage as a prophecy of Jesus's betrayal by Judas for thirty pieces of silver and of the priests' purchase of the 'potter's field' with the thirty pieces of silver when Judas had thrown them into the treasury of the Temple. But Matthew attributes this prophecy to Jeremiah instead of Zechariah. Possibly a copyist's error may have substituted the first name for the second in certain texts. It is also possible that the evangelist wished to tie in the passage from Zechariah to chapter 18 of Jeremiah: 'Arise, and go down to the potter's house, and there I will cause thee to hear my words', etc.

55   See the preceding note.

56   We have already mentioned the fact that most modern critics consider the 'Book of Isaiah' to be a collection of passages by various authors. The passage read at Sext on Holy Friday belongs to the section of the 'Book of Isaiah' which has been called the 'Songs of the Servant of Yahveh'. The identity of the 'Servant' is one of the most discussed questions in the exegesis of the Old Testament. Early Jewish exegesis as well as that of the Fathers applied these texts to the Messiah. Mediaeval Jewish and modern western exegesis see in the 'Servant' perhaps some historical person, perhaps a personification of the people of Israel. But, even if it were not originally so, the Church, under the inspiration of the Holy Spirit, would have the right to apply these texts to Jesus. And it is difficult, moreover, to understand the poems which apply to the Servant if one does not relate them to a personal Messiah. However, nothing hinders us from admitting that these various interpretations need not be mutually contradictory. There may be several superimposed symbols in these texts: the allusion would be, in differing degrees, to a certain king, to Israel, and to the Messiah. The Messianic interpretation seems to us to have the soundest base and to be the most satisfying.

57   In the original Hebrew, the Book of Job ends at verse 12 of chapter 42. The supplementary verses read by the Church at this service are taken from a Syriac version.

58   Matt. 27. 1-38; Luke 23. 39-43; Matt. 27. 39-54; John 19. 31-37; Matt. 27. 55-61.

59   The period that Jesus spent in the tomb coincided with the feast of the first sheaves. The day after the Passover (called the Sabbath of the Passover and not to be confused with the Sabbath of the seventh day), the first fruits of the harvest were solemnly reaped in the fields and offered to Yahveh the following day in the Temple (Lev. 23). The first sheaves of the Passover were a prelude to the festival of the harvest at Pentecost. These rites have a deep symbolic meaning for

Christians. The true first fruits of the Passover during which Jesus died were not the sheaves which the priest waved about in the Temple, but waited with him — in the tomb — for the coming of a new feast of the harvest, Pentecost.

60   And naturally with all the sufferings of the Passion: the scourging, the crowning with thorns, etc.

61   Let us pause for a moment to consider the theology of redemption. Sin is a disorder introduced into the divine order by created beings; it is more than a disorder, it is an affront to the glory and love of God. This affront could be pardoned without being atoned for, but, if this were so, sin would not have been annulled and the divine order would remain violated. The transgression which has been committed must be compensated for in a way that is adequate. It is not possible for a created being to offer an atonement which is sufficient for this, for a finite being cannot atone for an outrage which has taken on infinite proportions, because he addresses himself to infinite being. This is why the infinite itself wished to offer, in our place, an atonement which is infinite. This atonement consists in the death of Jesus on the Cross. In what sense does this death make reparation for sin? To start with, let us set aside the 'moral' and purely subjective theory of redemption which finds so many supporters in modern Protestantism: that the death of Jesus saves us because the spectacle of such generosity touches our hearts, and thus excites our repentance and leads to our conversion. This is profoundly true, but insufficient. The death of Jesus on the Cross has, in itself, an objective redemptive value. Let us also set aside another theory, which is diametrically opposed to the preceding one and which, incomprehensibly, found much favour in early Protestantism: the 'penal' theory, according to which the death of Jesus was a 'punishment' inflicted by the Father as necessary to atone for transgressions. The Cross would then become a reprisal, a veritable divine vengeance. We draw nearer to the truth with the theory of 'expiation' from which all idea of vengeance is eliminated and according to which the reparation is made not by suffering as such, but by the generous acceptance of suffering, of sacrifice. The theory of 'satisfaction' is a step forward from the preceding one. Jesus makes adequate satisfaction (*satis facit*) through the love and obedience of his homage to God in His Passion. This theory differs from the theory of expiation in two ways. On the one hand, the emphasis is placed not on the *acceptance of suffering*, but on the *homage* given *in* suffering. On the other hand, it does not consider suffering itself as necessary: what is necessary is that satisfaction be offered to make full reparation for sin. Now Jesus's whole life already had incomparable worth as a reparation; it already constituted a superabundant reparation, even without the Passion. Through His Incarnation, Jesus had healed and sanctified human nature. If our Lord chose the Cross as the supreme form of this satisfaction, it is because the Cross implied a maximum of generosity and love: 'Greater love hath no man than this, that a man lay down his life . . .'. Moreover, in choosing the Cross, Christ was not alone in 'obeying'. The three divine Persons both desired and accepted the sacrifice of the God-Man on the Cross because all three were moved by what one could call obedience to their own nature, by their 'inordinate' and essential love. The Father and the Spirit oriented the Son towards the Cross because of the maximal requirements of their 'glory', that is to say, of the dazzling manifestation of divine Love; with infinite compassion, they said 'yes' to the Passion of Jesus. Finally, on the Cross, Jesus gained credit for us in the sense that, because men are incorporated into his mystical Body, he did more than substitute for us; he

carried us with him on the sacred wood.

62   Contrition consists essentially in the grief of soul that results in a sinner when he is aware of having offended God. For this grief to be real, it need not take on an emotional aspect. If God grants us tears of repentance, we must thank Him for them, but contrition can be real without an emotional or sentimental element. True and deep repentance is independent of emotional fluctuations. It is an act of mature reflection, of high intellectual lucidity, of humility and of obedience. It implies, first of all, a judgement by the intelligence through which a sinner realises that, in some particular way, his behaviour has offended God. Then, following this, an act of will by which the sinner decides that, as much as he can, he will exclude sin. This act of will is equally directed to the past, the present and the future: in as much as it concerns the past, the sinner, in condemning his action and condemning himself, asks for divine mercy and pardon, and decides to atone, as far as he can, for the evil he has committed; in what concerns the present, he unites his will to the will of God, and decides to adhere and submit himself to him; in what concerns the future, he forms a firm resolve not to sin any more, and even to avoid the risk of certain opportunities which might be dangerous. The sort of regret for sins that results from purely human feeling (for example, fear of dishonour, or of the consequences of breaking the law) is useless as regards salvation. Regret based on the fear of divine judgement or on the hope of eternal bliss, begins to have a place in salutory contrition, but belongs to an imperfect contrition. Contrition becomes perfect when it is united to charity, or love towards God, and when sin is hated because of its antagonism to divine goodness. The contrition of salvation is supernatural; it is not of our contriving, although it needs our co-operation; it comes about through the inspiration of grace. It invokes and presupposes the redemptive merits of Christ. The contemplation of the Cross, especially on Holy Friday, must evoke more than an emotional gratitude when faced by the suffering which saves us (although we should seek to attain compassionate and grateful adoration of Jesus crucified): in front of the Cross, we must allow contrition to penetrate our whole being deeply and completely, and let it be sovereign in us. This is what we tried to express when we spoke of a 'violent movement of contrition' which 'throws us to the feet of Jesus', and it has nothing in common with a superficial exaltation of one's feelings.

63   *Today*: Jesus imposes no period of waiting on the repentant thief. *With me*: there are two Greek words which translate 'with'; one of them expresses a relationship of vicinity, of nearness, of juxtaposition, as when one puts an object 'with' another; the other expresses a relationship of participation, of shared and common existence, as when a friend desires to live 'with' another; and it is the second of these words that the gospel uses here. Jesus not only invites us to be close to him, he wants to enter intimately into our existence. Jesus's words to the thief also apply to us, and, now, in the time of our earthly life. Today – this very hour, this minute – I, too, can be in paradise with Jesus (which is heaven on earth) if, this moment, I unite my will as perfectly as possible with that of our Lord.

64   All sacramental confession should be a sinner's personal and direct encounter with the Cross and with the blood of the Redeemer. In the ecclesiastical rite of Penitence, the Church does not usurp the unique place of Jesus Christ, but brings the soul into the presence of its Saviour. A confessor's

predominant concern is to establish this real contact between the penitent and the Lord Jesus. The penitent should feel inwardly, at the moment when the priest covers his head with the stole, that the blood and the grace of Christ flows over him.

65   To begin with, no service was celebrated either in the morning or the afternoon on Holy Saturday. Until the seventh century, the service on Holy Saturday began in the evening. This was the great paschal vigil, which consisted of prayers, of hymns and readings which lasted until the dawn of Sunday, when the Resurrection was announced by alleluias. The blessing of the new fire, the lighting of the lamps and the candles, and the baptism of numerous catechumens took place during this vigil. In the eighth century, these same ceremonies were advanced by several hours; from then on, they took place during the course of Saturday afternoon. Even later on, the rites for the nocturnal vigil of Holy Saturday began during the morning. This strange anachronism was sanctioned by both the Latin and Byzantine Churches during the middle ages. Holy Saturday was the only Saturday of the year for which the early Church authorised a fast; in the time of St Irenaeus, from the second half of the second century, believers prepared for the feast of Easter by a total fast lasting forty hours.

66   An allusion to the dogma of 'the descent into hell': starting in the fourth century, the formula for this found a place in several ecclesiastical documents and in the tradition of the Fathers. The dogma is based principally on St Peter's affirmation: ' . . . he went and preached unto the spirits in prison' (1 Pet. 3. 19). These 'spirits in prison' were not demons or the souls of the damned, they were those of the righteous under the Old Covenant; immediately after his death, Jesus filled them with the light of glory and granted them the divine vision. An even greater hope is permissible to us: we can be confident that the same blessing has been (and is) extended to all those souls who, without having had explicit knowledge of the divine revelation, have acted in accordance with the measure of light that God has accorded them, and who have thus been invisible members of the Church. To believe in the descent into hell is to believe that salvation is offered to those who, while living, did not know the Gospel, but lived according to the spirit of the Gospel.

67   The tree plays an important role in the symbolism of salvation: the tree of life, the tree of the knowledge of good and evil, the tree of Jesse, and the tree of the Cross.

68   The piercing of Jesus's side by the lance and the blood and water that gushed forth have great symbolic and mystical importance. In the Byzantine rite, the priest commemorates this fact through words and by a special action during the *proskomedia* (or the preparation of the eucharistic gifts). The Latin devotion to the Sacred Heart has its origins in this episode of the Gospel. Certain representatives of Protestant piety have used (and perhaps abused) the term 'the Blood of Christ' so much that many modern Christians prefer to avoid this expression altogether, perhaps from a certain modesty, but also, we fear, because the meaning of the Precious Blood is perhaps no longer felt by them with intensity. The blood of Jesus, which was shed for us, never ceases to flow, in the sense that at each moment the grace he acquired is communicated to various men, under different conditions. Somewhere on earth, every minute, a child is baptised, a heart repents, or the Lord's Supper is celebrated, and, under these varying forms, salvation is conveyed through the blood of Christ. The shedding

of this blood gives the history of the world its true meaning, for the divine history of the world is the history of the Precious Blood. It is this which matters supremely. The most noble painting of the Flemish school, the masterpiece of the Van Eycks – which shows the universe gathered round the divine Lamb, whose blood is flowing – gives striking expression to the meaning of all existence. 'Who is this that cometh from Edom, with dyed garments from Bozrah? . . . Wherefore art thou red in thine apparel . .?' (Isa. 63. 1-2). The victorious hero of whom the prophet speaks was red with the blood of his enemies; but the wine that Christ, represented by this hero, extracts from the winepress – 'I have trodden the winepress alone; and of the people there was none with me' (Isa. 63. 3) – and which stained his garments, is the Redeemer's blood itself. Certainly, the victorious Christ seated at the right hand of the Father, transfigured and raised from the dead, is clothed in a garment of a white more dazzling than snow, and similarly, the righteous who are glorified 'have washed their robes, and made them white in the blood of the Lamb' (Rev. 7. 14). The world, however, does not yet have access to the white of Easter, it is still under the sign of crimson – in the process of being washed.

69   Such words show how inaccurate and superficial it is to assume that a passionate tenderness towards the God-Man, so frequently encountered in Western religious literature, is foreign to the Byzantine east. In fact, the Roman liturgy is conspicuously more sober in this respect than are the Eastern prayers.

70   The Jewish Passover was the feast of unleavened bread, symbol of renewal and of purity. Two days before the Passover, every morsel of leavened bread, be it only a crumb, was thrown out of Jewish homes.

71   Luke 23. 55-56.

72   Rom. 6. 4, 11.

Chapter VI
THE TIME OF EASTER AND OF PENTECOST

SUMMARY

Holy Saturday and the first announcement of the Resurrection. Easter Sunday. The Time of Easter. Thomas. The Myrrh-bearing Women. The Blind Man. The Ascension. The Holy Fathers. Saints of the Time of Easter. Vigil for Pentecost.

Holy Saturday and the First Announcement of the Resurrection

As we have already said, Holy Saturday shares both in the mourning of Holy Week and in the joy of Easter. It is partly turned towards the Lord's tomb, and partly towards the risen Jesus. Matins for Holy Saturday, which we have already described and which are generally celebrated on the evening of Holy Friday, express the waiting and sorrow of 'Jesus's friends' — the disciples and the holy women — whose attention is now concentrated on the tomb where Joseph of Arimathea has laid the body of the Lord. But vespers and the liturgy which are celebrated on the morning of Holy Saturday anticipate the events of Easter Sunday, and bring us a first message of the Resurrection.

The chants at vespers announce Christ's victory: 'Today hell laments and cries out: Better that I had not welcomed Him who is born of Mary. He has put an end to my power, He has broken my doors of bronze . . . . Glory to Thy Cross and Resurrection, O Lord . . . . The Crucified One empties all the tombs, the power of death is overcome . . . . O Lord, glory to Thy Cross and to Thy Resurrection'.

Three passages from the Old Testament are read after the 'Little Entrance'. The first is the account of the creation (Gen. 1. 1-13), for the resurrection of Jesus will in some way be a new creation. The next (Exod. 12. 1-11) describes the institution of the Mosaic passover and speaks of the lamb, the blood sprinkled on the doors which averts death, the unleavened bread — all those elements of the old passover which prefigure a better Passover, a 'passing over' of the Lord through which an infinitely greater grace is communicated to us. Let us therefore prepare ourselves ('with girded loins') for this new Passover. Then the reading from the Book of the prophet Daniel brings us once again the story of

175

the three young men thrown into the furnace because they had refused to worship the statue of the king (Dan. 3. 1-88, Sept.). Miraculously protected from death, they symbolise the victory of the risen Christ. Their song of thanksgiving[1] enjoins all nature to praise God: ' . . . O ye waters . . . O ye, fire and heat . . . O ye, ice and cold . . . earth, mountains and hills bless the Lord'. Thus we will include the entire universe in the joy of the Resurrection.

The epistle for the liturgy[2] develops the great theme, which is familiar to St Paul (Rom. 6. 3-11): 'so many of us as were baptised into Jesus Christ were baptised into his death . . . that like as Christ was raised up from the dead by the glory of the Father, even so we also should walk in newness of life'. The gospel (Matt. 28. 1-20) is the first account of the Resurrection that the Church lets us hear at this time of Easter; it describes the visit of the women to the sepulchre and the angel's declaration of the Resurrection, the council held by the Jewish priests, and, finally, Jesus's appearance to the disciples in Galilee. At the 'Great Entrance', instead of the 'cherubic hymn', we sing the *troparion*: 'Let all mortal flesh be silent, let it be still, let no earthly thing occupy its thought, for the King of Kings comes, the Lord of Lords . . .'. But the final blessing does not yet mention the fact of the Resurrection. Holy Saturday has announced Easter, but as if in an undertone. On this Saturday morning, the message of the Resurrection still has something intimate and secret about it. Meanwhile the day draws on and the hour approaches when the Church, with the full power of its voice, will proclaim that Jesus Christ is risen from the dead[3].

Easter Sunday

'Unique and holy day, king and lord of days, feast of feasts, solemnity of solemnities . . . .' Thus we sing at matins for Easter, in the eighth tone. The Sunday of the Resurrection is called the 'solemnity of solemnities'[4]. It would be theologically inexact, speaking absolutely, to say that Easter is the greatest of all Christian feasts. Easter Sunday is a much more important feast than Christmas and Epiphany, but one cannot say that Pentecost is less important than Easter. Yet the paschal solemnities — and here Holy Thursday and Friday must be joined to the feast of the Resurrection — endow the mystery of Christmas with the fulness of its meaning and are the prerequisite condition for Pentecost. Easter is therefore the centre, the heart of the Christian year. It is on its date that the whole liturgical cycle depends, because this determines the movable feasts of the calendar[5].

The Resurrection of Christ is solemnly proclaimed during matins for Easter Sunday. This service takes place either very early on the Sunday morning, or towards the middle of the night of Saturday to Sunday. Before the service starts, the *epitaphion*, which is on the 'tomb' in the middle of the church, is carried without any special ceremony into the sanctuary and placed on the altar. Some prayers are read. Then the celebrant appears at the royal doors of the iconostasion. In his hand he holds a lighted candle. The choir sings: 'Come, take light from the Light that has no evening, and glorify Christ, risen from the dead'. Once more, the eastern Church represents the Christian mystery in terms of a mystery of light; this Light, whose birth was marked by the star of Bethlehem, has been shining among us with growing intensity; the darkness of Golgotha could not extinguish it; now it reappears among us, and all the candles which the congregation hold in their hands, and that they now light, proclaim its triumph. In this way, the deeply spiritual meaning of Easter is indicated. The physical Resurrection of Jesus would be without value to us if the divine light did not shine at the same time among us, within us. We cannot worthily celebrate the Resurrection of Christ if, in our soul, the light brought by the Saviour has not completely overcome the darkness of our sins.

A procession forms. It leaves the sanctuary and stops outside the church, in front of the door. Often — though this custom is not universal — the account of the Resurrection taken from the gospel according to St Mark is read (16. 1-8). Then the great triumphal antiphon for Easter is sung: 'Christ is risen from the dead, trampling down death by death, and to those in the tomb He has given life'.

This antiphon is repeated several times. In between the repetitions, verses taken from the psalms are interpolated: 'Let God arise, and let his enemies be scattered . . . . This is the day which the Lord hath made; we will rejoice and be glad . . .' etc. The procession re-enters the church. The priest recites the great litany, then the Easter canon, attributed to St John of Damascus, is sung. These are some of its verses:

'Day of the Resurrection . . . . Jesus has risen from the tomb, as He foretold; He has given us eternal life, and His great mercy.'

'Come, let us drink a new drink; it is not drawn from a rock but springs from the tomb of Christ in Whom is our strength . . . .'

'Shine, shine, new Jerusalem, for the glory of the Lord shines on thee! Exult and adorn thyself, Zion! And thou, pure Mother of God, rejoice in the Resurrection of thy Son . . . .'

'O Great and most holy Passover, O Christ, Wisdom, Word, and Power of God, grant that we may partake more truly of Thee in the day without evening of Thy kingdom . . . .'

'Day of the Resurrection! . . . Let us embrace one another in joy . . . and call each other brothers . . . . The Passover of Beauty, Passover of the Lord. The glorious Passover has dawned for us . . . .'

The congregation kiss one another. They greet each other, saying: 'Christ is risen', to which the response is: 'He is risen indeed'.

Matins are followed by the liturgy of St John Chrysostom. The epistle, which consists of the first verses of the Acts of the Apostles (1. 1-8), speaks of the fact of the Resurrection: 'Unto the apostles . . . to whom also he shewed himself alive after his passion by many infallible proofs, being seen of them forty days, and speaking of the things pertaining to the kingdom of God'. It might seem strange that the gospel is not one of the accounts of the Resurrection. The Church, at this feast of Easter, gives us the beginning of the Gospel according to St John: 'In the beginning was the Word . . .'. Perhaps the reason for this choice is the predeliction of Greek Christianity for what takes place 'in the spirit': beyond the Resurrection of the body of Christ, there is the victory of light over the dark. For the verse, 'And the light shineth in the darkness; and the darkness comprehended it not' does not mean that the darkness did not accept and receive the light, but rather that the darkness was powerless to overcome and extinguish the light, this light whose triumph we see today: 'and we beheld his glory'. Perhaps too, because this feast is the one which means most to the soul of eastern Christians, the Church wanted to take advantage of this unique opportunity to let them hear the deep and striking abridgement of the whole Christian message which is set out in the prologue to the fourth gospel. At the end of the liturgy (or, in many churches, at the end of matins), the celebrant reads the very beautiful homily of St John Chrysostom for the Easter feast. We will quote some extracts from it:

'If any have wrought from the first hour, let him today receive his just reward . . . . If any have arrived at the sixth hour, let him have no misgivings; because he shall in nowise be deprived therefore. If any have delayed until the ninth hour, let him draw near, fearing nothing. If any have tarried even until the eleventh hour let him, also, be not alarmed at his tardiness; for the Lord,

who is jealous of His honour, will accept the last even as the first .
. . . Wherefore, enter ye all into the joy of your Lord . . . . Ye
sober and ye heedless, honour ye the day. Rejoice today, both ye
who have fasted and ye who have not kept the fast. The table is
full-laden; feast ye all sumptuously. The calf is fatted; let no one
go hungry away. Enjoy ye all the feast of faith: Receive ye all the
riches of loving-kindness. Let no one bewail his poverty . . . . Let
no one weep for his iniquities, for pardon hath shone forth from
the grave'.

These marvellous words raise a problem. St John Chrysostom
seems to place those who have not prepared themselves spiritually
for the feast on an equal footing with those who have. He invites
both one and the other. He seems not to differentiate between
them, and speaks as if the same grace had been granted to them.
And yet we know that only those who have carried the Cross and
have died with Christ can share in the grace of his Resurrection.
We know that the grief of Holy Friday is a necessary condition for
the joy of Easter. This is true. All the same, our Lord, in his mercy, reserves to himself the right to invert the order of these two
terms. He revealed his triumph to his apostles before including
them in his Passion. All except one had abandoned him during
the harrowing hours of Golgotha, yet, nevertheless, he admits
them directly to the joy of his Resurrection. It is not that the
economy of salvation has altered: without the Cross, the glory of
the Risen One cannot become our share. But the Lord Jesus deals
gently with the weakness of his disciples. He includes them, today, in the joy of Easter, even though they are little prepared for
it. Later, tomorrow, he will include them in his Passion. 'When
thou wast young, thou girdedst thyself, and walkedst whither
thou wouldest: but when thou shalt be old, thou shalt stretch
forth thy hands, and another shall gird thee, and carry thee
whither thou wouldst not.'[6] Our Lord spoke these words to Peter,
when he appeared to the apostles on the shore of Lake Galilee,
after the Resurrection. And the evangelist explains the meaning
of this saying: 'This spake he, signifying by what death he should
glorify God'[7]. Peter and the other apostles will share, through
their own martyrdom, in the Passion of their Master, but only
after the power of his Resurrection has been communicated to
them. Our Lord acts in the same way with us. We are far − at
least most of us are − from having drunk of the chalice of the
Passion. We have not helped Jesus to carry his Cross. We have not
died with him. We have slept during his agony and abandoned

him; we have denied him by our many sins. And yet, poorly prepared and impure as we are, Jesus invites us to enter into the paschal joy. If we truly open our heart to the forgiveness which flows from the empty tomb (the fact that the tomb is now empty is, in itself, the visible pledge of our forgiveness), if we allow ourselves to be penetrated by the light of Easter, if we adore the presence of the risen Lord, we, too, will receive the power of the Resurrection — which the gift of Pentecost will make perfect. Then, only then, will we understand what the Cross signifies and be able to enter, to our limited capacity, into the mystery of Christ's Passion. This is how the call, or rather the promise of St John Chrysostom to those who are not ready, to those 'who have not kept the fast' is to be understood. The Church has chosen the sermon for Easter day admirably. Let us read and reread this homily: we shall not find a better meditation for the day of the Resurrection.

The final blessing given at the liturgy for Easter Sunday begins thus: 'May He who is risen from the dead, who by His death has overcome death and has given life to those in the tomb, Christ, our true God . . .' etc.[8].

In the afternoon of Easter Sunday, very short vespers are celebrated. The gospel account of Jesus's appearance to the disciples, in the room whose doors were locked (John 20. 19-25), is read — in several languages if possible[9]. The risen Jesus overcomes all obstacles. He can even enter into souls which, up till now, have remained closed to him. Let this be our prayer on this evening of Easter. May Jesus enter where doors are shut — first of all in our own selves — and bring his message of mercy: 'Jesus . . . stood in the midst, and saith unto them, Peace be unto you'.

The Time of Easter

The liturgical season which is called the 'time of Easter' begins on Holy Saturday and ends on the eve of Pentecost. There are forty days between the Sunday of Easter and the Thursday of the Ascension, fifty between Easter and the Sunday of Pentecost, and six Sundays in this period of fifty days[10], not including the Sunday of Easter.

The time of Easter contains several special features of ritual. The chief one is that at the beginning and end of each liturgy, the *troparion* of the Resurrection — 'Christ is risen from the dead . . .' — is sung. During the week that follows Easter, the doors of the iconostasion remain constantly open: in this way we symbolise the free access to the Holy of Holies that Jesus Christ, our great high priest, opened to us with his blood. The *epitaphion* remains on the altar, so that the liturgies are celebrated on the image of the 'life-giving tomb' of the Saviour. One must neither fast nor prostrate oneself during the week of Easter. Friday of this week is specially dedicated to the Holy Virgin under the title of the 'Fountain of the Mother of God', in allusion to a tradition in Constantinople[11].

Easter week, in Greek, has a very beautiful name: 'The week of Renewal'[12], which in fact suits the whole of the paschal time. Jesus wished to die and to rise again at the threshold of spring. In the same way that Christmas coincides with the victory of sunlight over darkness, when the days begin to lengthen, so Easter coincides with the renewal of nature, when greenery and flowers appear. the universe itself is a symbol of spiritual realities. Springtime speaks to us — if we know how to interpret God's creation — of inner renewal. There is a springtime of the soul. Easter, like springtime in nature, brings us a message of hope. The Resurrection of Jesus tells us that we can be changed. We need to feel the 'new green' of the paschal season, to which some sayings in Holy Scripture apply very well:

'Purge out therefore the old leaven, that ye may be a new lump, as ye are unleavened. For even Christ our passover is sacrificed for us. Therefore let us keep the feast, not with old leaven . . . but with the unleavened bread of sincerity and truth.'[13]

'Therefore if any man be in Christ, he is a new creature: old things are passed away; behold all things are become new.'[14]

'. . . that like as Christ was raised up from the dead . . . even so we also should walk in newness of life[15] . . . that we should serve in newness of spirit, and not in the oldness of the letter.'[16]

'As newborn babes, desire the sincere milk of the word, that ye may grow thereby.'[17]

Thomas

The two Sundays which follow Easter are dedicated to commemorating certain episodes that relate to the Resurrection of Christ. The second Sunday of the Easter season is called, in the Byzantine ecclesiastical calendar, the 'Sunday of Thomas'. As this designation indicates, the Church wants to draw our attention to the attitude of the apostle St Thomas on this Sunday[18], an attitude which was provisionally disbelieving, and then deeply believing. The episode is told in the gospel which is read at the liturgy (John 20. 19-31).

In the evening of the day of the Resurrection, our Lord appeared to his disciples as they were gathered together. The doors were shut and yet, suddenly, Jesus was in their midst: thus he penetrates even into those souls that seem most shut away from him. Twice he says to the disciples: 'Peace be unto you'. There is a nuance between these two wishes. The first time, Jesus brings peace to the troubled minds of the disciples themselves. The second time, he gives them peace so that they may transmit it to others, for he immediately adds: 'So send I you . . .'. Then he breathes on them: 'Receive ye the Holy Ghost. Whose soever sins ye remit, they are remitted unto them . . .'. They have therefore already received the Holy Spirit, even though it is not yet Pentecost: the Spirit is in them, but as if latent; Pentecost will be its manifest coming, its coming with power. In the same way, the Spirit may lie quiescent in our soul without showing its working or its power: the soul still needs the grace of Pentecost. Thomas, however, was not there. The report of the Lord's appearance that he hears later from the other disciples leaves him incredulous: 'Except I shall see in his hands the print of the nails, and put my finger into the print of the nails and thrust my hand into his side, I will not believe'. A week passes, and Jesus appears once again to the disciples. He invites Thomas to put his finger into the mark of the nails and to thrust his hand into his side. He exhorts him not to be faithless, but believing. Thomas answers with an act of faith and adoration: 'My Lord and my God'. Jesus goes on to say: 'Blessed are they that have not seen, and yet have believed'.

Christ, in truth, does not blame Thomas. Moreover, the other disciples were no less to blame, for neither did they believe the Resurrection until they had seen the Risen One. Jesus allows for the fact that the human spirit needs credible grounds for belief before it can make the act of faith. It is right that we should know how to convince others that our faith, even if it goes beyond reason, is not, in itself, unreasonable. This is theology's task. It 'thinks out' the revelation. But Jesus proclaims the special blessedness of those who, without debate, believe as soon as they inwardly hear the word of the Master, for they have recognised a unique and loved tone of voice in this word.

Today's gospel also puts us on guard against any presentation of the Christian message which seeks to eliminate the Cross and the crucifixion. The danger of such a falsification comes from two different sides. There are those who wish to soften and humanise Christ so that he becomes a mild and likable teacher of morals: the mystery of the Cross seems too harsh to them, and unacceptable to the 'modern spirit'. Then there are gnostics and pseudo-mystics who are so filled with ideas of Incarnation, of transfiguration, and of deification that, in their notion of salvation, there is no place for the Cross. Both the former and the latter — the humanists, the theosophists, anthroposophists, etc. — share an aversion to what the Cross represents in practical life, that is to say to repentance, asceticism and sacrifice. We reject the false Christs that they set up, and shall insist on looking at and touching the wounds of our Lord. We know that a Christ who does not carry the imprint of the nails is not authentic, and we shall reserve our adoration for the Crucified One alone.

The episode with Thomas suggests another line of thought. Can we, today, touch the wounded flesh of the Saviour? Can we, who are not granted ecstasies or visions, be sure that it is a living being and not a phantom that we worship? We can, and this possibility is given to everyone. Jesus is invisibly, but really, alive in the flesh and blood creatures who exist all around us. We can estimate the wounds of the crucifixion today, and worship them in the sick, the poor, in all men and women who suffer, in all those who continue Jesus's agony — members of the mystical Body who share in the Passion of their divine Head. Jesus says to us: 'If thou dost doubt that I was crucified for thee and that I was raised from the dead, pay attention to the suffering members of my body. Touch me in stretching out a rescuing hand to them. In giving to them, thou shalt find me. Do something for them which is costly for thee. Sacrifice thyself for them as much as thou canst. And, behold, in them thou shalt discover me. I shall answer thee with special grace, for thou shalt feel me living and present. Thou shalt experience the reality, the power of my Resurrection'. It is not given to us to see the Blessed Face constantly, but, like an evanescent vision, the face of Christ will appear to me behind the face of my brother, and, through compassion, I shall meet the Passion[19]. I shall touch my brother who suffers, and say: 'My Lord and my God'.

The epistle for this Sunday is taken from the Book of the Acts of the Apostles (5. 12-20). This text is fairly short, but its few verses evoke vividly the atmosphere of miracles and fervour at Jerusalem in the early days of the Church's existence. 'By the hands of the apostles were many signs and wonders wrought among the people . . . .' The sick are brought out so that when Peter passed by, his shadow might fall on them and heal them. The high priest has the apostles arrested; but, during the night, an angel of the Lord opens the doors of the prison. These happenings belong, chronologically speaking, to the time after Pentecost. All the same, the Church, in beginning to read the Acts at Easter, shows us the underlying unity between the triumph of the Son and the reign of the Spirit. The miracles performed by the apostles after Pentecost are, if one may dare to use such a comparison, the small change of the central miracle — the Resurrection of Christ — which itself was brought about by the power of the Holy Spirit.

The Myrrh-bearing Women

The third Sunday of the Easter season is called the 'Sunday of the Myrrh-bearing Women', or the 'Myrrhophores'. This Greek name means 'the spice-bearers'. It refers to the women who came to anoint Jesus's body in the tomb, and to whom the Resurrection was first announced. The episode is related in the gospel for the liturgy (Mark 15. 43-16. 8), and the Church makes it the special object of our meditation for this Sunday.

At daybreak on the Sunday, Mary of Magdala, Mary the mother of James, and Salome go to the sepulchre. Our days would indeed be blessed if, every day 'very early in the morning' and more particularly on 'the first day of the week', our thoughts turned to Jesus's victory over death. It was at 'the rising of the sun' that the women went to the sepulchre. Jesus is the true sun, who should light our day from its first moments. The whole day becomes different when it starts with Jesus.

The women do not know how they will be able to get to the body of Jesus: 'Who shall roll us away the stone from the door of the sepulchre?'. The gospel makes it clear that it 'was very great'. Many of us might feel that the women's question applies to ourselves. For, in many souls, Jesus seems to be buried as if in a sepulchre. He seems to be paralysed, immobilised — even dead. He is covered by a heavy stone; the stone of sin, of ignorance, of indifference, the stone of bad habits that have accumulated over the years. Perhaps we may desire to take away this stone and reach the living Lord, but we do not have the strength. 'Who shall roll us away the stone?'

The women's undertaking – humanly speaking – seems to have no hope of success. And yet, they have set out. Without knowing how they will be able to get into the sepulchre, they walk towards him. In the same way, without knowing how the obstacle which may prevent us reaching the Saviour can be removed, let us trust. We can make a first move: we can get up; we can set out. Let us walk towards Jesus who is separated from us by the heavy stone, and allow faith and hope to guide us.

The women are not going empty-handed to the sepulchre. They 'had bought sweet spices, that they might come and anoint him'. We, too, can bring something to the sepulchre. Even if we are stained with very serious sins, we can bring a beginning of good will, the little we have of love, some generosity towards another, our feeble prayer. Doubtless our poor gifts will not bring about the removal of the stone, for our access to the risen Jesus and to the power of his Resurrection remains the magnificent and entirely free gift of divine mercy, but the fact that we do not journey towards the sepulchre with hands that are quite empty will show that our hearts are not quite empty too. Where are the 'spices' with which we wish to 'anoint' Jesus?

And, behold, a miracle has taken place. 'They saw that the stone was rolled away.' The women would never have been able to move such an obstacle. But God himself has provided for this. The gospel that we read this Sunday does not tell us exactly how the stone was rolled away from the entrance to the sepulchre. Another gospel is more explicit: 'And behold, there was a great earthquake: for the angel of the Lord descended from heaven, and came and rolled back the stone from the door . . . .'[20]. This verse is rich with meaning. When the angel of the Lord comes to take away the stone from the sepulchre, he does not roll it gently away. It is not an operation which can be accomplished without effort, without a deep and violent upheaval. An earthquake is necessary. In the same way, the removal of whatever obstacle separated us from Jesus cannot be thought of as a partial adjustment. It is not a matter of taking off or rearranging some loose stones, of modifying some details and leaving the whole as unchanged as possible. In this case too, an earthquake is needed. It is to say that the change must be total, reaching into every aspect of our being. Conversion is a spiritual 'earthquake'.

The angel clothed in white, seated on the sepulchre[21], says to the women: 'I know that ye seek Jesus . . . . He is not here: for he is risen, as he said. Come, see the place where the Lord lay'. Not only is the risen Jesus no longer in the tomb, but all attempts to limit, to localise, to circumscribe his presence from now on, are in vain. Human piety sometimes imagines that it can bind the Saviour's presence to certain conditions or circumstances – of time, place or action – or to certain intangible formulae. But Jesus Christ is now accessible at all times and in all circumstances. He goes beyond, and shatters, the frames within which certain Christians would like to enclose him – 'the place where the Lord lay'. They will say to us 'He is here', or 'He is there'; and he is, though perhaps in a rather different way than the faithful who adore him in 'this' or 'that' place think; but he is also elsewhere, and we can discover his presence everywhere. 'Why seek ye the living among the dead', as another gospel account of the Resurrection says[22].

The angel also says to the women: 'Go your way, tell his disciples and Peter that he goeth before you into Galilee: there shall ye see him, as he said unto you'. What is the significance of this meeting in Galilee, which is mentioned several times in the gospels? Does Jesus simply want to shield his disciples from the curiosity and hostility of the Jews? Does he, after these past days of trouble and anguish, want to assure them of an interval of tranquility, in an atmosphere very different from that of Jerusalem? Perhaps this is so. But perhaps, too, we would not be mistaken in giving Jesus's words a deeper interpretation. It was in Galilee that most of the apostles had their first, their unforgettable, meeting with their Master. It was there they first heard him and followed him, and had given him their hearts. Now that their faith has been submitted to a harsh test – in which they were found wanting – it would be good for them to be plunged once again into the Galilean atmosphere and to find Jesus there again, also to recapture the freshness and joy of the first encounter, and to renew their act of faith and obedience. This is true for us too. There is a Galilee in the lives of most of us (we think particularly of those who read these lines). A Galilee: that is, a moment, perhaps already long past, when we met Jesus personally and when, for the first time, we listened to him and tried to follow him. Since then, much that is sinful, forgetful, and negligent may have separated us, perhaps, from the Lord. At the hour of decisive crisis, we may, like the apostles, have abandoned the Master. The risen Jesus seeks to meet us, too, in Galilee. He asks us to let the memory and fervour of the first meeting live again. If we try to become again what we were then, we shall again find

him. We need not say: 'It is too difficult', for he has made ready
the way: 'He goeth before you into Galilee . . .'. Invisibly present,
he walks in front of us towards that Galilee of the soul; if we
follow him, each step will become easier for us, and a moment
will come when, if not with the eyes of the body, at least with the
eyes of faith and love, we will attain an unshakeable certainty of
his Presence: 'There shall ye see him'.

At the liturgy, in place of an epistle, we continue reading from
the Book of Acts. Today, it is the account (Act 6. 1-7) of appoint-
ing the first seven deacons. They are chosen to ensure the 'daily
ministration', that is, the distribution of material help which
would allow the apostles to concentrate on 'prayer and the
ministry of the word'. This episode contains a double teaching.
On the one hand, it is necessary to 'serve tables', and this should
be organised on a regular basis in a Christian community. A
Church which neglected the material needs of men and did not
exert itself to be a source of help could not be an authentic
Church of Jesus Christ. On the other hand, the Gospel involves
more than philanthropy; discipleship must not become simply
social work; 'It is not reason that we should leave the word of God,
and serve tables'. In our human condition, we cannot escape this
division of work: one will be called to contemplation, another to
the apostolate, yet another to works of mercy. There is only One
who is able not only to multiply the loaves and to preach on the
mountain, to wash the feet of the guests and to address them after
the Supper, and that One alone, infinitely above all the apostles
and all the deacons, is the perfection and fulness of the Church.
When, at times, we do not know how to combine the demands of
'external works' and those of the divine Word — whether we hear
it or speak it — he alone, if we will but consult him, can show us
the right proportion in which to unite the obedience of Martha to
that of Mary.

The Paralytic

The first two Sundays after Easter Sunday gave us the mystery of
the Resurrection to contemplate, from various aspects. The
third, which is called the 'Sunday of the Paralytic', seems — as do
the two Sundays after it — foreign to the cycle of the Resurrection. This Sunday is dedicated to commemorating a miracle
which, historically, belongs to the early days of Jesus's ministry.

But the Church meditates on it today because it is one of the 'very great' miracles (if we can be allowed to distinguish between major the minor miracles): we mean that, from the seriousness of the illness that was cured, from the length of time it had lasted, from the circumstances which surround the healing, the miracle worked on the paralytic's behalf bears witness to the Saviour's authority over the human body in a particularly impressive way. On the Saturday evening, at vespers for this Sunday, the choir sings: 'O Christ, compassionate God, Thou didst come and heal the afflicted man'. Moreover, Jesus's power to heal is intimately linked with the Resurrection; for it proclaims that he who can overcome death in his own body has power over all human flesh. Our Lord can heal the paralytic, because he himself can rise from the dead. And that is why the commemoration of this healing can, if not chronologically, at least spiritually, find a place at Easter time.

The account of the healing of the paralytic is read at the liturgy, as the gospel for Sunday (John 5. 1-15). In Jerusalem, near the pool of Bethesda, Jesus sees a crowd of the ill and infirm who are waiting for the water to be moved by an angel of the Lord: this phenomenon happened at certain intervals, and, after its occurrence, the first sick person to step into the water was healed. Amongst these sick people is a man who has suffered from paralysis for thirty eight years[23]. Jesus asks him if he wants to be healed. He answers that he has no one to help him down to the pool and that he is always overtaken by others. Jesus says to him: 'Rise, take up thy bed and walk'. The man is healed immediately. The Jews protest because the healing has taken place on the Sabbath. Jesus finds the man in the Temple and says to him: 'Sin no more, lest a worse thing come unto thee'.

The immediate significance of this gospel is Jesus's sovereign power over illness. A secondary significance which the gospel points to is the connection between physical illness and sin: we are not told clearly that this man was ill because he had sinned, but Jesus says that he has and that if he sins again, a more terrible consequence will follow. We can indeed be thankful that God, in his mercy, does not always allow our repeated sins to have such distressing repercussions on our bodies! Finally, the gospel for today suggests a certain relationship between two orders of things. On the one hand, there is this periodic and expected descent of the angel to the pool, this moving of the waters and possibility of healing opened to him who can get to the pool first. On the other hand, there is the immediate healing of a man, effected by Jesus

himself, without any descent into the water. One could say that
the first type of healing corresponds to the 'institutional' element
in the Church, to the various channels of grace (sacraments, rites,
vocations, disciplines, etc.) that the Christian community makes
available to all its members and which it would be as dangerous as
it would be impious to deny or underestimate. The second type of
healing corresponds to the direct contact, without intermediary,
of the soul with its Saviour: it would be equally dangerous and impious to deny or underestimate the possibility of this contact.
However holy and useful the ecclesiastical institutions may be, no
institution is strictly speaking, *indispensable*; for the Lord can,
when he sees fit, act directly on men, without making use of
them [24]. The spiritual realities are not limited to their external
signs. The reality matters infinitely more than the sign.

Once again, it is a portion of the Acts of the Apostles (9. 32-42)
that is read today instead of an epistle. Two miracles are worked
by Peter. Passing through Lydda, he heals a man named Aeneas
who, for eight years, has been sick of the palsy. Then, at Joppa,
he brings back to life a woman named Tabitha or Dorcas, whose
life had been rich in good works. Each one of these belonged to
the Christian community. This passage from the Book of Acts
harmonises deeply with the gospel for this Sunday. The healing of
Aeneas forms a parallel to that of the paralytic in the gospel; not
only is the infirmity the same, but Peter uses words which are
similar to Jesus's: 'Arise, and make thy bed'. The resurrection of
Tabitha fits well into the context of the Easter season: every
human resurrection is an effect and a special implementation of
the Resurrection of Christ.

The epistle and the gospel for today are united in their concentration on the healing of the sick. On the Saturday evening, in the
chants for vespers, the Church recalled three cases of healing:
that of the Canaanite woman, of the centurion's servant at Capernaum, and of the paralytic at Bethesda. 'Thou didst take pity . . . .
Thou didst not decline . . . . That is why we implore Thee, O
all-powerful God, and cry: Glory be to Thee.' We will enter into
the spirit of the Church by praying especially, this Sunday, that
our Lord will succour the sick and the infirm.

The Samaritan Woman

The fifth Sunday of the Easter season is called the 'Sunday of the
Samaritan Woman'. It may seem puzzling at first that this Sun-

day is dedicated to the commemoration of an episode – the meeting between Jesus and the Samaritan woman near Jacob's Well – which has no connection with Easter time and which contains no miracle which could be linked, even indirectly, with the Resurrection. The reason for this dedication is, if one may say so, of remarkable liturgical subtlety. The Wednesday which precedes the fourth Sunday after Easter is called 'Wednesday of mid-Pentecost'; in fact, it falls in the middle of the fifty day period which separates Easter and Pentecost, and divides these fifty days into two periods, each of three weeks. Now the Church has established a symbolic correspondence between this date of 'mid-Pentecost' and the 'midst of the feast' mentioned in a verse of the fourth gospel[25], although this was concerned not with the feast of the Jewish Pentecost, but with the feast of Tabernacles (the transition from one to the other of these feasts being facilitated by the fact that both had an agricultural aspect, the one the harvest, the other the greenery of the booths set up in the fields for the feast). Because of this symbolic correspondence, the Church reads, at the liturgy of 'mid-Pentecost', the portion of the gospel[26] that begins with these words: 'Now about the midst of the feast Jesus went up into the temple . . .'. If we read a few verses more of this gospel for the Wednesday, we come to these words: 'In the last day, that great day of the feast, Jesus stood and cried, saying, If any man thirst, let him come unto me, and drink. He that believeth on me, as the scripture hath said, out of his belly shall flow rivers of living water. (But this spake he of the Spirit, which they that believe on him should receive . . .)'[27]. Here we meet both the Pentecostal theme of the Spirit and the theme of living water, which Jesus develops in his encounter with the woman of Samaria. The *troparion* for 'mid-Pentecost' also says: 'At the mid-feast, O Saviour, give to my thirsty soul drink from the waters of true praise . . .'. This is a new allusion to the meeting with the Samaritan woman, in which Jesus speaks of those who worship 'in spirit and in truth'[28]. In this way, the week of 'mid-Pentecost' leads us towards Jacob's Well. On the fifth Sunday after Easter, we will hear Jesus announce to the woman of Samaria the doctrine of water and of the spirit. The chants at vespers on the Saturday evening introduce the commemoration of this episode: 'Behold we come to the half of those days which begin with the saving Resurrection and end with the divine feast of Pentecost . . . . Thou didst come to the wells at the sixth hour, O Thou, most wonderful Fountain'.

Everyone remembers the episode of the woman of Samaria, which is told in the gospel read at the liturgy (John 4. 5-42). Its beauty — we could even say its poetry — and its spiritual richness speak almost uniquely to souls. We shall now attempt to interpret some of its aspects.

Jesus, weary after a long walk, sits on the wall of Jacob's Well, which is near Sychar. It is mid-day. He knows who will be coming, and he waits[29]. Sometimes Jesus goes out to meet souls, especially when he foresees that, left to themselves, they will not know how to look for him: thus the Good Shepherd will go through thorns to rescue a stray sheep and will carry it back on his shoulders. But sometimes he sits and waits for the natural course of life to bring a journeying pilgrim to him. And even when he is with me, Jesus also awaits me a little further on, a little later on. Christian life combines both the constant presence of Jesus and a series of encounters with him. Jacob's Well moves with me, and never ceases to offer me opportunities for a meeting with the divine.

In order to meet the Samaritan woman, Jesus chose a place which is particularly associated with the national tradition and religion of Samaria. The Samaritans liked to be connected with the patriarch Joseph. Now the land on which Sychar stands is near the portion that Joseph's father, Jacob, gave him, and it is Jacob himself who dug the well. Jesus, in his relationship with us, places himself willingly along the line of our origins, our traditions and our habits. And this, a disciple of his must also do, if he wishes to practise his discipleship. A common ground, a common language, with the person one is speaking to must first of all be found. Then dialogue becomes possible.

Jesus knows that the Samaritan woman will come to draw water at this well. A material human need can be a starting point for dialogue. The material will lead to the spiritual. Often, in order to intervene in my life, Jesus waits for some need on the material level to give him that opportunity. In the same way, if I wish to meet another man on the spiritual level, it helps to meet him first on the material level of everyday life and its humble needs and labours.

Jesus asks the Samaritain woman for a drink. He himself could have given this woman living water. But he, who could have been the giver, puts himself in the position of one who asks. Letting oneself be indebted to someone is often an effective way of opening the other one's heart. It makes one smaller than them.

Humility and charity call reciprocally to each other.

'Give me to drink . . .'. The water that Jesus gives men to drink is the life of the soul carried to its highest potential. We all desire a certain intensity or fulness of life. But Jesus asks us to give him something of our own life. He wants us to seek in him that intensity to which we aspire. If to live is to love, he is thirsty for our human love. He is so close to us, and so humble, that he asks us to love him — 'Give me to drink . . .'.

He will respond to our love, which is so poor, with love that is infinite: 'If thou knewest the gift of God, and who it is that saith to thee, Give me to drink; thou wouldest have asked of him, and he would have given thee living water'. We seek to quench ourselves, to satisfy our thirst for love and intensity, our desire to live, by multiplying the objects we desire and that we possess. We run, gasping for breath, after sensations, after emotions, thoughts, beauty — and yet, ever and again, our thirst is unassuaged. 'Whosoever drinketh of this water shall thirst again . . .'. But he to whom Jesus communicates his life stops being tortured by thirst — 'shall never thirst' — and even finds, O miracle! that this water in him becomes a living source: 'The water that I shall give him shall be in him a well of water springing up into everlasting life'. Not only does he drink at the source, but he becomes a source for others.

The woman of Samaria asks Jesus for this water: 'Give me this water, that I thirst not . . .'. Jesus answers: 'Go, call thy husband . . .'. The Saviour puts his finger on her sore spot. He knows that the woman has had five husbands and that she now lives with a man who is not her husband [30]. Our Lord cannot communicate his life and his grace to us as long as we do not overcome those moral obstacles which stand between him and us. Spiritual life is not separable from moral life. When we are tempted to forget this, Our Lord immediately puts a stop to our pseudo-mystical transports, and says to us simply: 'Go, call thy husband'. Which means: 'First, repent of your sin — not of sin in general — but of the actual sin which is your own and that dominates you. Put right in your life what needs to be put right. Free your soul from its idolatries, its adulteries — its five husbands (and yet more) — and let it come to me, who will at last be its rightful husband' [31]. Often we try to illude ourselves: not having the courage to renounce our 'husbands', we substitute for this renunciation thoughts about God (Oh, such beautiful ones!), theological systems and discussions, schemes for good works (only in rough

outline, though, for good works that will last call for the purity of
a diamond), 'ecumenical' preoccupations. And Jesus cuts these
lies short: 'Where is thy husband? I did not entrust thee with the
universe: what about thy soul?'

The Samaritan woman admits her own situation with humility
and frankness. Surprised at Jesus's perspicacity, she sees him as a
prophet. But still she hesitates: this prophet is Jewish; now the
Jews worship at Jerusalem, whereas the Samaritans worship on
Mount Gerizim[32]. Jesus's answer offers something of great importance to those preoccupied with the divisions and the unity of
Christians, for we can transpose the Judaeo-Samaritan problem
onto this plane. 'The hour cometh, when ye shall neither in this
mountain, nor yet at Jerusalem, worship the Father . . . . The
hour cometh, and now is, when the true worshippers shall worship the Father in spirit and in truth.' A strange answer, which
seems to indicate something which is both in the future — 'the
hour cometh' — and exists already — 'and now is' — the moment when our differences will be united in a perfect spiritual
adoration. How can this hour be both to come, and have already
arrived? The antithesis is remarkable. The hour still belongs to
the future, for Jesus (and this is the lesson for 'ecumenism') is far
from minimising or putting on a level of equality the dissimilar
beliefs of the Samaritans and the Jews. He says this clearly: 'Ye
worship ye know not what: we know what we worship: for salvation is of the Jews'. And nevertheless, both Jerusalem and Gerizim
(and in this is a lesson for all 'orthodoxy') will be outstripped; the
hour of adoration in spirit is come. The 'and now is' is explained
by the presence of Jesus himself. The Samaritan woman, standing
before Jesus, finds herself facing the reality of which Jerusalem
and Gerizim are but pale shadows. Jesus is the essence and the
consummation of our faith. His presence is the reality of that unity which, when we do not see the Saviour, seems so distant. Of
course we can in no way compromise with the message we have
received from the apostles; the hour is still to come when this
message will be wholly accepted by all. But already, in specially
blessed moments, or when we feel ourselves (as much as we can
feel this) united to Jesus Christ, we find in him the whole, un-
divided Church. This, when Jesus is talking with the Samaritan
woman, is neither at Jerusalem nor at Gerizim: it is at Jacob's
Well, with him.

And this is the great declaration which Jesus addresses, from
Jacob's Well, to believers of all times: 'God is a Spirit: and they

that worship him must worship him in spirit and in truth'. Adoration which is in spirit and in truth is neither dogmatism, nor emotionalism, nor ritualism, nor legal formalism. It is a constant effort to think and say what is true, to unite our will to that of God, to let the Holy Spirit direct our soul supremely. These words of Jesus's have been hated by every human authority that has ever tried to substitute itself for divine authority. They have been, and will remain, eternally loved by those who wish to free themselves from all the lies and the bondage which intervene between the Saviour and the soul[33].

The woman of Samaria says to Jesus that she knows that the Messiah will reveal all things. Jesus says to her: 'I that speak unto thee am he'. The contrast between the solemn affirmation 'I . . . am he'[34], and the intentionally familiar form of 'who speak unto thee', is worth noticing. If we meditate on this phrase, we shall understand better the abyss of grandeur and of condescension that is implicit in every meeting of the human soul with Jesus. On the one hand, it is the Christ-God who speaks. The Creator addresses his creature. On the other, he gives his words the form of an intimate and friendly conversation. All prayer, unless it has reached the great silence of the 'state of union', should resolve itself into an affectionate exchange.

The Samaritan woman goes off, leaving her waterpot behind. She goes to her fellow countrymen: 'Come, see a man, which told me all things that ever I did: is not this the Christ?'. Faith in Christ has not only begun to shine in her soul, but she now takes upon herself a certain ministry, an apostleship. This apostleship is fruitful, because the Samaritans leave the city and come out to meet Jesus. The woman's apostleship takes the form of personal witness. Witness is quite different from preaching. The preacher says: 'Believe this' or 'Do this'. The witness says: 'This is what happened to me'. There is much greater efficacy, much greater persuasive power, in bearing witness than in preaching. We are not all called to preach, but each person can, in his own sphere, bear simple and humble witness to the graces that have been granted to him. This testimony will be all the more striking when the witness sincerely admits his sins: 'a man which told me all the things that ever I did', said the Samaritan woman. Often it needs considerable courage to 'share' our faults and our graces with others, but the best testimony is that 'sharing' which takes place under the guidance of the Spirit[35]. Am I a good witness of Jesus Christ?

The disciples, who had gone to the city to buy provisions, return. They urge Jesus to eat. He answers: 'My meat is to do the will of him that sent me'. In this lies the perfection of obedience. It is one thing to say: 'I carry out God's will', and quite another to say: 'My meat is to do the will of God'. Obedience to the Father constitutes Jesus's very food and life. Every disciple sent by Jesus should, also, be able to say: 'My meat is to do the will of him that sent me'. How far from that am I, who do not even have the strength to keep the divine precepts in a simple way.

Jesus invites the disciples to look around them: 'Lift up your eyes, and look upon the fields; for they are white already to harvest'. He reminds them that they will reap where they have not sown; they will enter into the labour of others; and yet the reaper will receive his wages and will rejoice with the sower. The allusion to the conversion of the Samaritans is apparent; the disciples will get followers solely because of Jesus. The harvest — the mission — is ready waiting. But, in a more general way, Jesus's words call us to recognise with humility that others have already laboured where we think we are doing something for God and, in any case, that our Lord alone is the sower.

And now the harvest starts. 'And many of the Samaritans of that city believed on him for the saying of the woman . . . . And many more believed because of his own word; And said unto the woman, Now we believe, not because of thy saying: for we have heard him ourselves . . . .' We see here two forms of faith, of which the second is more perfect than the first. One can believe in Jesus because of someone else's testimony. But one can also believe in Jesus because one has heard his voice oneself. We can believe because of the testimony of the apostles, the martyrs, the saints and the whole Church. We shall be fortunate indeed, however, if it is given to us to believe because of an inner and personal experience of the Saviour's words[36].

For the epistle at the liturgy this Sunday once again a portion of the Book of Acts (11. 19-30) is read. It describes the dispersion of the disciples as a result of persecution, and tells of their evangelising work in Cyprus and Phenice, and of the success of Saul and Barnabas's mission at Antioch, where disciples were 'called Christians first'. Here again we find the theme of mission, which was also indicated in the gospel for the day, when Jesus announced the good news near Jacob's Well and in the city of the Samaritans.

The Blind Man

Last Sunday – the Sunday of the Samaritan woman – at the liturgy, the following antiphon for communion was sung: 'Rejoice and be glad, door of the divine Light (that is to say, the Virgin Mary), for Jesus, after being hidden from sight in the tomb, has risen again more brightly than the sun, and thereby illumines all believers'. Here, there is a return to the theological and liturgical theme of light, which, as we have already said, is so characteristic of Byzantine spirituality; here, too, more particularly, there is a reminder of the link between the Resurrection of Christ and the light that shines into our consciousness. An external event, be it even the Resurrection of our Lord, has no practical value for souls unless it translates itself, in them, into an increase of that inner Light which must direct our whole life. The light of Christ is an essential paschal theme. It is this theme which is developed on the sixth Sunday of the Easter season, called the 'Sunday of the Blind Man', when the healing of a blind man is commemorated and leads to the idea of our own blindness and healing.

At the liturgy, we hear the gospel account of the healing of the blind man (John 9. 1-38). Jesus meets a man who was born blind; having applied a mixture of clay and spittle to his eyes, Jesus sends the man to wash in the pool of Siloam[37]. The man receives his sight, and becomes the object of hostile curiosity and insidious questions from the Pharisees. But however much they declare that Jesus is a sinner, the man protests that a sinner has not the power to give sight to a blind man. Expelled by the Pharisees, the man who was blind is found by Jesus (it is not he who finds Jesus, but Jesus who finds him, and this is rich in meaning). Jesus asks him if he believes in the Son of God. 'Who is he, Lord, that I might believe on him?' Jesus answers: 'Thou hast both seen him, and it is he that talketh with thee' (we remember the very similar words spoken by Jesus to the Samaritan woman). 'And he said, Lord, I believe. And he worshipped him.'

This episode illustrates the words of the Prophet Isaiah: 'Then the eyes of the blind shall be opened'[38], and what Jesus himself said: 'The Spirit of the Lord . . . hath sent me . . . to preach . . . recovering of sight to the blind'[39]. It is certain that physical blindness, while being the immediate object of Jesus's solicitude (and one knows how much suffering is caused by eye disease in the Middle East), here symbolises the spiritual blindness from which

Jesus heals men. But the healing, in the gospel we have just read, cannot be separated from the good will and the sincere faith of the blind man himself. The most authoritative commentary on this episode is that given to us by the Church itself, which, in two of the antiphons for this Sunday, expresses it thus:

'Christ, our God, Sun of Righteousness beyond all understanding, O Thou who, in touching him, didst open the eyes of the man born blind, open the eyes of our souls and make us children of light . . . .'

'I come to Thee, O Christ, the eyes of my soul blind as the eyes of the man born blind, and, in repentance, I cry to Thee: Thou art the Light of supreme brightness for all those who are in darkness.'

In place of the epistle at the liturgy, the reading is from the Book of Acts (16. 16-34) and tells of what happened to Paul and Silas at Philippi (or perhaps at Thyatira, for the question of place is not made clear). Paul and Silas heal a young girl who was possessed. At the instigation of her masters who were making money from the predictions she made, Paul and Silas are arrested for disturbing public order, beaten and imprisoned. In the middle of the night, there is an earthquake which shakes the foundations of the prison. The doors open and the chains fall off. The gaoler, thinking that the prisoners have escaped, wants to kill himself. Paul stops him. The gaoler is converted, is baptised, and then takes Paul and Silas into his own home. The two central verses of this portion of Acts seem to us to be the short dialogue between the gaoler and his prisoners: 'Sirs, what must I do to be saved? — Believe on the Lord Jesus Christ, and thou shalt be saved, and thy house'. Paul does not ask the gaoler to accept an intellectual doctrine that later will be explained to him ('And they spake unto him the word of the Lord, and to all that were in his house'). What he asks for, immediately, is an act of faith, not in the word — of which the gaoler is still ignorant — but in the person of Jesus. The gaoler must recognise that 'Jesus Christ is the Lord'. The formula is very vague intellectually. Practically, it is very precise, for it calls for homage and unreserved submission of the will. This act of faith is an act of obedience and of trust by which the distressed person throws himself at Jesus's feet — as the gaoler had just thrown himself, trembling, at the feet of Paul and Silas. Before explaining all the intellectual consequences of our faith in Christ, we must first, we must above all, believe in Jesus as him who is the Lord, and whose rights over us are absolute. The most scrupulous Orthodoxy would not be able to save us if this was not our attitude towards Christ, and if this attitude did not bear its fruits. We will not miss the comparison between the act of faith proposed by Paul to the gaoler and that which Jesus himself called for, in today's gospel, from the blind man whom he had healed.

The Ascension

The Wednesday which follows the fifth Sunday after Easter is the day when, in liturgical terminology, we 'take leave' of the Easter feast. We commemorate the last day of the physical presence of the risen Christ amongst his disciples; and to honour this presence, to honour the Resurrection once more, the Church on this Wednesday repeats the service for Easter Sunday in its entirety. And now we have come to the fortieth day after Easter, the Thursday on which the Church celebrates the feast of the Ascension[49].

Three lessons from the Old Testament are read at vespers for the Ascension, on the Wednesday evening. The first lesson (Isa. 2. 2-3) speaks of a mountain: 'It shall come to pass in the last days, that the mountain of the Lord's house shall be established in the top of the mountains . . . and all nations shall flow unto it . . . . Come ye, and let us go up to the mountain of the Lord'. This alludes to the Mount of Olives, from which Jesus ascended to his Father. The second lesson (Isa. 62. 10-63. 3, 7-9) was chosen because of the following words: 'Go through, go through the gates; prepare ye the way of the people . . . . In his love and in his pity he redeemed them; and he bare them, and carried them . . .'. Jesus, ascending to heaven, opens the gates to his people, he prepares a way for them, he carries them and raises them up with him. The third lesson (Zech. 14. 1, 4, 8-11) also speaks of the mountain which was the scene of Jesus's final triumph: 'Behold the day of the Lord cometh . . . . And his feet shall stand in that day upon the mount of Olives, which is before Jerusalem on the east . . . . And it shall be in that day, that living waters shall go out from Jerusalem.'

The chants at matins for the Ascension are already filled with allusions to the Spirit, the Comforter, whom Jesus will send. Ascension is the prelude to Pentecost.

At the liturgy, the beginning of the Book of the Acts (1. 1-12) is read. Jesus, after a last meeting with His apostles, is taken up, and disappears in a cloud[41]. The gospel for the liturgy (Luke 24. 36-53) takes up the account of events from the first appearance of the risen Jesus to the assembled disciples[42] and continues with it right up to the Ascension itself.

It is rare, if one has lived through the joy of Easter time sincerely, that one does not experience a certain constriction of the heart when the day of the Ascension comes. We know perfectly well that it is one of the very great Christian feasts, and yet, despite ourselves, it seems like a parting, a separation, and that after it, our Lord is not with us in quite the same way any longer. The disciples did not react like this. They could have been overwhelmed with grief but, on the contrary, they 'returned to Jerusalem with great joy'[43]. We, too, can try and enter into this joy of the Ascension. Why does the Ascension bring joy to Christians?

First of all, the glory of our Lord must be very precious to us, and the Ascension is the crown of his earthly mission. He has accomplished on earth the whole mission which he had received from the Father. It is to the Father that his whole being reaches out. Now he will receive from the Father the welcome that his victory over sin and death — a victory gained so grievously — has merited for him. Now he will be glorified in heaven. The glory and the desire of our Lord are surely more important to us than the sort of 'perceptible consolations' that we might receive from his presence. Let us know how to love our Lord enough to rejoice in his own joy.

Then the Ascension marks God's acceptance of the Son's whole work of reparation. The Resurrection was the first dazzling sign of this acceptance, and Pentecost will be the last sign. The cloud which today envelopes Jesus and ascends with him to heaven represents the smoke of the sacrifice rising from the altar to God. The sacrifice is accepted, and the victim is admitted to God's presence where it will continue to be offered in an eternal and heavenly manner. The work of our salvation has been accomplished and is blessed.

Jesus does not return to his Father in isolation. It was the incorporeal Logos which came down among men. But today it is the Word made flesh, both true God and true man, who enters the kingdom of heaven. Jesus brings into it the human nature which he had assumed. He opens the door of the kingdom to humanity. As if by proxy, we take possession of the benefits which are offered and made possible to us. '(God) hath raised us up together, and made us sit together in heavenly places in Christ Jesus'[44].

There are places destined for us in the kingdom, if we are faithful. Our presence is desired and awaited.

The Ascension makes thoughts of heaven more immediate, more actual to us[45]. Do we think of our permanent home often enough? For most Christians, life in heaven is no more than a supplement – of which they have but a very hazy notion – to life on earth. Life in heaven is seen somewhat as a postscript, an appendix, to a book whose text is formed by earthly life. But it is the opposite which is true. Our earthly life is but the preface to the book. Life in heaven will be its main text, and this text is endless. To make use of another image, our earthly life is but a tunnel, narrow, dark – and very short – which opens onto a magnificent, sunlit landscape. We think too much of what our life now is. We do not think enough of what it will be. 'Men have not heard, nor perceived by the ear, neither hath the eye seen, O God . . . what he hath prepared for him that waiteth for him.'[46] At matins for this feast, we sang: 'We who live in this world, let us feast like the angels . . .'. That is to say: let us open our minds more to the angels, and try to enter into their feelings, experiencing something of what they experience when the Son returns to the Father; let us go ahead in spirit and be near the Blessed Virgin Mary and the glorified saints, who will be our true co-citizens: 'For our conversation is in heaven; from whence also we look for the Saviour, the Lord Jesus Christ'[47]. Our lives would be transformed if, from now on, we threw our hearts over the barrier, beyond this world, into the kingdom where is found not only our own true good but also the true good of those whom we love.

When the disciples had been separated from Jesus, they remained full of hope, for they knew that they were to receive the Spirit. '(He) commanded them that they should not depart from Jerusalem, but wait for the promise of the Father'[48]. The cloud surrounds Jesus, but this cloud is coloured already by the fire of Pentecost. Jesus, in going away from us, leaves in us an attitude which is one not of regret, but rather of joyous and trustful awaiting.

Jesus's departure has been both an act of benediction and an act of adoration, the one corresponding to the other: 'And it came to pass, while he blessed them, he was parted from them, and carried up into heaven. And they worshipped him, and returned to Jerusalem with great joy'[49]. This is what the feast of the Ascension should be to us. If Jesus withdraws with an act of blessing, and if we adore Jesus as he withdraws (we speak figuratively), we will get up filled with new power — which comes from this adoration, this blessing — and we, like the apostles, will return 'with great joy'.

The Holy Fathers

The Sunday which follows the Ascension — sixth Sunday after Easter Sunday itself — is called 'Sunday of the Holy Fathers'. It commemorates the bishops who sat at the Council of Nicaea, the first in date of the seven ecumenical councils[50].

The councils, and, independently of each council considered by itself, the idea of council in itself, have a great importance for the Orthodox Church[51]. But the Council of Nicaea holds a very special place in the history of Christian doctrine: for, in affirming the divinity of Christ, it laid the foundation of all subsequent definitions. The great temptation of 'modern' theology, since the sixteenth century, has been, if not a return to Arianism, at least a sliding towards a 'humanist' conception of the person of Jesus Christ, who is seen as a more or less divinised creature. The Nicene Creed, in proclaiming that our Lord is truly God, equal to the Father, safeguards the integral message of love and of the divine gift: God so loved the world that he gave himself to us, and became man in the person of the unique Son. To change a single iota of the Nicene Creed[52] is to diminish the grandeur and generosity of God's gift, it is to alter the essence of Orthodox Christianity radically.

The commemoration of the Fathers of Nicaea, this Sunday, does not mean that the Church proclaims or honours the personal sanctity of each one of the bishops who took part[53]. Rather, the Church pays homage today to the collective witness that the Assembly of Nicaea bore to Christian truth. The epistle read at the liturgy (Acts 20. 16-18, 28-36) alludes to the duties of pastoral care, especially to the duty of combating doctrinal deviations: 'Take heed therefore unto yourselves, and to all the flock, over which the Holy Ghost hath made you overseers, to feed the church of God, which he hath purchased with his own blood. For I know this, that after my departing shall grievous wolves enter in among you, not sparing the flock. Also of your own selves shall men arise, speaking perverse things, to draw away disciples after them. Therefore watch . . .'. Thus spake Paul to the elders of the church at Ephesus[54]. The gospel for the liturgy (John 17. 1-13), taken from the words spoken by our Lord after the Last Supper, expresses the same pastoral and doctrinal care: 'This is life eternal, that they might know thee the only true God, and Jesus Christ, whom thou hast sent . . . . I have given unto them the words that thou gavest me; and they have received them, and have known surely that I came out from thee . . . . I pray for them . . . .'.

This Sunday already belongs to the sphere of ideas connected with Pentecost rather than with the Ascension, for the catholic Church believes that the Council of Nicaea, like the other ecumenical councils and the apostles themselves gathered at Jerusalem, taught under the inspiration of the Holy Spirit[55]. And the first verse of the epistle for today already orients our thoughts towards Pentecost: 'For he (Paul) hasted, if it were possible for him, to be at Jerusalem the day of Pentecost'. To be with the apostles at Jerusalem, in spirit, at next Sunday's great feast – is not this what we, too, desire and humbly ask for?

Saints of the Time of Easter

Before coming to the end of the forty days of Easter time, let us take a quick look at the saints whose feasts normally fall into or near this period. We will only mention three feasts: that of St George (April 23rd), of Constantine and Helena (May 21st), and of St Cyril of Alexandria (June 10th). These three commemorations have one feature in common: they shed light on an idea rather than on a person. Almost nothing is known about St George himself[56], but, in him, we venerate a martyr for Christ; popular piety has even made him a symbol of martyrdom. Constantine and Helena[57] were honoured under very different heads: Helena because certain traditions have associated her name with the worship of the Cross; Constantine, because he gave peace to the Church and even, to a certain extent, Christianised the empire. What one could call 'Constantinian Christianity' is difficult to judge without bias: whether it be in Rome, in Byzantium, or in Russia, the idea of the 'Holy Empire' and of State Christianity has been sullied by so much blood and persecution, so much servility towards Caesar, so many ambitions both ecclesiastical and political, so many compromises between the Gospel and the world, that many historians (or even simple Christians) think of the reign of Constantine as the principal factor responsible for deviation in the evolution of the Church. All the same, there is in 'Constantinian Christianity' a very true and fundamental idea, a very proper intention: to know that Christ Jesus is, the King not only of individual souls, but of human society, and that the Gospel must inspire the social and political life of peoples[58]. We can commemorate Helena — whatever we may think about the wood of the true Cross — in celebrating the Cross of Christ, the instrument of Redemption. We can commemorate Constantine in rejecting caesaro-papism (and no less, papo-caesarism), but in celebrating the universal Majesty of Christ. In St Cyril of Alexandria[59], the adversary of heresy and champion of the faith which was proclaimed at Nicaea, we honour an integral orthodoxy which does not allow the person of the God-Man to be diminished.

The Vigil of Pentecost

The Saturday which follows the sixth Sunday after Easter Sunday is the vigil of the feast of Pentecost. In the Byzantine liturgical tradition, this Saturday has a double character.

On the one hand, it bears the name of 'Saturday of the Dead'. It is dedicated to prayer for the departed. On the Saturday which follows the Sunday of the Prodigal Son, at the threshold of Great Lent, we have already had a special commemoration of the faithful who have departed this life[60]. On this last day of the Easter season, once again we pray for them, so that they are in some way associated with the Resurrection of Christ, the cause and first fruit of the resurrection of all flesh. The services for this day are identical with those of 'Memorial Saturday' before the beginning of Great Lent. The epistle for the liturgy (1 Thes. 4. 13-16) exhorts us, 'concerning them which are asleep', not to sorrow 'even as others which have no hope. For if we believe that Jesus died and rose again, even so them also which sleep in Jesus will God bring with him'. The gospel (John 5. 24-30) brings us Jesus's words: 'Verily, verily, I say unto you, he that heareth my word, and believeth on him that sent me, hath everlasting life, and shall not come into condemnation; but is passed from death unto life . . . . The hour is coming, and now is, when the dead shall hear the voice of the Son of God: and they that hear shall live . . . they that have done good, unto the resurrection of life; and they that have done evil, unto the resurrection of damnation'. We would also refer the reader to the gospel for the resurrection of Lazarus, read on Saturday, eve of Palm Sunday[61]. The Orthodox Church has not dogmatised on the way in which the souls of the departed, who have not yet been admitted to the divine vision and joy, will be purified, but it does invite us to pray for souls; it does not doubt that our intercession is able to help them to progress from light to greater light. Let us therefore join the Church in saying this text from matins for today: 'O Lord, give rest to Thy servants in the city of the living, where there is neither sorrow, nor sadness, nor sighing. And forgive them, Thou lover of mankind, the sins they have committed in this life, for Thou alone art without sin and Thou alone art merciful, Lord of the living and of the dead'.

The prayer for the dead must not allow us to forget the other aspect of this Saturday. It is both the last day of Easter time, and the eve of Pentecost. The biblical readings at the liturgy (readings which belong to the day itself and are distinct from those that commemorate the dead) have a certain 'finality' about them – they mark an end, a conclusion. Instead of an epistle, we read the last chapter (ch. 28) of the Acts of the Apostles: Paul, after his shipwreck at Malta, reaches Rome to be judged by Caesar and, while waiting, preaches Jesus Christ 'with all confidence, no man forbidding him'. These are the last words in the Book of Acts. Similarly, at the liturgy, the last chapter of the gospel according to St John (ch. 21) is read. We will draw attention to Jesus's last words, as they are reported by John. Jesus, risen from the dead, and standing on the shore of the lake, says to Peter, who is curious about John's destiny: 'What is that to thee? follow thou me'. These last words are the same as the first words Jesus once addressed to Simon and Andrew, on the shore of the same lake: 'Follow me'[62]. Between this first invitation and the final injunction, many months have passed, many events have taken place – and what events! Now Simon knows what he did not know at the beginning: what has taken place at Jerusalem during the last few weeks has shown him the full implication of 'following the Lord'. And in our lives, too, when we are mature or old and hear Jesus repeat the word he perhaps spoke to us in the time of our youth, we now understand more fully what is implied by these last words that are quoted in the gospels. For several saints, these words have been the stimulant which committed them to the 'way', to following the Master. As long as we live, there is still time to make the essential decision and obey the word which tells us, as it told Simon Peter, not to be concerned with what others do, but to concentrate ourselves wholly on the only true essential: 'Follow thou me'.

Notes to Chapter VI

1   This canticle, which occupies an important place in the prayers of the Greek, the Roman and the Anglican church rituals, does not belong to the original Hebrew text of the Book of Daniel. The verses 24-30 of Chapter 3 of Daniel, as they are read in the Greek and Latin versions of the Bible and in the modern translations that derive from them, constitute an insertion which belongs to the Septuagint. In the Hebrew text and the translations made from the Hebrew, verses 24-30 of this chapter correspond to verses 91-96 of the Greek and Latin texts derived from the Septuagint.

2   Today the liturgy of St Basil is celebrated. At the beginning of the liturgy, the liturgical colours are changed. Those vestments and ornaments which signify mourning or are of a penitential character, and which have been used during Lent and Holy Week (although there are a certain number of exceptions), are changed and replaced by joyful colours. Unlike the Roman Church, the Byzantine Church does not allocate a strictly determined colour to particular liturgical celebrations. The most ancient custom is that materials of a dark shade are used on penitential days and of a light shade on feast days, regardless of the actual colour of the material. Nevertheless, the use of red gradually became characteristic of celebrations for the departed or in honour of martyrs. In our day, many Orthodox churches use black in services for the departed and for those during Lent. This is a Latin infiltration which, like many others (as, for example, the formula of absolution in the Russian Church), came about in the seventeenth century, via Poland.

3   The Church which, from the tenth Sunday before Easter, has read the liturgical texts for the variable feasts from the *Triodion*, closes this book on Holy Saturday. These texts will be taken from the *Pentekostarion* until the first Sunday after Pentecost.

4   It is beyond doubt that Easter is historically the most ancient of the Christian feasts. From the year 120, the feast of the Resurrection of Christ has been celebrated in Rome as well as in the East, but the Churches differed as to the date and the methods of this celebration. In the last years of the second century, a lively controversy about the date of Easter brought Pope Victor and the Churches of Asia into opposition. In the fourth century, the Council of Nicaea laid down certain rules that we shall look at further on, but this did not prevent a certain amount of discussion and dissent. The Byzantine Church and the Roman Church have many points in common in the celebration of Easter, among them, the emphasis placed on the theme of light (the solemn blessing of the paschal candle in the Roman rite). One often hears it said that the Roman liturgy does not celebrate the Resurrection with as much joy as do the oriental liturgies. This is one of those superficial generalisations which should be absolutely rejected. An attentive reading of the Latin texts will show that the paschal joy is the same, both in the East and the West. Nevertheless, it is true to say that Easter does not occupy as central a place in the popular piety of the Latin and Germanic nations as it does in that of the peoples of the East.

5   The Council of Nicaea, in 325, laid down that the Resurrection of Christ should be celebrated on the Sunday following the full moon that comes after the spring equinox (the equinox is on 21 March). This rule appears to be simple, but leaves the door open to certain difficulties and uncertainties which we will not go into here. It is the basis of the computation', or calculation which is specially designed to determine the date of Easter and the movable feasts, and to fix the

ecclesiastical calendar for each year. We know that the Julian calendar, which is still adhered to by some Orthodox Churches, is thirteen days behind the Gregorian, which has been adopted by the west. However, those Orthodox Churches which follow the Gregorian calendar remain faithful to the Julian calendar in regard to the calculation of the date of Easter. The result is that the Orthodox and Roman feasts of Easter normally fall on different dates, but that occasionally they coincide.

6 John 21. 18.

7 John 21. 19.

8 After the Easter service, the blessing of the eggs, meats, breads, cakes, etc., which are proper to this feast, takes place in Orthodox parishes. The custom, in itself, is excellent. It associates the life of the home with the life of the Church. But one cannot protest too much against the deviation which it causes in certain Orthodox countries where many of the faithful are so absorbed with the cleaning of their houses, the decoration of eggs, the making of cakes, in short, with the material preparations for the feast, that they miss the services. Religion thus becomes an adopted national or familial custom which is no longer animated by the breath of the Spirit.

9 In some Orthodox Churches, this reading of the Gospel in several languages – which is designed to underline the universality of Christ's message – takes place at the liturgy of the night or on the morning of Easter. In other churches, it takes place on Easter Monday.

10 The term 'the time of Easter' is fairly elastic. During the course of history, this period has sometimes been shortened, sometimes lengthened. A canonical basis for thinking of it as lasting from Easter till Pentecost is the custom that fish is allowed on all Wednesdays and Fridays during this period. Usually, not only meat, but dairy produce, eggs, oil and fish are forbidden on Wednesdays and Fridays; but, except in monasteries, practice usually falls far behind theory. During Easter week itself, one can eat meat even on the Friday. So to think of the time of Easter as comprising fifty days corresponds to certain canonical regulations as well as to the idea of the fifty days which end with Pentecost (moreover, the Greek *Pentekoste* means 'fiftieth day'). Nevertheless, there is both a theological and a historical basis for dividing the fifty days that follow Easter into two quite distinct periods: the time of Easter, which in fact ends on the day of the Ascension; and Ascension tide which lasts from Ascension day to the eve of Pentecost.

11 Around the middle of the fifth century, in a suburb of Constantinople called the Seven Towers, and close to a spring where many healings attributed to the Mother of God had taken place, the Emperor Leo the Thracian had built a rich church dedicated to her. Later on, the church was destroyed. On its ruins, the Turks built the mosque of the Sultan Bayazid. The crypt and the spring survived, however. In 1821, the remains of the church were totally demolished. The spring itself sanded up and somehow disappeared. In 1833, the Sultan authorised the building of a new church of considerable dimensions, near to the site of the first.

12 The Russians call Easter week 'Bright Week'.

13 1 Cor. 5. 7-8.

14 2 Cor. 5. 17.

15 Rom. 6. 4.

16 Rom. 7. 6.

17   1 Peter 2. 2.

18   Historically, we know nothing of the life of Thomas after Pentecost. There exist the *Acts of Thomas* and the *Gospel of Thomas*, but these compositions are of Gnostic origin and their contents are somewhat extravagant. The tradition according to which Thomas went and preached in India is not proved, but it contains nothing either impossible or even improbable. The evangelising of India seems to have taken place very early. It is certain that there were Christians in India from the fourth century, and certain communities in Malabar claim to derive from St Thomas.

19   Allow us here to quote an incident from the life of G. F. Andrews, who was a great disciple of Christ and an agent of reconciliation in the Indies – and whom we had the privilege of knowing. A native of the Fiji Islands had been cruelly beaten and wounded by a European. He was so terror-stricken that, when Andrews tried to speak gently to him, he fled. Andrews had a sort of vision: he first of all saw this disfigured and battered man before him, then he saw the figure of Christ substitute itself gradually for that of the man. The result of this was that Andrews left for the Fiji Islands and gave himself to the work of improving conditions for the native peoples.

20   Matt. 28. 2.

21   The fourth gospel (20. 12) speaks not of one angel only, but of 'two angels in white sitting, the one at the head, and the other at the feet'. This description, especially coming from the pen of a symbolist such as the author of the fourth gospel, naturally evokes the memory of the 'mercy seat', the long golden cover of the ark of the covenant at each end of which was a golden cherub (Exod. 25. 17-18). The 'Mercy Seat' was in some way a meeting-place between God and man: 'And there I will meet with thee, and I will commune with thee from above the mercy seat, from between the two cherubims . . .' (Exod. 25.22). Let us take note: it is not on the ark itself, which contained the tables of the law, that God wishes to manifest himself to men (if the place of our meeting with God was under the sign of the law, who could survive?). God, in order to allow us to draw near to him, covered the tables of the law with his mercy; the meeting could take place under the sign of mercy, not that of justice. In the New Covenant the empty tomb, representing the victory of Jesus's resurrection over sin and death has become the mercy seat. Golgotha was also a mercy seat, with the two criminals replacing the two cherubim; but the mercy seat of the Resurrection is greater than that of the Passion, because the defeat of Jesus was only temporary and his triumph is eternal. Let us draw near to the tomb of our Lord (which, in Byzantine liturgical symbolism, is represented by the altar) in the same way that we draw near to the Cross, that is to the mercy seat where we receive the forgiveness and the word of God.

22   Luke 24. 5.

23   It is not necessary to try to find a secret meaning in this number. Here the figure 'thirty eight' simply indicates that the paralytic is not suffering from a temporary illness, but from an infirmity which has beset him for a long time: the sudden healing will therefore be all the more remarkable. Those who like a symbolic exegesis – which, after all, has often been the exegesis of the Apostles themselves and of the Fathers of the Church, and which has its legitimate place – will see a relationship between the thirty eight years of the impotent man's suffering and the thirty eight years of the people of Israel's wanderings before reaching the brook Zered (Deut. 2. 14), and they will relate the words: 'Rise,

take up thy bed, and walk', spoken by Jesus to the impotent man to the word of God to the Israelites: 'Rise up, said I, and get you over the brook Zered' (Deut. 2. 13).

24   Let us remember the Thomist saying: *Deus non alligatur sacramentis,* 'God is not bound to the sacraments'. We have recourse to the witness of the Thomistic school, because one could not suspect it of minimising the objective elements of religion.

25   John 7. 14.

26   John 7. 14-31.

27   John 7. 37-39.

28   John 4. 23.

29   The liturgical prose *Dies irae, dies illa,* which the Latin Church sings at services for the dead, contains an allusion to this episode: *Quaerens me sedisti lassus,* 'Thou wast wearied seeking for me and didst sit . . .'.

30   Some exegetes have wondered whether there may not be a symbolic allusion in this: Samaria was peopled by settlers who had come from five areas of Assyria, and each of these five groups had brought with them their local idols (2 Kings 17). In Jesus's time, the Samaritans mixed the worship of Yahveh with the worship of their ancient divinities: there was in this a sort of spiritual adultery. It is also possible that Jesus was alluding to real events in the Samaritan woman's life. Her situation was not only not impossible, but not even strictly incompatible with what religious custom allowed in those times. Nevertheless, it is clear that Jesus considered the Samaritan woman's state to be morally irregular. It is also possible that this passage alludes both to the biographical elements which were personal to the woman and to historical elements which belonged to the Samaritan people as a whole.

31   The conjugal tie between the Christian soul and Jesus is not the invention of a sentimental piety. The concept is based on scriptural material, notably on the Church's interpretation of the Song of Songs, and on the very ancient and authentic tradition of the Fathers. It is completely erroneous to reject this concept, as some Orthodox do, on the pretext that it is a late, emotional, and somewhat suspect product of Roman mystics.

32   The Samaritan temple on Mount Gerizim was built in about 400 B.C., and destroyed by the Jewish prince John Hyrcanus in about 129 B.C. The separation between the Jews and the Samaritans took place after the return from the Babylonian captivity.

33   One cannot take this saying as authorising one to reject the Church. In the Church there is both a divine element — which coincides with the breath of the Spirit — and a human element which is imperfect and sinful. But there is need of constant striving to make the human element more subject to the divine element and more in conformity with it. In this sense, the Church needs a continual Reformation, which can, however, in no way be identified with the work of the Reformers of the sixteenth century (though we do not ignore the positive aspects of their work).

34   Contemporary exegesis has emphasised the importance and the implications of the formula 'I am' in the fourth gospel. The same formula is often used by Jehovah in the Old Testament, and its use is always marked by particular solemnity and majesty.

35   These terms may remind some of our readers of the language used by a contemporary religious movement, Moral Rearmament. Orthodoxy must be prepared to recognise what is to its benefit, wherever it finds it.

36 The question has been asked how Jesus's meeting with the Samaritan woman, which took place in the absence of the disciples, could have been reported as it is in the fourth gospel, and one conclusion reached is that the meeting has a fictional aspect. But, in reading this episode, we are struck by its feeling of reality. Perhaps one of the disciples had stayed behind, and it was he who described the meeting; or perhaps the woman provided the information – or even Jesus Himself.

37 The gospel itself tells us that the Hebrew word *Shiloah* or *Siloam* means 'sent'. The waters of Siloam, which, as Isaiah says (8. 6) 'go softly' in contrast to the turbulent waters of Assyria, had been connected by an underground channel to what is now called 'the well of the Virgin'. These names provide a source of meditation for those who care for symbols; we are free not to accept this, and have no right to condemn it.

38 Isa. 35. 5.

39 Luke 4. 18.

40 This feast has been celebrated throughout the whole Church since the beginning of the fifth century. In those days, Christians from Jerusalem went to celebrate the Ascension at Bethlehem, in the church built above the traditional site of the cave. This custom expressed the desire to bring together the last and the first day of Jesus's earthly life.

41 The presence of the cloud shows clearly the symbolic character of what might be called the physical aspect of the Ascension. The cloud which enveloped the tabernacle and guided Israel in the desert constituted the visible sign of the divine presence. Jesus's disappearance in a cloud is not rough imagery: it signifies that the end of our Lord's earthly life is the absorption of his glorified Body into the bosom of God.

42 Let us notice the simplicity of our Lord's return to his disciples. Jesus does not begin by addressing them either with reproaches or with sublime teachings. He wishes them peace, and then straightaway asks whether they have anything for him to eat. The disciples offer him broiled fish and honey, which he eats in front of them. It is only afterwards that he teaches. In the same way, when somehow we have become separated from the Saviour, we should not worry about the way in which the link can be re-established, but simply call Jesus to us; we can offer him our fish and honey – that is, we can take him straight away to the centre of our life and of our daily preoccupations. We can pick up life's threads again at the point where they were broken off. He will say and do the rest.

43 Luke 24. 52.

44 Eph. 2. 6.

45 What exactly is heaven? Theologically, there would be nothing impossible in heaven being a 'place', transcending our empirical space. But, in any case, heaven is a state: a state of perfect happiness. Primarily and essentially, this happiness consists in the vision of God – the 'beatific vision' – and in intimate union with the Persons of the Holy Trinity and their life of love. Being part of the divine life, source of all perfections and of all bliss, is an ocean of infinite joy. Then, we shall find in God and near him all those people and those things whose principle he is. This is what we can say with certainty about heaven – which remains a mystery. More simply, let us think what it would be like to have constant sight of our Lord, to be close to him always, living a life penetrated by his and for ever fixed in his.

46   Isa. 64. 4.

47   Phil. 3. 20.

48   Acts 1. 4.

49   Luke 24. 51.

50   The Council of Nicaea (in Asia Minor) met in 325, at the instigation of the Emperor Constantine. It drew up the canons which became the foundation of the Church's discipline. It formulated the Creed which, retouched by a later Council held at Constantinople, has become the Creed recited in the Byzantine liturgy. But its principle task, and the reason for its being called, was to condemn the Arian heresy. This heresy, which attacked the co-equality of the Word and the Father and also the divinity of Christ, threatened to ruin the Christian faith.

51   The Orthodox Church recognises that supreme authority resides in the ecumenical Councils – that is to say those Councils to which, by right if not in fact, all bishops are called to take a seat. Orthodox theologians, however, have different concepts of the authority that stems from the ecumenical Councils. The most traditional, followed by Greek theologians, is that the doctrinal definitions drawn up by the Councils are infallible (whereas the disciplinay canons can be subject to revision) and demand adherence from the faithful precisely because they are the work of the ecumenical Councils. For many recent Russian theologians, a Council does not call for adherence from the consciences of believers because it is ecumenical but, on the contrary, it becomes ecumenical to the extent that it has been accepted by the collective conscience of the Church; the bishops, from this point of view, are not judges and doctors of the universal faith but only the witnesses and the mouthpieces of the faith in their local Churches; the Council is the organ, the instrument which gives expression to the unanimity of the faithful. These two very different concepts of the nature of authority in the Church nevertheless unite in their notion of divine inspiration: it is the same Holy Spirit which directs a Council to declare the truth and which prompts the faithful to acknowledge this truth, and thus to give recognition to the Council.

52   The iota is the smallest letter of the Greek alphabet, and, in the fourth century, passionate debates were provoked by an iota. The Council of Nicaea had proclaimed Jesus Christ to be *homoousios* with the Father, that is to say 'of the same nature' as the Father, 'consubstantial' with the Father. Others asserted that the Son was not *homoousios*, but *homoiousios* to the Father (the two differ by only an iota), that is to say of a nature 'similar' to that of the Father. This is not just a quarrel about words. It is obvious that if the second formula had triumphed, Christians would have had their Saviour, the God become man, taken away.

53   In fact, the history of the Councils is not edifying: too much of it consists of politics, manoeuvring, intrigues and personal rivalries. But despite this, in the ecumenical Councils, the divine element has always finally carried the day over the human element of mediocrity or evil. The dogmas promulgated by these Councils, however painful may have been the circumstances of their elaboration, have always been signposts marking the true road on which the Christian Church goes towards its Lord.

54   The Greek text says that Paul addresses himself to the *presbuteroi*, 'elders'. But, in speaking to them, the apostle calls them *episcopoi*, 'guardians, overseers, stewards'. From these two words, *presbuteroi* and *episcopoi*, which here seem us-

ed in much the same way, are derived the words 'priests' and 'bishops'. In the early days of the Church, the ideas of episcopacy and of priesthood still had a fluidity which they have since lost.

55   'It seemed good to the Holy Ghost, and to us', said the Apostles at Jerusalem (Acts 15. 28). Similarly, the Councils, in the preambles to the dogmatic definitions they promulgated, have always insisted on the certainty of their being inspired by the Holy Spirit.

56   Liturgical texts qualify Saint George as a 'great martyr'. Popular legend has made him out to be a military saint who overcame a dragon or at least some monstrous and dangerous animal. Nations and towns have chosen him as their patron. However, the only thing that seems historically certain is that a martyr named George suffered near Lydda, in Palestine, at an unspecified date before the time of Constantine.

57   Constantine (280-337) put an end to persecutions by the Edict of Milan in 313. As ruler of the empire, not only did he assure the liberty of the Church, but also favoured it, without suppressing the pagan cult of which he remained titular head. Constantinian legislation relating to slaves and to women bears the mark of Christian influence. On the other hand, Constantine was ambitious and cruel. Although he assumed the role of protector of the Church, he only chose to be baptised at his death. Helena (died *circa* 330), wife of the Caesar, Constantius Chlorus, and mother of Constantine, was the daughter of an inn-keeper. She became Christian, visited Palestine, had churches built in Bethlehem and on the Mount of Olives, and, according to a dubious historical tradition, instigated searches which led to the discovery of the wood of the Cross.

58   Frequently in the course of history, and even nowadays, we find pastors of the Church who declare that the Church must not express her views on questions that concern public life: the Church may reserve prayer and the sacraments to herself; she must leave to the State — yesterday to the 'prince', today to 'popular democracy' — all that touches on the existence of the city. This is a monstrous aberration. No doubt the Church should not take sides in matters that are purely political or economic, but she should and must intervene when politics or economics raise ethical questions. She must defend the essential rights of the human being. She must fight for natural law to be respected, whether between individuals or between states. History proves how those Churches are chastened which choose to flatter Caesar and to oppose real progress in the intellectual and social order, so that this progress is accomplished despite the Church, against the Church. Of course the kingdom of God is within us — but we have the duty to make it shine around us.

59   Cyril died in 444, after having been Bishop of Alexandria for 32 years. He was one of the first great theologians of the Incarnation; he contended with Nestorius, and the doctrine of the mystical Body of Christ owes a lot to him. Certain aspects of his activities — his persecutory attitude towards the Jews, his mobilisation of the monks of Egypt during uprisings of the people in Alexandria, his connivance in the riots during which the celebrated woman philosopher, Hypatia, a neo-platonist, was killed — do not win him our sympathy.

60   See ch. IV.

61   See ch. V.

62   Matt. 4. 19.

Chapter VII
PENTECOST AND THE TIME AFTER PENTECOST

SUMMARY

The Days of Pentecost. The Feast of All the Saints (1st Sunday after Pentecost). 'They immediately left the ship and their father' (2nd Sunday after Pentecost). 'Take no thought for your life' (3rd Sunday). The Centurion (4th Sunday). 'The Word is nigh thee' (5th Sunday). 'Having then gifts differing' (6th Sunday). The Blind and the Dumb (7th Sunday). 'And I of Christ' (8th Sunday). Walking on the Water (9th Sunday). The Grain of Mustard Seed (10th Sunday). 'As we forgive them' (11th Sunday). 'By the grace of God' (12th Sunday). Some Minor Feasts of the Summer. The Holy Apostles Peter and Paul (June 29th). The Transfiguration (August 6th). The Falling Asleep of the Mother of God (August 15th). The End of the Liturgical Year.

The Days of Pentecost

'Behold we now celebrate the feast of Pentecost, the coming of the Spirit, the fulfilment of the promise and also of our hope.' It is in these terms that the Church, at vespers for Pentecost on the Saturday evening, invites us to enter into the atmosphere of this very great feast celebrated on the seventh Sunday after Easter[1], which is not inferior to Easter itself.

During these vespers, three readings from the Old Testament prepare us for the feast. The reading from the Book of Numbers (11. 16-17, 24-29) tells us how Moses, at God's command, chose seventy elders to whom God would communicate part of the spirit he had given to Moses. They stood round the tabernacle 'and when the spirit rested upon them, they prophesied . . . '. And, when Joshua asked Moses to silence two men who prophesied without having come to the tabernacle, Moses answered: 'Enviest thou for my sake? would God that all the Lord's people were prophets, and that the Lord would put his spirit upon them!'[2]. The reading from the prophet Joel (2. 23-32) predicts what will happen at the first Christian Pentecost: 'It shall come to pass afterward, that I will pour out my spirit upon all flesh; and your sons and your daughters shall prophesy, your old men shall dream dreams, your young men shall see visions: And also upon the servants and upon the handmaids in those days will I pour out my spirit'. The reading from the prophet Ezekiel (36. 24-28) also an-

212

nounces an inner renewal: 'A new heart also will I give you, and a new spirit will I put within you: and I will take away the stony heart out of your flesh, and I will give you an heart of flesh. And I will put my spirit within you . . .'.

At matins for Pentecost, which are celebrated on the Saturday evening or Sunday morning, we read a gospel account of one of the appearances of the risen Jesus. In this passage (John 20. 19-31), we see a first descent of the Spirit on the disciples: 'He (Jesus) breathed on them, and saith unto them, Receive ye the Holy Ghost . . .'. This first coming of the Spirit is no less real than on the day of Pentecost. The difference is that, on the day of Pentecost, the Spirit descended on them with 'power'. There is the same difference in this between the coming of the Holy Spirit on a baptised Christian at the moment when he receives the sacrament of chrismation or confirmation, and that baptism of the Spirit which we shall speak of again, and which certain Christians receive at an advanced stage of spiritual life.

At the liturgy, on Sunday morning, instead of an epistle, the account of the events of Pentecost, as they are described in the Book of the Acts of the Apostles (2. 1-11), is read. Certain aspects of this account call specially for our attention.

'And when the day of Pentecost was fully come . . .'. Pentecost is both a culmination and a start. A new way was opening to the disciples, but they had prepared themselves for it. Somehow, we cannot enter into Pentecost without preparation. We need first to have assimilated the whole spiritual substance that the fifty days between Easter and Pentecost have offered us. Before that, we need to have experienced the risen Christ: the days of the Passion, too, need to have been lived through. In short, one must have matured.

'They were all with one accord in one place.' Some other verses in Acts picture for us the eleven assembled 'in the upper room' with Mary, mother of Jesus, and the women. It was the Church being born. They all prayed together. We find in this the necessary conditions for receiving the Holy Spirit. At certain moments we need to retire from the world and to shut ourselves in the upper room of our soul. There we must pray. And we must unite ourselves to the prayer and the faith of the whole Church. We must be 'together' with the apostles and with the mother of Jesus. Whoever seeks to ignore the authority of the apostles, or to do without the maternal presence of Mary, cannot receive the Holy Spirit.

'And suddenly there came a sound from heaven as of a rushing mighty wind . . . .' The Holy Spirit is a breath, a wind. What mat ters for us is not to stand amazed at the power of this breath, but to submit ourselves to it completely and allow ourselves to be 'guided' by the Spirit, like Jesus during his earthly life. May this breath direct us where it wills. And let us remember that this breath itself is 'guided': it is not an independent and incoherent force. Jesus breathed the Holy Spirit on his disciples, but this breath proceeded first from the mouth of the Father [3]. It is an obedience to God. In obeying the impulse of the Spirit (the sound of the wind is but an external, and a rare, symbol — the inner impulse is the reality), we become part of the Spirit's own obedience, proceeding from the Father, sent by the Son.

'And there appeared unto them cloven tongues like as of fire, and it sat upon each of them.' The Holy Spirit appears under the form of tongues. Pentecost heals the dispersion and confusion of languages brought about by the proud effort of the tower of Babel. It re-establishes the unity of human language. The disciples will be understood by all the strangers then in Jerusalem, Parthians, Medes and Cappadocians, who are astonished to hear the speech of these Galileans, as if in their own languages. The language of the Spirit — at least in its inner meaning — is still accessible today to all men, to all races, to all nations; the same Spirit transmits a universal message that each soul nevertheless recognises as its own. And also, even in our day, someone in whom the Holy Spirit is active becomes capable, even if he cannot express himself in languages that are foreign to him, at least of finding the psychological 'language' which will echo in, and open the heart of, each person. Thus 'dialogue' becomes possible. The tongues which alighted on the disciples are tongues of fire, and imply a burning charity. The words seem conditioned by the flame. Lastly, these tongues are evenly distributed. They are not the privilege of Peter, or of Mary, or the eleven. They alight on all those present in the upper room — yet these tongues of flame are one and the same fire. Thus the problem of unity and of the person finds itself resolved in the Church. Neither the one nor the other is sacrificed.

'And they were all filled with the Holy Ghost . . . .' This sudden and complete invasion of the whole soul by the Holy Ghost, accompanied by a new and extraordinary power, constitutes the 'baptism of the Holy Spirit', which differs both from the baptism by water and from the anointing by which the Church bestows the

Spirit. There is a reality in this which we have, to a great extent, lost sight of, but on which Scripture insists and towards which our attention should be redirected[4].

'And began to speak with other tongues, as the Spirit gave them utterance . . .' We have already drawn attention to the importance of the word 'given' with reference to the Spirit[5]. But, in a more general manner, this raises the question of extraordinary, or Pentecostal, graces, of gifts[6]. One danger would be to desire them in a disordered way. Another danger would be to neglect them, to forget about them, to think that all those things belong to the past, when in fact they have been given — or rather they are given — to the Church for all time.

The gospel for the Sunday of Pentecost (John 7. 37-52, 8. 12) tells of the debates of the Jews concerning the person of Jesus. Only the first three verses have a direct bearing on the Holy Spirit: 'Jesus stood and cried, saying, If any man thirst, let him come unto me, and drink. He that believeth on me, as the scripture hath said, out of his belly shall flow rivers of living water. (But this spake he of the Spirit, which they that believe on him should receive: for the Holy Ghost was not yet given; because that Jesus was not yet glorified)'. The meaning of these words is clear. On the one hand, the outpouring of the Holy Spirit depends on belief in Jesus. On the other hand, the Holy Spirit will be given when the visible presence of Jesus will have withdrawn from this world. These are the two fundamental points of doctrine concerning the relationship between the Son and the Spirit in the life of Christians.[7]

As soon as the liturgy is over, vespers, which have a special structure, begin. During this service, the congregation, kneeling, sings with solemnity the *troparion* 'Heavenly King, Comforter, Spirit of Truth, thou who art everywhere present and fillest all things . . .'. We know that this *troparion* is said at the start of every liturgy and the majority of services in the Byzantine rite; and it is, if we are not mistaken, the only prayer addressed directly to the Holy Spirit in this rite[8]. On the morning of the Sunday of Pentecost, this prayer is of cardinal importance: singing it marks the moment when the Church concentrates its whole aspiration towards the Spirit, and entreats its coming; at this moment, each believer who is kneeling can, if he truly asks the One who is the supreme 'gift', receive in his heart the renewal of Pentecostal grace and the descent of the dove[9]. While the congregation kneels, the priest reads seven long prayers: two of them are addressed to God, without distinction between the three divine Persons; two are addressed to the Father, and three to the Son. At first glance, these may seem a bit diffuse; but an attentive analysis will reveal that in them is contained a summary of Orthodox doctrine. They recapitulate the whole divine economy of salvation; they indicate all that God has done for men since the creation, and they earnestly entreat the gifts of which we have need. Although they make certain allusions to the Holy Spirit, they mark a shift from the mystery of the Spirit to the mystery of the Trinity. One sentence from the fifth of these prayers says: 'O Thou, who, on the last and great day of our salvation, the day of Pentecost, hast revealed to us the mystery of the Holy Trinity, consubstantial and co-eternal . . .'. This 'trinitarian' aspect of the feast of Pentecost explains why, amongst Orthodox peoples, this Sunday is often called the 'day of the Trinity'[10]. It also explains why the Churches of the Byzantine rite have thought it fitting to consecrate the Monday of Pentecost more particularly to the Holy Spirit. On this Monday, the liturgy and the greater part of the service of the previous day (except for the seven prayers of which we spoke) are repeated. Actually, to call the Monday of Pentecost 'day of the Holy Spirit', as is done, is an anomaly, for the real feast of the Holy Spirit is the Sunday of Pentecost, and it is certainly to be wished that, on this Sunday itself, believers should address their devotion very specially to the third person of the Trinity, whose existence and action remain so veiled to many of us. On the other hand, it is also good that the mystery of the Trinity itself should be brought to our attention. To think of the dogma of the Trinity as an abstract, distant, speculation, which had no connection with our practical life, would be a great mistake. The living and reciprocal love of the three divine Persons is the eternal fact, the greatest fact, infinitely greater and more important than everything that concerns ourselves[11]. Man was created because the three divine Persons wished to communicate to him some measure of their own intimate life. Here on earth, already, the life of grace is participation in this life of the Trinity. The soul which dies united to God is called to enter into the circulation of love between the three Persons. Their relationship constitutes the supreme model — albeit transcending them infinitely — for the relationships that should exist between men. Pentecost, which is the final event in the history of our salvation (for the gift of the Holy Spirit will not be followed, in this world, by any superior or new dispensation), leads us into the heart of the mystery of the

Trinity — that ocean which is both the source and the end of the flood of divine love which carries men towards God[12].

In order to mark that, at Pentecost, the liturgical cycle has reached its fulness, the Orthodox Church calls all the Sundays which follow 'Sundays after Pentecost'. They are referred to in this way right up the first Sunday of preparation for Great Lent. When the liturgical year starts (September 1st), there results from this a curious split between the series of Sundays which belong in a certain way to Pentecost — to the time of fulness — and the feasts of Our Lord (Advent, Christmas and Epiphany) — which are times of awaiting, of birth and growth. In fact, during the first five or six months of the liturgical year, believers will know how, in their worship, to relate the Sundays, spiritually, with the mystery of Christ awaited, appearing, and growing in the midst of men. On the other hand, it is good that we should know how to maintain the Sundays from Pentecost till the end of the liturgical year in the framework of the 'time after Pentecost', or, rather, 'the time of Pentecost', which will last right up to the beginning of September. These Sundays are celebrated in the spirit of Pentecost: at the liturgies we shall hear episodes from the gospels which take place long before Pentecost, and belong to the earthly life of Jesus before his Passion and his glorification. But we can interpret them in terms of the Spirit, for it is under the breath and through the power of the Holy Spirit that Jesus spoke and acted.

We have already underlined the importance of the theme of light in the Byzantine liturgical year: this divine light first appears with the birth of Christ, it grows with him; on Easter night it triumphs over the darkness; at Pentecost it reaches its full zenith. Pentecost is 'the midday flame'. But this development, which the liturgical year expresses, must correspond to a growth of the inner light in our soul. The riches and symbolism of the liturgical year are worth nothing if they do not help this 'inner light' to guide our life.

We have said, too, that in spiritual life three stages can be discerned which are comparable to three conversions. The first conversion is the meeting of the soul with our Lord, when he is followed as a Friend and as a Master. The second conversion is a personal experience of pardon and salvation, of the cross and of resurrection. The third conversion is the coming of the Holy Spirit into the soul like a flame and with power. It is by this conversion that man is established in a lasting union with God. Christmas or Epiphany, then Easter, and finally Pentecost correspond to these three conversions. Alas! it is probable that we have not yet been transformed into living flame by the many Pentecosts with which already, year after year, we have been liturgically associated. But at least it is good never to lose sight of what graces, what possibilities each Pentecost brings us.

The Feast of all the Saints

The first Sunday after Pentecost is dedicated to the commemoration of all the saints[13]. Sanctity is the work of the Holy Spirit; all Christian holiness[14] is a fruit of Pentecost. There is therefore a logical link between today's feast and that of last Sunday.

At the liturgy a portion of the epistle to the Hebrews (11. 33-12.2) is read which evokes the sufferings of the 'cloud of witnesses', that is to say the prophets, the martyrs, the righteous, those who were stoned, put to the sword, or tortured, 'of whom the world was not worthy'. We know this passage well, for the Church has already given it to us to hear twice during the liturgical year: first on the Sunday before Christmas[15], then on the first Sunday of Great Lent[16]. It seems that the Church, in calling our attention to this text before the Nativity, before Easter, and immediately after Pentecost, wants to emphasise that we draw near to these great mysteries 'catholicly', surrounded by the saints and helped by their prayers; she wishes above all to tell us that saintliness is not an abnormal or exceptional state: that, on the contrary it is the normal flowering of every Christian life. The call to holiness is addressed to each one of us.

The gospel for the liturgy (Matt. 10. 32-33, 37-38, 19. 27-30) is a selection of the sayings of Our Lord which relate to the actual conditions of holiness: 'He that loveth father or mother more than me is not worthy of me . . . . And he that taketh not his cross, and followeth after me, is not worthy of me . . . . Everyone that hath forsaken houses, or brethren, or sisters, or father, or mother, or wife, or children, or lands, for my name's sake, shall receive an hundredfold and shall inherit everlasting life'. Once again, our Lord brings us into the presence of his Cross and the personal renunciations that it involves. There is, however, a great difference between the way we read these words today and the way we read them (or similar texts) during the preceding months: read after Pentecost, this invitation to sacrifice is now clothed in fire, in the light and power of the Holy Spirit. The apostles did not really follow their master on his painful road until after the coming of the Paraclete; the saints, whose collective feast we celebrate today, only carried the cross when they were under the inspiration of the Spirit. The cross that Jesus sets before our eyes, on this first Sunday after Pentecost, is a cross of fire — the fire of the Spirit descending on the disciples[17].

'They immediately left the ship and their father'

The second Sunday after Pentecost shows us the practical application of the great call to renunciation formulated by Jesus in the gospel for the first Sunday. The gospel read today at the liturgy (Matt. 4. 18-23) tells of the calling of the first apostles. On the shore of Lake Galilee, Jesus sees Simon and Andrew fishing. He says to them: 'Follow me'. He wants to make them fishers of men. 'And they straightway left their nets, and followed him'. Further on Jesus meets James and John, also fishermen, in the company of their father, Zebedee. Jesus calls them. 'They immediately left the ship and their father, and followed him.' The new disciples abandoned their nets and their ships: Jesus sometimes asks us to renounce our profession, our instruments of work, whatever we possess. But some sons, at the call of Jesus, abandon their father too: sometimes he wants us to abandon family affections, human friendships, created love. This is not a purely negative attitude. Jesus's call has a very positive aspect: one must follow the Master. But the first apostles could not have followed the Master if they had not first of all left their ships, and their nets, and their father. And what have I abandoned in order to follow Jesus? What does he want me to leave?

The epistle (Rom. 2. 10-16) deals with themes of the law and of faith that we will continue to consider on the following Sundays. Today, we hear St Paul compare the state of the Jews and of the Gentiles in relation to the law. The Jews have received the law; they will be judged by it. But the Gentiles, who do not know the mosaic law, nevertheless are not without law. 'When the Gentiles, which have not the law, do by nature the things contained in the law, these, having not the law, are a law unto themselves: which show the work of the law written in their hearts . . . .' In any case, what is important, is not simply to hear the law, but to fulfil it. 'For not the hearers of the law are just before God, but the doers of the law shall be justified.' This is why the apostle pays homage to whosoever does good, whatever (as one would say today) his 'persuasion' or 'denomination' might be: 'Glory, honour, and peace, to every man that worketh good, to the Jew first, and also to the Gentile'. Paul resolves this problem with great breadth of spirit. We can apply what he says of the Greeks and the pagans to those who do not know the Gospel of Christ. They will be judged according to the measure of their faithfulness to the inner light which has been granted to them. They have a law to which their conscience bears witness. Do not let us be too quick, therefore, either to exclude from the kingdom of God those who do not share our faith, or to think that our faith dispenses us from doing good. Let us rather give thanks to God that no man is left entirely in darkness, and examine in ourselves our own faithfulness to the light.

'Take no thought for your life'

The Gospels for the last two Sundays have shown us that, in order to follow Jesus, earthly preoccupations must be abandoned. We may ask: 'But how then shall we live?' The gospel for the third Sunday after Pentecost (Matt. 6. 22-33) puts us on guard against this anxiety. Jesus tells us that we must unify our inner life: 'If therefore thine eye be single, thy whole body shall be full of light . . . . No man can serve two masters . . . . Ye cannot serve God and mammon. Therefore I say unto you, take no thought for your life, what ye shall eat, or what ye shall drink; nor yet for your body, what ye shall put on'. If the heavenly Father feeds the birds of the air, if he clothes the lilies of the fields, which 'toil not neither do they spin', with colours more glorious than those of Solomon himself, how much more will he see to our needs! These words must be understood with discernment. There are men whom our Lord calls to follow him in absolute poverty. The majority of men have family and social responsibilities, and have to face them through work. As far as earthly goods are concerned, our Lord does not condemn the prudence which is called for by both justice and charity, but he does condemn avarice and the anxious care which indicate a lack of faith. 'Your heavenly Father knoweth that ye have need of all these things . . . . But seek ye first the kingdom of God, and his righteousness; and all these things shall be added unto you'. Let both him whose special vocation it is to strip himself of everything, and him whose duty is to care for the material welfare of his family, be confident: the Father will not abandon them, but they must — the one and the other − seek, before all else, the kingdom of God and its righteousness in their own consciences and round about them [18]. These are the two main ideas − first of all, the search for the kingdom of God, and then trust in the Father's goodness for life's necessities − to take away with us this morning from the church in which we heard the gospel read.

The epistle (Rom. 5. 1-10) starts with this phrase: 'Therefore being justified by faith, we have peace with God through our Lord Jesus Christ'. Indeed, 'God commendeth his love toward us, in that, while we were yet sinners, Christ died for us'. But the death of Christ carries no assurance of salvation to someone who does not conform his life to Christ. If we have been reconciled to God through the death of his Son, 'much more, being reconciled, we shall be saved by his life'. Justification by faith (and not by our personal merits) is a principle we must never lose sight of. This justification must always make itself known through a patient and active charity. 'We glory in tribulations also . . . because the love of God is shed abroad in our hearts by the Holy Ghost which is given unto us.' Faith that justifies is not a final result. It is a starting point, the root of good works.

The Centurion

Last Sunday, we heard St Paul tell us that we are 'justified by faith'. The gospel for the fourth Sunday after Pentecost (Matt. 8. 5-13) shows us what sort of faith it is that justifies. At Capernaum, a Roman centurion obtains from Jesus the healing of his servant who is sick. The healing is in answer to his act of faith: 'Go thy way; and as thou hast believed, so be it done unto thee . . .'. This centurion is not one of the children of Israel. Nor does Jesus ask him for any profession of intellectual belief; he puts him to no test of doctrine. Yet, nevertheless, it is in the centurion, and not in the most 'orthodox' Jews that Jesus finds the sort of faith he looks for: 'Verily I say unto you, I have not found so great faith, no, not in Israel'. What goes to make up the centurion's lived and saving faith? It is not identified with adherence to any dogma, nor with the performance of rites or the carrying out of legal precepts. It is based, first of all, in profound humility: 'Lord, I am not worthy that thou shouldest come under my roof . . .'. Then, it is all tensed to hear the Lord's word: 'But speak the word only . . .'.

The word of the Lord, here, is not only received with respect and faith, but it is desired and sought, as a principle of power and salvation. This word, which the centurion awaits with his whole being, he does not intend to separate from everyday life, by placing it in a 'religious' setting. 'Speak the word only, and my servant shall be healed.' The centurion believes that Jesus's word will enter his life, will erupt into its domestic realities, and bring about a definite result. Lastly, the centurion's faith is a predisposition to obedience. He says: 'I am a man under authority', I command soldiers and servants; what I tell them, they do. He, himself, is under the command of superior officers, and he carries out their orders. He thus finds it natural that Jesus should command and that he should be obeyed instantly. He awaits Jesus's command. This, then, is the centurion's faith, the faith that Jesus praises. And this is the sort of faith that Jesus looks for in us: a confident giving of our whole selves to the word which saves and gives life. This faith does not exclude either a clearly defined belief in revealed truths, or a meticulous practice of the divine law; but a faith which relied entirely on such belief or practice, and lacked the inner dynamic that sends the centurion to Jesus, would be a dead faith. The living faith of the centurion – 'a man under authority' – implies submission of the will to Jesus's word. As soon as the centurion puts his request to our Lord, he places himself under his authority, 'between his hands'. I, too, must become a 'man under authority', a man who, having placed his whole life under the direction of the Lord, finds in this obedience and trust, at every moment, the security and certainty of which those who are a law unto themselves can know nothing.

The epistle for this Sunday (Rom. 6. 18-23) is also a commentary on the true nature of justification by faith (without the Church having sought specially to make the epistle and the gospel for this day accord). Paul continues to expound to the Romans what the new justice in Christ means. 'For as ye have yielded your members servants unto iniquity; even so now yield your members servants to righteousness unto holiness . . . . Being made free from sin . . . ye have your fruit unto holiness.' We are justified by faith, but faith is nothing unless it transforms our life, unless it bears fruit, and leads to holiness [19]. 'Holiness': Paul does not hesitate to set this great word, this great thing, before the assembled community in Rome: he thinks of holiness as being natural to a Christian, as attainable by all who are faithful. He does not make holiness depend on extraordinary ascetic exploits:

the 'fruit unto holiness' is simply to serve God attentively, and to
conform our will to his.

'The Word is nigh thee'

The gospel for the fifth Sunday after Pentecost (Matt. 8. 28-34,
9. 1) tells us how Jesus healed a case of diabolic possession, and how
the demons entered into a herd of swine which then hurled itself
into the Sea of Galilee. We have already come across this episode
in the gospel for the twenty-third Sunday after Pentecost (Luke 8.
27-38), at the start of the liturgical year, and we would ask the
reader to refer to that[20]. The same episode is also found in the
gospel according to Mark (Mark 5. 1-20). Although there are
some differences of detail in these three accounts, their substance
is identical.

Let us come back to the great doctrine of justification by faith.
In the epistle for today (Rom. 10. 1-10), St Paul continues to
enlarge on this theme. He deplores the blindness of the Israelites
who, 'going about to establish their own righteousness, have not
submitted themselves unto the righteousness of God'. This
'righteousness of God' is Christ himself. 'For Christ is the end of
the law . . .'. Such a phrase must be correctly understood. Paul
certainly does not intend to say that the content of the moral law
has been abolished. Crimes that the law condemns remain
crimes; the good that it commands continues to be good. But we
are no longer tied by an external and institutional law, by a written text. The person of Jesus Christ has become our law. It is no
longer a matter of knowing whether this or that action is prescribed or forbidden by a text, but of asking ourselves it if does or
does not conform to Christ. This new law, Christ Jesus, 'the word
of faith, which we preach', is not difficult to remember or to for-
mulate; it is not a remote text, it is not even to be found
somewhere outside ourselves. 'The word is nigh thee, even in thy
mouth, and in thy heart . . . if thou shalt confess with thy mouth
the Lord Jesus, and shalt believe in thine heart that God hath
raised him from the dead, thou shalt be saved.' Let us always
remember that, unless it bears the fruits of holiness, a belief kept
safe in our heart is no more than an empty formula. And let us
give thanks to God that we have been delivered from multiple and
burdensome outward observances: he has established us in liberty; instead of submission to the letter, he asks us to act in a certain
spirit, in accordance with a certain meaning. But, because the

apostle Paul is making use of a text from the Old Testament, let us read the phrase again in the original and pay attention to the last words: 'But the word is very nigh unto thee, in thy mouth, and in thy heart, *that thou mayest do it*'[21].

'Having then gifts differing'

The gospel for the sixth Sunday after Pentecost (Matt. 9. 1-8) describes Jesus healing the man sick of the palsy. It throws light on the relationship between the forgiveness of sins — 'Son . . . thy sins be forgiven thee' — and physical healing — 'Arise, take up thy bed'. Jesus, who is able to heal the man's palsy therefore also has, despite the indignation of the scribes, the right to forgive sins. This episode has already been read as the gospel for the second Sunday in Lent (Mark 2. 1-12); we refer the reader to it[22].

We continue the reading from the epistle to the Romans (12. 6-14). St Paul, after his long discourse on the nature of faith and justification, goes on to practical questions. All of us, he says, have 'gifts differing according to the grace that is given to us'. One is called to prophesy, another to teach, another to preach, another to administer. These different ministries must be exercised in a spirit of faith and loyalty to the particular grace received. We see that Paul does not limit the individual gifts to the high functions we have just listed: he considers that giving alms and works of mercy are also ministries which correspond to a special grace. 'He that giveth, let him do it with simplicity . . . he that sheweth mercy, with cheerfulness.' These last two points, simplicity in almsgiving, and cheerfulness in works of mercy deserve to be meditated on seriously by everyone. From this, Paul goes on to the duties that are common to all: love, zeal, hope, patience, perseverance in prayer, hospitality. He concludes by advising us to bless, and not to curse, our persecutors. This epistle, besides the general duties to which it calls us, raises the question of our own special 'gift' or 'ministry'. I must examine before God what my own particular vocation is, what gift I have received to share with others. But I can also bear in mind that every action which immediate circumstances necessitate, and every situation in which I am placed by the divine will at any moment, constitutes in itself a sort of temporary vocation and ministry. There is a special grace corresponding to each minute of my life, if that minute is offered to God. No detail of life is without importance or without a blessing, as long as one knows how to see, in that detail, the reflection of a divine gift calling, on man's part, for a loving and trustful response.

The Blind Man and the Deaf Man

It is again Jesus as healer who is shown to us by the gospel for the seventh Sunday after Pentecost (Matt. 9. 27-35). Our Lord opens the eyes of two blind men and He gives speech to a dumb man possessed by the devil. Many details of this episode — especially the question that Jesus asks the blind men, 'Believe ye I am able to do this?' — deserve our attention. All the same, we will concentrate on the nature of the two miracles. Blindness and dumbness: these are both also great spiritual infirmities. The man who is spiritually blind does not see the Light of the World. He moves about in darkened space. Not only does he not see the divine reflection, but he does not know how to see men — for it is only possible to see men properly by the Light from above; too often, our own imagination, when it is not purified and illumined by God, makes us see other men as monstrously deformed. And he who is spiritually dumb cannot speak to other men; real dialogue, the exchange of the supreme values between a 'thou' and an 'I', is inaccessible to him; he is condemned to a continual and sterile monologue, for, basically, he seeks only himself, in an egoistical way. All the more reason for him not to be able to tell others what comes from God. He cannot even speak to God; prayer bothers and exasperates him. He who does not receive the Word made flesh is deprived of all words; he who does not receive the Light of the World is deprived of all light. O my Saviour, open thou my eyes, and free thou my speech.

The passage from the epistle that is read today (Rom. 15. 1-7) contains, as did last Sunday's, practical advice. St Paul stresses the need for patience and concern for those who are weak. 'We then that are strong ought to bear the infirmities of the weak, and not to please outselves'. He starts as if he was simply going to write a chapter of straightforward human morals, but his thought soon flies to Jesus, who remains the inspiration and the model in all circumstances. ' . . . wherefore receive ye one another, as Christ also received us to the glory of God.' This attitude towards men is not possible unless Christ himself, who still heals the blind and the dumb, has opened our eyes and loosened our tongues.

'. . . And I of Christ'

On the eighth Sunday after Pentecost we read one of the gospel accounts of the multiplication of loaves (Matt. 14. 14-22). With five loaves and two fishes, Jesus feeds a crowd of more than five thousand. This account throws light on the Saviour's human concern and kindness: 'And Jesus . . . saw a great multitude, and was moved with compassion toward them'. It also throws light on the way men can collaborate in God's work: Jesus makes use of his disciples — and wants to use us — in distributing bread to the multitude. 'He . . . gave the loaves to his disciples, and the disciples to the multitude.' But above all, the multiplication of the loaves is the sign of a spiritual reality: Jesus is the food of our soul, the living bread come down from heaven. Nor do we speak only of the gift that Jesus makes of himself in the Eucharist. His presence, his word, his invisible action are already a food, the true manna, of which we can say, as did the disciples in another part of the gospels[23]: 'Lord, evermore give us this bread'.

In the epistle which is read at the liturgy (1 Cor. 1. 10-17), St Paul speaks out against the divisions and the growth of factions which he finds in the bosom of the Christian Church. Some say they are of Paul, others of Apollos[24], others still, of Cephas[25]. But Christ is not divided, and it is not Paul — as he himself says — who was crucified for us. Let us then hold on to the attitude, ' . . . and I of Christ', of those who did not wish to say 'I am of Paul', or 'I of Cephas'. Ecclesiastical groups must not be allowed to veil from us the face of Christ Jesus. We can develop our hidden life with Jesus and keep it aloof from all such theological 'side-taking'. The more a serious and humble work for the Church — which is the body of Christ — is blessed by Our Lord, the more any ecclesiastical 'agitation' becomes dangerous to us and spiritually sterile. Paul thanks God that very few people have been baptised by him, so that they will not associate his name with the baptismal rite. And let us, too, avoid linking our spiritual life to the name of any man, or to any human institution, 'lest the cross of Christ should be made of none effect'.

Walking on the Water

The gospel reading for the ninth Sunday after Pentecost (Matt. 14. 22-34) follows straight on from that of last Sunday. After feeding the multitude, Jesus sends them away. He tells his disciples to get into a ship, and he himself retires to a mountain, alone, to pray. Meanwhile the ship in which the disciples are crossing the Sea of Galilee is shaken by waves; the winds are contrary. But suddenly the disciples see Jesus, walking on the sea: terrified, they think it is a ghost. Jesus reassures them: 'Be of good cheer; it is I'. To Peter's request, 'Lord . . . bid me come unto thee on the water', Jesus answers: 'Come'. Peter gets out of the ship: 'And when Peter was come down out of the ship, he walked on the water, to go to Jesus. But when he saw the wind boisterous, he was afraid; and beginning to sink, he cried, saying, Lord, save me'. Jesus stretches out his hand to him, and saves him: 'O thou of little faith, wherefore didst thou doubt?'. Jesus and Peter get into the ship, and the wind drops; the disciples worship their Master: 'Of a truth thou art the Son of God'.

This account contains precious information that applies to our own spiritual life. The wind-tossed waters on which Peter wants to walk could be compared to our difficulties and, especially, to our temptations. Why does Peter sink? Is it a sign that he was presumptuous, and should not have attempted to walk on the water? But Peter had asked Jesus for permission. He did not leave the ship without a positive invitation from the Lord: 'Come!'. We can learn from this that we should never undertake anything extraordinary without a call, an order from the Master. But the centre of gravity of this episode lies elsewhere. As long as Peter goes towards Jesus, as long as his attention remains fixed on that goal, he is able to walk on the sea. It is when his attention is distracted from his goal, when he notices the storm surrounding him, that he starts to be afraid and, so, to drown. Thus, in our moments of temptation, we must look directly, constantly, at the person of Jesus. We must fix in our minds the image of the Saviour and pay no attention to the surrounding storm. If we look back at our spiritual defeats, we will see that it is always at the instant when we stopped looking at Christ and going straight towards him that we have begun to be beaten. As soon as we allow our attention to be distracted by the wind and the waves, as soon as we delay in order to consider the temptation and discuss it, instead of going straight towards Jesus, we are lost — for we always find ourselves weaker than the adversary. We are saved from temptation (and all distress) only when we make up our minds to look at Jesus alone, and not at the obstacles. Briefly, instead of facing the temptation and fighting it head-on, what matters is, instead, to face the Saviour, and to substitute his person for the temptation. Many storms surround and threaten us. 'Lord . . . bid me come *unto thee* on the water.'

In the epistle for this Sunday (1 Cor. 3. 9-17), the apostle Paul compares our soul to a divine edifice: 'Ye are God's building'. He develops this idea in two ways. First of all, God has given all the buildings that we are the same foundation: 'For other foundation can no man lay than that is laid, which is Jesus Christ'. Then, it is up to us to continue to build on from the foundation of Christ. 'But let every man take heed how he buildeth thereupon.' According to the spiritual value of each existence, men may build with gold, silver, precious stones, wood or straw. These constructions will be tried by fire on the day of judgement. If what we have built withstands the fire, we shall be rewarded. If our structure perishes, the builder 'shall suffer loss: but he himself shall be saved; yet so as by fire'. This phrase is not easy to interpret. Perhaps one should understand it in this way: if, during his earthly life, a man was attached to eternal values, his building will last; but if he was attached to earthly and transitory things, if he builds with wood or with straw, this will all be destroyed, and nothing left. The man himself, as long as he does not die separated from God, will not be condemned for ever, he will see God annihilating the vain objects of his affections, and he himself will, in some way, be affected by this destructive test: but, because of Christ, the foundation, he will pass through it and finally achieve salvation. Paul then considers a different aspect of this theme of the divine building. We are the temple of God not only because Jesus Christ is its foundation but also because the Spirit of God dwells in us. This presence of the Holy Spirit in our soul is the most intimate aspect of Christian life. Are we going to defile the temple that we are?

The Grain of Mustard Seed

On this tenth Sunday after Pentecost, we read at the liturgy the gospel account of the healing of a young epileptic (Matt. 17. 14-23); a different version[26] of this same episode was read on the fourth Sunday of Great Lent. We would ask the reader to refer to that. Today, we shall restrict ourselves to commenting on some of Jesus's words which are not found in the gospel for the fourth Sunday in Lent. They are these: 'If ye have faith as a grain of mustard seed, ye shall say unto this mountain, Remove hence to yonder place; and it shall remove; and nothing shall be impossible unto you'. It seems to us that, in this saying, the emphasis is not placed on the extraordinary physical phenomenon, on the possibility of removing a mountain[27], but rather on the contrast between the mountain and the grain of mustard seed, on the infinite possibilities (of which the displacement of a mountain is only a symbol) open to faith − even if it is very new − provided that it is authentic. It is evident that, here, Jesus intends by 'faith' something other than a simple intellectual adherence to a revealed truth. As in the case of the centurion at Capernaum[28], Jesus speaks of faith as being a humble and total trust in the all-powerful goodness of God. If I have but a grain of such a faith, I can risk making that faith the basis of my life in all circumstances, confident that God will not necessarily give my difficulties the precise solution I may have in mind, but that he will give them their true, their best, solution − the one he wants. That would be my way of removing mountains. And, furthermore, I should always bear these words of St Paul's in mind: 'And though I have all faith, so that I could remove mountains, and have not charity, I am nothing'[29].

In the epistle for today (1 Cor. 4. 9-16), Paul attacks the self-importance, the lack of humility and obedience of some of the Christians of Corinth ironically: 'We are fools . . . but ye are wise . . . we are weak, but ye are strong; ye are honourable, but we are despised . . .'. Although Paul first speaks of this inferiority of the apostles ironically, he then goes on to speak of it with the utmost seriousness, vindicating it as a reality and a privilege. Yes, the apostles are all that the Corinthians have said, and still more. Indeed, they are madmen. Their share is poverty, persecution, being defamed: 'We are made as the filth of the world'. He does not want to hurt the Corinthians: 'I write not these things to shame you, but as my beloved sons I warn you'. Let them be meeker towards him who, with regard to them, is more than an instructor and has the right to say: 'I have begotten you through the gospel'. Let them not be afraid to lower themselves to the level of the apostles and to share their sufferings: ' . . . be ye followers of me'. This recommendation is addressed to all Christians − just as much as to those of Corinth. The apostles lived in abasement and misery, 'as it were appointed to death'. Will we be seeking honour, comfort, or security?

'As we forgive them'

'... Forgive us our trespasses, as we forgive them that trespass against us.' This petition from the Lord's Prayer is illustrated by the parable from the gospel for the eleventh Sunday after Pentecost (Matt. 18. 23-35). A king calls his servants to account: one of the servants owes him ten thousand talents[30] and, as he cannot pay the debt, he will be sold, together with his family and all his possessions. The servant begs the king to allow him time to repay, and the king mercifully forgives him the whole debt. However, the servant, on meeting another servant who owes him a very small sum, takes him by the throat and has him thrown into prison. Other servants report this to the king who, in his wrath, hands the servant over to the tormentors until the debt is fully paid off: 'Shouldest not thou also have had compassion on thy fellow-servant, even as I had pity on thee?'. Jesus ends: 'So likewise shall my heavenly Father do also unto you, if ye from your hearts forgive not every one his brother their trespasses'. We shall underline two very striking points in this parable. God does not forgive our debts *because* we forgive those of our debtors. Certainly, there is a continuity, a sequence, a parallel ('*as* we forgive . . .') between the forgiveness which we receive from God and that which we accord to men, but the second is not the cause of the first. God, in his generosity, takes and keeps the initiative of forgiveness. When we ourselves forgive others, it is not 'our' own forgiveness we grant them. We allow the divine forgiveness which we ourselves have received to 'pass through' and beyond us, we make ourselves its instruments: for all forgiveness comes from God. And also, we do not only forgive others because they are men, just as we are, but because we are all servants of the same King. Let us, today, examine every fold of our heart, every corner of our mind, lest some trespass, some injustice that we have not forgiven lies there. We have no right to try to bring to a halt in ourselves the forgiveness that flows from the Cross with the blood the Saviour. We must allow it to flow freely, we can make it flow on to others, and especially on to those who may have harmed us. If I do not, how shall I dare to say the Lord's Prayer through to its end? The forgiveness that God grants me, I can send on beyond myself. May it reach those to whom I would extend it, and then come back and remain with me.

St Paul, in the epistle for today (1 Cor. 9. 2-12), speaks out frankly on the rights of apostles; one feels he is answering personal criticisms. He and Barnabas, he says, have the same rights as have Cephas and the other apostles; they would be quite justified in asking the believers to take care of their material well-being. 'Who goeth a warfare anytime at his own charges?' Nevertheless, Paul declares, 'we have not used this power; but suffer all things, lest we should hinder the gospel of Christ'. The question that is raised here, is still raised in our day, and in the same terms. It concerns knowing when it is appropriate to renounce the exercise of a right. Not all the things that we have the right to do serve the 'Gospel of Christ' equally well, and the service of the gospel must take precedence over everything else.

'By the grace of God'

The gospel for the twelfth Sunday after Pentecost (Matt. 19. 16-26) tells us again of the rich young man whom Jesus advised to sell all his goods and give them to the poor, if he would achieve perfection; he did not have the courage. We have already considered this episode [31] on the thirtieth Sunday after Pentecost, and invite the reader to refer to this [32].

The epistle read at the liturgy (1 Cor. 15. 1-11) contains first of all a summary of Paul's preaching, which the apostle himself makes with some solemnity. 'I declare unto you the gospel which I preached unto you . . . I delivered unto you first of all that which I also received . . . .' This essential message is that Christ died for our sins and rose again. Paul lists here all those who were witnesses of the Resurrection [33]. Then he adds: 'And last of all he was seen of me also, as of one born out of due time. For I am the least of the apostles . . .'. Nevertheless, Paul does not underestimate what he is, but attributes it all to grace: 'By the grace of God I am what I am . . . . I laboured more abundantly than they all: yet not I, but the grace of God which was with me'. We cannot say, as Paul does, that we have laboured more than others; far from it. But yet, with him, we can pay homage to the sovereignty of grace. If we have done anything, if we are not spiritually dead, we owe it to grace alone. We can even hope — hope humbly — that Jesus will let himself be seen by us too, with the eyes of the soul, 'as one born out of due time'.

Here we will bring to an end the series of Sundays after Pentecost included in this chapter. The Sundays that follow are dealt with in the first chapter of this work. Because of the uncertainty that the variation in the dates of Easter introduces into the cycle of Sundays after Pentecost, it may be that this or that Sunday should be eliminated from this chapter and added to the first chapter, or, perhaps, taken from the first chapter and added to this one. The reader will be able to make this adjustment easily if he has in front of him an Orthodox calendar of the current year.

Some Minor Feasts of the Summer

We will now speak of some feasts which, without being of first importance, the Orthodox nevertheless observe with special reverence.

The Sunday which falls between July 13th and 19th is dedicated to the memory of the 'Holy Fathers' who took part in the first six ecumenical councils [34]. What we have already said concerning the commemoration of the Fathers of the Council of Nicaea [35] is relevant here. It is not the personal holiness of these bishops which is affirmed and honoured, but their collective witness to Orthodox belief. The meaning of the feast is well expressed by these words, which are sung at vespers: 'You have become, O Holy Fathers, worthy guardians of the apostolic traditions'. The gospel read at the liturgy (Matt. 5. 14-19) contains the phrase: 'Let your light so shine before men', which is very apposite here.

On July 20th, we celebrate the feast of the prophet Elijah [36], whose memory is particularly honoured in the Churches of the Byzantine rite in the Middle East [37]. The *troparion* for the feast calls Elijah 'Pillar of the prophets and their foundation stone, the precursor of the Second Coming of Christ'. His life in the mountains, in the desert, and his austere fast, are an ascetic protest against the corruption of the world. In his conflicts with the rulers of Israel, he is the voice of conscience, the champion of the outraged rights of God and of men. The chants at vespers call our attention especially to three episodes in Elijah's life, which have a spiritual meaning for our own lives. First of all, the prophet's extraordinary experience of the presence of God. ' . . . And behold the Lord passed by, and a great and strong wind rent the mountains, and brake in pieces the rocks before the Lord; but the Lord was not in the wind: and after the wind an earthquake; but the Lord was not in the earthquake: And after the earthquake a fire; but the Lord was not in the fire: and after the fire a still small voice . . .' [38]. God must not be looked for in some overwhelming manifestation of his power, but in the 'still small voice' which speaks to our conscience. And, if sometimes God judges it good to cast us down and break us, it is only so that we should become able to hear this sound. Let us beware lest certain forms of noise and agitation, which we might wrongly interpret as being religious, cover over this inner voice; and be careful not to confuse the various emotional and external forms of religion – however impressive they may be – with adoration in spirit and with listening for the Word. The second episode is the competition between Elijah and the priests of Baal: although they cry out loudly and inflict cuts on themselves with knives, the divine fire does not fall on the dry wood of their sacrifice but on the drenched wood of Elijah's sacrifice: the people who witnessed this marvel, massacre the priests of Baal[39]. 'O wise Elijah, thou hast massacred the priests of confusion . . . .' say the chants at vespers. Rather than dwell on this massacre, which corresponds to a given period in the evolution of customs rather than to the spirit of the New Covenant, we shall turn our attention to the fact that even wet wood, green wood, can be set on fire by the divine flame: we, ourselves, who are wood made very damp by human passions and weakness, can receive as a totally gratuitous gift, the fire of divine charity which purifies, illumines and warms. The third episode is the taking up of Elijah by a chariot of fire[40]. The more we allow ourselves to be consumed by the divine fire, the less we belong to earth and the closer we shall live – in anticipation – to God, in our true country. Another episode, which is not mentioned in the service, indicates the way we should intercede for others. When the widow of Zarephath told Elijah of her desolation at the death of her son, the prophet took the child's body and carried it to his own bed, where he stretched himself out on it three times and called on God: the child came to life once again[41]. We must not think that we have really prayed for someone because we have mentioned their name, without too much attention, either in the liturgical litanies, or in our private intercessions. To pray for another is to take them in our arms up to God, it is to stretch ourselves over them in spirit; to communicate to them the life and power we have received; it is to implore God for them with our whole being. The epistle for the liturgy (Jas. 5. 10-20) alludes to the rain obtained by Elijah after a three years' drought, for 'the effectual prayer of a righteous man availeth much'. The gospel (Luke 4: 22-26, 28-30) recalls the words of our Lord directed against national exclusivism: 'Many widows were in Israel in the days of Elias . . . . But unto none of them was Elias sent, save unto

Sarepta, a city of Sidon, unto a woman that was a widow'.

July 22nd is the feast of St Mary of Magdala, 'Myrrhophore and equal to the apostles'. We know that in Byzantine liturgical usage the various Maries mentioned in the gospels are differentiated: Mary who brings precious ointment, Mary the sister of Lazarus, Mary the sinner. There are strong historical reasons against this distinction. If, all the same, we accept it by hypothesis, the gospel accounts of the anointing at Bethany, before the Passion [42], and of the myrrh-bearing women, the second Sunday after Easter [43], constitute the best commentary for the feast which is celebrated on this day. They remind us that we must bring to the feet of Christ the fragrance, which is necessarily costly and precious, of a life made holy by grace.

On August 1st, the feast for 'The Procession of the Honourable and Life-Giving Cross' [44] is celebrated. We have already seen that there are two other feasts dedicated to the commemoration and the adoration of the Cross of the Saviour, one on September 14th [45], the other on the third Sunday of Great Lent [46]. Today's feast does not have the importance of the other two, though it shares certain features with them – for example, prostration in front of the Cross and the kiss which is given to it. The gospel of the Passion according to St John is read, or at least its final episodes, those relating to Golgotha. If one wanted to give the three Byzantine feasts of the Cross a purely spiritual interpretation, one could say that the feast in September is the 'discovery' of the Cross, its encounter with the soul, our first contact with the Cross of Jesus – not only the historical Cross and the mystery of redemption, but also our own bearing of the Cross, the experience of sharing in the Cross of Christ which God gives us in our own life. The feast in Lent signifies that the Cross – the Cross of the Saviour as well as our own – is set up and adored in our hearts: we recognise its own supreme authority over ourselves. August's feast is really a 'procession': it concerns 'following' the Cross where it leads us, and thus forms the practical outcome of the previous feasts.

Twice during the summer, we commemorate the Precursor, John the Baptist. If we have placed the two commemorations among the 'minor' feasts, it is not because we fail to recognise the 'major' importance of the Precursor: we do not forget that the Church places him above the apostles themselves. But is seems that the great feast of John the Baptist is the feast of Epiphany: it is at the moment when he baptises Jesus that John reaches the climax of his human life and of his ministry. Moreover, the Church consecrates the day after Epiphany (January 7th) to the memory of the Precursor. The two feasts of the summer are on June 24th, the nativity of John the Baptist, and on August 29th, his martyrdom. The epistle (Rom. 13. 11-14. 4) and the gospel (Luke 1. 1-25, 57-58, 76, 80) for June 24th take us back to the atmosphere of Advent: the gospel describes Zacharias's vision in the Temple, and John's circumcision. Zacharias, who had not believed, was rendered temporarily dumb. A priest who receives the divine message with incredulity or with certain reservations cannot 'speak' (in the deep sense of this word) to his people. The meaning of the feast of August 29th[47] is expressed by the words sung at vespers: 'O John, thou wast beheaded for the sake of the law of the Lord'. For this feast does not celebrate so much the man who baptised Jesus and preached repentance as him who championed the moral law, and who was killed because that law was hated. The gospel read at the liturgy (Mark 6. 14-30) relates this episode in which impurity is mixed with cruelty. The daughter of Herodias, after she has danced for Herod, obtains from him the head of John on a charger, because John had said to Herod: 'It is not lawful for thee to have thy brother's wife'[48]. This passage from the gospel begins with the words: 'Others said, That it is Elias'. For Elijah's courage, in condemning the crimes of Ahab and Jezebel, lived again in John; and Jesus himself likened these two prophets to each other[49]. John before Herod remains a symbol and model of conscientious protest in the name of the eternal law, against its violation by the 'authorities'. Several times history has shown how far a Church can fall when its leaders acquiesce in a tyrant's will. On a more humble level, our conscience must sometimes lead us to protest against our own immediate surroundings, against our friends, against our family, against an institution or a superior. At the liturgy, instead of the epistle, we read a portion of the Acts of the Apostles (13. 25-33) chosen because of Paul's reference to John the Baptist at the start of his speech in the synagogue at Antioch in Pisidia. To end this feast — which falls only two days before the end of the liturgical year — let us recall how the memory of the Precursor mingles, several times throughout the course of the year, with the cycle of the Lord Jesus's life, and we can repeat these words from the *kathisma* for matins, which are a fitting summary of John's role: 'Let us, the faithful, unite in praise of him who was the mediator between the Law and Grace'.

The Holy Apostles Peter and Paul

We have considered some feasts of the period after Pentecost which are, liturgically, of secondary importance. We come now to the three great feasts that belong to this time. The first in date (June 29th) is that of the apostles Peter and Paul[50]. There is a strict spiritual link between this feast and that of Pentecost, for the witness of the apostles is the immediate fruit of the descent of the Holy Spirit on them[51]. In the liturgical cycle of the Byzantine rite, the importance of the feast of St Peter and St Paul is marked by the fact that a special fast — called the 'fast of the apostles' — prepares the faithful for this solemnity. This period of fasting, in practice quite a mild one, begins on the Monday which follows the first Sunday after Pentecost and ends on June 28th.

'Let us exalt Peter and Paul, those two great lights of the Church, for they shine in the firmament of the faith . . .', the choir sings at vespers for the feast on the evening of June 28th. At matins, as at vespers, praise seems to be shared equally between the two apostles, to whom we address ourselves by turn. However, the gospel read at matins (John 21. 14-25) of course applies to the apostle Peter. We hear our Lord ask Peter three times: 'Lovest thou me?' The first time, Jesus says: 'Lovest thou me more than these?' Three times, Peter answers with a humility that is both saddened and fervent: 'Yea, Lord; thou knowest that I love thee'. And three times Jesus tells him to feed the flock of the Good Shepherd: 'Feed my lambs . . . . Feed my sheep'. Then Jesus predicts in a veiled way 'by what death he should glorify God'. This gospel text has two things to say to us. First of all it asks the one real question clearly, the question to which we have, and will have to answer: 'Lovest thou me?'[52]. Everything, in Christian life, comes down to this question. Can we answer, like Peter, 'Yea, Lord; thou knowest that I love thee'. Would our actions not prove that such an affirmation was lamentably untrue? But to answer simply that we do not love the Lord would be to misunderstand and to stifle those longings — however faint they may be — that the Holy Spirit puts in our hearts and that guide us toward Christ. We, too, could therefore say to Jesus: 'Lord, thou knowest all things; thou knowest that I love thee. I can expect nothing from myself; I rely for everything on grace'. The second teaching given by this gospel concerns the nature of authority in the Church. Here, the Lord confers a special authority on Peter. It will be noticed that this authority is based on the primacy of love —

'lovest thou me more than these?' — and then that it consists of service that is both humble and disinterested — 'Feed my lambs . . .'. All pre-eminence amongst Christians that is not the pre-eminence of love and of service goes against the intention of our Lord. All authority in the Church which seeks to express itself in terms of prestige, or of material possessions, or of domination is hostile to this truly pastoral solicitude to which Jesus calls Peter. All those who claim some authority at the heart of the community of believers will be judged on these words of the Lord to Peter[53].

The texts which we hear at the liturgy for June 29th show how the ministries of Peter and Paul are both necessary and complementary. The gospel (Matt. 16. 13-19) contains Peter's confession at Caesarea Philippi: 'Thou are the Christ, the Son of the living God . . .' and Jesus's answer: 'Thou art Peter, and upon this rock I will build my church; and the gates of hell shall not prevail against it. And I will give unto thee the keys of the kingdom of heaven: and whatsoever thou shalt bind on earth shall be bound in heaven: and whatsoever thou shalt loose on earth shall be loosed in heaven'. This text has raised many controversies[54]. But what is certain is that Jesus wished to recognise and to sanction the act of faith which Peter had just formulated by bestowing on him high spiritual power. The epistle (2 Cor. 11. 21-12. 9) — of which we have already heard the greater part on the nineteenth Sunday after Pentecost[55] — enumerates the claims that Paul — whose call to the apostolate was direct from Christ — has to be considered as equal, or even superior, in authority to those ministers of the Gospel who were already appointed and recognised on a regular basis. 'Are they ministers of Christ? . . . I am more'. Paul bases this affirmation partly on the sufferings he has endured, partly on the graces and revelations granted to him. An attentive study of the relations between Paul and the eleven can teach us a lot about the question of authority in the Church. Paul never rose up against the 'institutional' element represented by the 'historical' apostolate of the eleven. He received the laying on of hands from those who were already recognised as possessing the Holy Spirit, and he submitted his own methods of apostolate to the approval of the Church which was gathered at Jerusalem. But he never admitted either that his extraordinary vocation was in any way inferior to the more normal vocation of the other apostles, or that his knowledge of Christ, although entirely spiritual and received through grace, was less than the knowledge which the first disciples had of Jesus; or, even, that he should

238 THE YEAR OF GRACE OF THE LORD

sacrifice his own opinions to the most authoritative view of the apostles: 'When Peter was come to Antioch, I withstood him to the face, because he was to be blamed'[56]. The more the Church is ruled by the Holy Spirit, the more will all tensions between authority acquired through the regular channels and spiritual liberty be overcome. A synthesis must be found between tradition and inspiration. Peter and Paul cannot be separated; and that is why the Church celebrates them both on the same day. 'Rejoice, O Peter the Apostle, thou who art the great friend of the Master, Christ our God. Rejoice, well-beloved Paul, preacher of the faith and doctor of the universe. Because of this, may you both intercede with Christ our God for the salvation of our souls'[57].

The Church wants to associate all the other apostles in the homage which she pays to Peter and Paul. So the day of June 30th is dedicated to the collective commemoration of the twelve. As is said in the *kontakion* for the day: ' . . . in commemorating their memory today, we glorify Him who glorified them'[58].

The Transfiguration

The second great feast of the summer is the Transfiguration of Our Lord Jesus Christ, which is celebrated on August 6th[59].

The texts from the Old Testament which we hear during vespers for the feast, on the evening of August 5th, prepare us to understand the mystery of the Transfiguration. First of all, comes the account (Exod. 24. 12-18) of Moses on Mount Sinai, where he spent forty days and forty nights. The reasons for choosing this text are easy to understand. Moses is one of the figures of the Old Covenant who, according to the gospel acount, is seen with the transfigured Jesus. Then there is the theme of the mountain: 'Come up to me into the mount, and be there', and it is also on a mountain that Jesus is transfigured. There is the parallel — and the contrast — between the two modes of revelation received on the mountain: in the first, God gives Moses the law written on tables of stone; in the second, God reveals the living person of his only Son. Finally, there is the light, or cloud, of the divine presence, that 'glory' which, for the Hebrews, had a physical reality — 'A cloud covered the mount. And the glory of the Lord abode upon Mount Sinai . . . . The glory of the Lord was like devouring fire on the top of the mount . . .' — and which already presages the light of the Transfiguration. The next reading Exod.

33. 11-23, 34. 4-6, 8) gives us an episode each word of which applies marvellously well to our own spiritual life. God says to Moses: 'My presence shall go with thee, and I will give thee rest'. Moses asks God: 'I beseech thee, shew me thy glory'. God answers: 'I will make all my goodness pass before thee . . . . Thou canst not see my face'. Moses comes to the meeting place fixed by God; he stands on Sinai with the tables of the law in his hands. 'And the Lord descended in the cloud . . . . And the Lord passed by before him, and proclaimed, The Lord, The Lord God, merciful and gracious, longsuffering, and abundant in goodness and truth . . .'. God speaks to us inwardly as he spoke to Moses, 'face to face, as a man speaketh unto his friend'. As with Moses, he makes his goodness rather than his glory pass before us. But we are more fortunate than Moses, for we know that we can contemplate the face of God in the person of the Son. Finally, two episodes from the life of Elijah (Septuagint, 3 Kgs. 19. 3-16) are read. First, his taking refuge for forty days on Mount Horeb, where an angel brings him bread and water; then, the revelation of the divine presence which was not in the fire, the wind or the earthquake, but in the 'still small voice'. Earlier in this chapter, we have commented on this[60], and so ask our readers to refer to that. These three readings from the Old Testament associate Moses and Elijah, for both of them will be witnesses of the Transfiguration of Our Lord.

At matins, we hear the account of the Transfiguration given in the gospel according to St Luke (9. 28-36). At the liturgy, the account is taken from the gospel according to St Matthew (17. 1-9). The epistle read at the liturgy is the second of Peter's epistles (1. 10-19): with James and John, he was one of the three witnesses of the Transfiguration. Also, his memory of this mystery is particularly moving: 'We . . . were eyewitnesses of his majesty . . . when there came such a voice to him from the excellent glory, This is my beloved Son . . . . This voice which came from heaven we heard, when we were with him in the holy mount . . .'. Peter compares these words to those of the prophets, which are yet 'more sure' (perhaps because his readers have not had his experience, or through humility he gives a higher standing to Scripture than to his own experience, or perhaps he wants to underline the divine authority of the whole body of prophecies). The prophetic word, like the light of the Transfiguration 'shineth in a dark place', says Peter, 'until the day dawn, and the day star arise in your hearts'.

Let us now try to consider some aspects of the gospel account of the Transfiguration.

Jesus takes his three most intimate disciples with him. Sometimes God reveals Himself to sinners in an extraordinary way, but, in general, the privilege of contemplating God, and of entering into the joy of the Transfiguration is reserved for those who have followed the Master long and faithfully.

Jesus leads His disciples to a high mountain[61]. Before attaining the light of the Transfiguration, the hard path of asceticism is necessary.

Jesus's normal appearance is changed. His face shines 'as the sun'. His clothes become 'white as the light'. It is in this that the Transfiguration consists. The Jesus that the disciples knew well and whose looks, in ordinary life, did not differ radically from those of other people, suddenly appears to them in a new and glorious form. In our inner life, a similar experience can happen in three ways. Sometimes our inward image of Jesus becomes (to the eyes of the soul) so luminous, so resplendent, that we seem truly to see the glory of God in his face: somehow the divine beauty of Christ becomes for us an object of our experience. Or, sometimes, we feel with great intensity that the inner light, that light which is given to all men born into the world as a guide to their thought and action, is identified with the person of Jesus Christ: the power of the moral law becomes fused with the person of the Son, and the attraction of sacrifice makes us glimpse the sacrificed Saviour, and hear his call. Sometimes, too, we become aware of Jesus's presence in some man or woman whom God has set in our path, especially when it is given to us to bring compassion to their sufferings: then, in the eyes of faith, that man or woman is transfigured into Jesus Christ. From this last example, one could evolve a precise spiritual method, a method of transfiguration which could apply to everyone, everywhere and always.

Next to Jesus appear Moses and Elijah. Moses represents the law. Elijah the prophets. Jesus is the fulfilment of all law and of all prophecy. He is the final completion of the whole of the Old Covenant; He is the fulness of all divine revelation.

Moses and Elijah speak with Jesus of his coming Passion. Usually, not enough attention is paid to this aspect of the Transfiguration. In Jesus's life, the glorious mysteries cannot be separated from the mysteries of suffering. It is when he is preparing to go to his Passion that he is transfigured. In our own life, we shall not enter into the joy of the Transfiguration unless we accept the Cross.

Peter wants to stay in the blessedness of the Transfiguration. He suggests to Jesus that three tabernacles be built. In the same way, someone at the beginning of their spiritual life often wants to prolong the 'consolations', the moments of intimate sweetness. Jesus leaves Peter's suggestion unanswered. Neither to the first disciples nor to us is it permitted to withdraw from the hard labours of the plain and to establish oneself now in a peace which belongs only to a future life.

The bright cloud covers the heights of the mountain. From the midst of it a voice is heard to say: 'This is my beloved Son, in whom I am well pleased: hear ye him'. The same words, or very nearly, had already been spoken by the same voice at Jesus's baptism. They give the scene of the Transfiguration its whole meaning. Why does Jesus's appearance change? Why is he clothed in light? This is not simply in order to provide the apostles with an impressive and comforting sight. It is to transmit outwardly the solemn testimony which the Father bears to his Son. And the Father himself gives a practical conclusion to the vision: 'Hear ye him'. Any out-of-the-ordinary grace is effectual only if it makes us more attentive and more obedient to the divine Word.

The disciples fall on their faces in fear. Jesus touches them and reassures them. 'And when they had lifted up their eyes they saw no man, save Jesus only'[62]. Different meanings can be found in these words that are equally true. On the one hand, the normal state of a disciple in this world is to attach himself to the person of Jesus without this being vested with the outer attributes of divine glory. The disciple must see 'Jesus only', Jesus in his humility. If, at rare moments, his image does seem to us to be clothed in light, and if we seem to hear the voice of the Father commending the Son to our love, these lightning flashes do not last; and we must immediately find Jesus again where he is normally to be found, in the midst of our humble and sometimes difficult everyday duties. To see 'Jesus only' also means: to concentrate our attention and our gaze on Jesus alone, and not to allow ourselves to be distracted either by the things of this world or by the men and women we meet, in short, to make Jesus supreme and unique in our lives. Does this mean that we must shut our eyes to the world that surrounds us and often needs us? Some of us are called to be absolutely alone with the Master: let them be faithful to this vocation. But most of Jesus's disciples, who live in the midst of the world, can give another interpretation to the words 'Jesus only'. Without renouncing a grateful contact with created things, and a loving and devoted contact with men, they can attain a degree of faith and love which will allow Jesus to become transparent through both men and things; all natural beauty, all human beauty will become the fringe of the beauty that is itself Christ's; we will see its reflection in everything which attracts and merits our sympathy in others; in short, we shall have 'transfigured' the world, and we shall find 'Jesus only' in all those on whom we open our eyes.

The mystery of the Transfiguration has yet another aspect which the scriptural texts for the feast do not indicate clearly, but which the liturgical chants underline. 'To show the transformation of human nature . . . at Thy Second and fearful Coming . . . Saviour . . . Thou didst transfigure Thyself . . . . O Thou, who has sanctified the whole universe by Thy Light . . . .' These words, which are sung at matins, allude to the cosmic and eschatological nature of the Transfiguration. The whole of nature − which now suffers the consequences of sin, the source of physical ills − will be freed, renewed, when Christ comes in glory at the end of time. This transformation of the world is suggested to our belief, to our hope, and to our expectation. But we must be careful not to exaggerate this aspect of the Transfiguration to the detriment of the others[63]. The gospels show us that the first, fundamental, meaning of the Transfiguration concerns the person of our Lord, whom his Father glorifies before letting him go to his Passion. Effusions about the mystery of the transfiguration of the 'earth' must not veil this truth: that, before all else, the Transfiguration is the Transfiguration of the well-beloved Son.

And finally, the Transfiguration is also a revelation of the Father and the Spirit. It lifts the veil which, in this earthly life, hides from us the intimate life of the three divine Persons. We can join the whole Church in saying, in the ninth canticle for matins, 'Let us stand in spirit in the city of the living God, and let us gaze with our minds at the spiritual Godhead of the Father and the Spirit, shining forth in the Only-begotten Son'.

The Dormition of Our Lady the Most Holy Mother of God

The third of the great feasts of the summer is the commemoration of the death of the Most Blessed Virgin Mary, which, in liturgical language is called the 'Dormition' of Our Lady[64]. This, from the liturgical point of view, is the most important of the feasts dedicated to the Virgin. It is preceded by a two weeks' fast, the "Lent of the Mother of God", analogous to that which precedes the feast of St Peter and St Paul; this fast begins on August 1st and lasts till August 14th inclusive. The feast itself is on August 15th.

Many features of this feast are taken from other feasts dedicated to the Virgin. Thus the gospel for matins tells of Mary's visit to Elisabeth (Luke 1. 39-56). The epistle (Phil. 2. 5-11) and the gospel (Luke 10. 38-42, 11. 27-28) for the liturgy are those which we read for September 8th, the day of Mary's Nativity; we ask our readers to refer to what was said there about these texts[65]. It will be noticed that the scriptural passages which are read on August 15th make no allusion to the death of the Blessed Virgin. It is in the chants for vespers and matins that one finds the special significance which the Church attaches to the feast of August 15th.

This significance is twofold, and is given exact expression by a phrase which is sung at vespers: 'The source of life is laid in the grave and her tomb becomes a ladder to heaven'. The first part of this − 'the source of life is laid in the grave' − indicates that we commemorate the death of the most Blessed Virgin. If, each year, we celebrate reverently the anniversaries of the deaths of the Precursor, the apostles and the martyrs, there is much more reason to celebrate the death of the Mother of God, who is also our mother, and whose holiness and glory go far beyond that of the elect[66]. But the feast of August 15th is more than the commemoration of Mary's death. The second part of the phrase says: ' . . . and her tomb becomes a ladder to heaven'. The tomb of anyone who has died in Christ is, in a certain way, a ladder which leads to heaven. All the same, Mary's case is exceptional. The liturgical texts which are sung imply something more: 'Open wide the gates and receive above the world the Mother of the everlasting Light . . . . For today heaven is opened to receive her . . . . The angels hymn thy most holy falling asleep . . . that we celebrate with faith . . . . Let all the sons of earth tremble in spirit . . . and celebrate with joy the venerable Assumption of the Mother of God'. This makes it clear that more is involved than Mary's soul being received into heaven. Although in the Byzantine calendar, the feast of August 15th does not bear the name of the feast of the Assumption (as it does in the Latin Church), our texts express belief in the bodily assumption of Mary. According to this belief, Mary's body did not suffer the corruption which follows death; it did not stay in the tomb. Mary, raised from the dead, was carried to heaven by angels (the Assumption differs from the Ascension in that Christ rose to heaven by himself).

The Assumption of Mary is outside — and above — history. Belief in the Assumption does not depend on any biblical account, or on any historical witness that is scientifically acceptable[67]. It is not the object of any dogmatic definition. The Church has not, up till now, imposed on any believer the need to affirm Mary's bodily Assumption. But even if the Church does not insist on such an (inner or outward) affirmation, one can say that the Orthodox conscience would consider any active negation of the Assumption not only as foolhardy, but also as a blasphemy. Moreover, how does one deny a fact which is not susceptible to any historical verification? Belief in the Assumption is not based on documentary proofs. Catholic thinking, enlightened by the Holy Spirit, has, little by little become convinced that if 'the wages of sin is death'[68], Mary gained a special victory over death[69]. In the same way as Jesus (while keeping a due sense of proportion), she was glorified in her body. It is this glorification of the all-pure and all-holy Mother of God in her soul and in her flesh — and not this or that material symbolism or historical circumstance — which constitutes the object of the feast of August 15th.

The Assumption is the feast, not only of Mary, but of all human nature. For, in Mary, human nature reached its goal. One week after the start of the liturgical year, we celebrate the birth of the most Holy Virgin. Two weeks before the end of the liturgical year, we celebrate the death and glorification of Mary. Thus, associated with and subordinate to the cycle of Jesus's life, the cycle of Mary's life manifests the destiny and development of a human nature which is entirely faithful to God. It is the human race which is carried up and received into heaven with her. Mary was granted privileges which cannot be ours. However, the perfect flowering of grace that we marvel at in Mary on August 15th suggests what the line of development could be in a soul which applied itself to making the great gifts received during the liturgical year — the gift of Christmas, the gift of Easter and the gift of Pentecost — bear their fruit.

The End of the Liturgical Year

Only two weeks separate the feast of the Dormition of the Mother of God and the end of the liturgical year. The cycle of the ecclesiastical year has nearly revolved completely. A new cycle starts on September 1st[70].

Many believers cannot see the cycle, during which they followed Jesus from his birth to his glorification, come to an end without a certain sadness. When one has been close to the glory of Easter and of Pentecost, a return to the humble beginnings, the anticipation of the Nativity, may seem like a diminution. If the fulness has been reached, why come back to the starting point?

The human condition is such that we are not able to remain permanently in a maximum state. We need to learn again the first elements of what we think we know. It is only through a constantly renewed and constantly attentive contemplation of the life of our Lord, in all its aspects, in its whole succession of human vicissitudes, that we will perhaps be able at least to glimpse some reflections of the mystery of Christ. Then there are our sins, our falls. A soul that is sullied could not endure the radiance of the glory of God. It is good, it is necessary, for it to come back to periods of penitence and expiation.

The return of the liturgical cyle reminds us, too, that 'salvation', in the Christian sense of the word, cannot be separated from a historical and a personal context. It does not belong to a purely metaphysical order. It is not the communication of an abstract doctrine. We are saved because 'something has happened', because certain events have taken place. The liturgical year commemorates and renews those events mystically.

We would be mistaken if we identified the fulness of the liturgical year with its glorious end. The mystery of liturgical time is the mystery of time itself: time 'distorts', and makes the eternal divine reality imperfect, multiple and successive. In God, there is but one moment, in which everything is included. The fulness of the liturgical year does not consist of the commemorative cycle of Christ's life being resolved or completed, for the completion of a series implies that there is a series, a succession of disjointed elements. The fulness of the liturgical year has to be thought of qualitatively and not quantitatively; it is achieved if, on any day whatever of the liturgical year, whichever it might be, we are capable of grasping – through the particular event which is commemorated – Christ as a whole, the whole of his life, the whole of his work, the whole of his word. Each feast, and even each day of the year thus becomes the fulness of the whole liturgical cycle. This cycle never repeats itself; each one of its aspects reflects the inexhaustible depth and fulness of Christ, and, as a result, becomes new for us to the extent that we understand it better. The liturgical year is a prism which receives the white light of Christ and splits it into different colours. Christ is the year.

Notes to Chapter VII

1   We know that, to begin with, Pentecost, like Easter, was a Jewish feast. It originated as the feast for the harvest of the first fruits (Exodus 23. 16). Later, under the influence of the Pharisees, this feast became more spiritual in character: it became the commemoration of God's giving the law to Moses. Christian Pentecost develops both these lines of origin: the conversions and miracles which took place at the first Christian Pentecost were the first fruits of Jesus's religion; the coming of the Spirit into the hearts of the disciples inscribed in them a new Law. We know from Tertullian that, by the third century, Christians celebrated their own feast of Pentecost, and from the so-called *Apostolic Constitutions* we learn that in the fourth century the celebration of Pentecost lasted for a week. Catechumens were baptised on the eve of the Sunday of Pentecost, as on Holy Saturday. Easter and Pentecost — the Easter of the Spirit — were accorded equal status.

2   This text ought to be meditated on, in our day, by those exclusivists who believe that God can only raise up prophets through their own tabernacles, and that because of this, those servants of God whose lives and words are approved by the Church have exceptional authority. But there exists no Church or group of Christians, there is no religion, even a pagan one, from which God cannot elect saintly and inspired servants.

3   The breath becomes a voice. The voice which pronounces and the word that is pronounced both proceed from the Father. The Son is the Word, the Word of God, the Holy Spirit is the voice which carries and pronounces this Word. When God speaks to our inner selves, the content of the message comes from the Father, the Son formulates and pronounces the text of the message, and it is through the power of the Spirit that the message reaches us. If the text of the message is the Son's, the intonation and the inflexions, so to speak, come from the Spirit. The same musical score can give rise, in its execution, to nuances which can be very delicate: the Holy Spirit is the divine transmitter of the words uttered by the Son; it plays the pedals on which depend the power or the gentleness of the message, and determines its impact on the human soul. May we be forgiven for using such lamentably inadequate comparisons. But we are *dealing with realities* that can only be represented by very rough analogies. Moreover, when we say that the Spirit, breath of the Father, was — and still is — breathed by Jesus on his disciples, we speak of the sending, of the mission, of the Spirit in this world. But first of all we must think of the Spirit as the breath of the Father on Jesus, the breath which Jesus transmits to men. In this, we are touching on the question of the procession of the Holy Spirit. Both the Orthodox and the Romans are today in agreement on one point: in the Trinity, the Father, alone, is the absolute mainspring of procession. Those who maintain

that the Spirit proceeds from the Father 'and the Son' nevertheless do not admit that the Son is, as is the Father, the source from which the Spirit proceeds; he is but the channel, the instrument. Those who think that the Son and the Spirit both proceed from the Father in an immediate manner, without the Son being an intermediary for the procession of the Spirit (although, in the outward missions of the Spirit, it is the Son that sends him), are perhaps implicitly concerned about this: to avoid the slightest appearance of making the invisible element (the Spirit) depend on the visible element (the incarnate Son). This anxiety has importance consequences for the concept of the Church, or, more precisely, for the relationship between the spiritual and the institutional elements in the Church.

4   Scripture shows us that the coming of the Spirit "with power" can take place without any human ministry or sacramental intermediary such as the laying on of hands, or unction. This is how Cornelius and others received the Holy Spirit (Acts 10. 44). Here, baptism by the Spirit took place before baptism by water. Paul also received the Holy Spirit before being baptised by water; in Paul's case, the coming of the Spirit took place through the laying on of hands, although we do not know what position in the Christian community the man who conferred it occupied (Acts 9. 17). It has also happened that the Spirit came a second time on a man or a group which had already received it (Acts 5. 31). We cannot therefore simply assume that this baptism of the Spirit, mentioned in Scripture, is to be identified with the ecclesiastical rites of 'confirmation' or 'chrismation', which come nearer to Jesus's gift of the Spirit to the apostles by breathing on them after the Resurrection – well before the flame and the power of Pentecost descended on them. Similarly, if asked the question that Paul put to the Ephesians: 'Have ye received the Holy Ghost?', it would not suffice for us to answer: 'I received the Spirit when, after I was baptised, I was anointed with the chrism'. What matters is to know if and how the seed of the Spirit which was sown in us then has developed and borne fruit. The coming of the Spirit with power, the inner Pentecost, sometimes develops gradually and imperceptibly, sometimes it constitutes a sudden event and brings about a radical break in the thread of life. It can take place without any human intervention; it can also come about through contact or through the prayer of someone, whoever they might be, who already possesses the power of the Spirit. Many souls live as strangers to this Pentecostal power although they may have been marked by the double seal of baptism by water and by unction. On the other hand, we would not dare to deny that in our day, as before, certain men who have not received the Spirit sacramentally have nevertheless received the reality of baptism by the Spirit and Pentecostal grace, for 'The wind bloweth where it listeth' (John 3. 8) and 'God giveth not the Spirit by measure' (John 3. 34). A Christian life in which the power of the Spirit (not just its latent presence) did not make itself felt would not have attained its normal development. But in how many Christians does baptism by the Spirit, Pentecost, constitute an active *power*? One recognises this power in the lives of saints.

5   Early Christianity knew the 'gift of tongues' under a double form: 'xenoglossy', which consists of speaking to a foreigner in his language though one does not know it oneself or, if the speaker is using his own language, being understood by foreigners; and 'glossolalia', which consists in uttering mysterious words that are incomprehensible in all languages, and which need an interpreter who is himself inspired to translate to those who hear them.

6   St Paul lists the principal gifts of the Spirit: healing, prophecy, speaking in

tongues, discerning of spirits, etc. (1 Cor. 12. 7-10). These extraordinary gifts have never disappeared from the Church, though this aspect of the apostolic succession has largely devolved on the saints, and constitutes the spiritual and prophetic ministry at the heart of the Christian community. The poverty of our faith is the reason why too often we consider these graces as exceptional. Jesus spoke to believers of all times when he said: 'And these signs shall follow them that believe; In my name shall they cast out devils; they shall speak with new tongues; they shall take up serpents; and if they drink any deadly thing it shall not hurt them; they shall lay hands on the sick, and they shall recover' (Mark 16. 17-18). Paul exhorted believers to desire these gifts of the Spirit which seem to us exceptional: 'Covet earnestly the best gifts' (1 Cor. 12. 31). But, at the same time, it must not be forgotten that beyond these gifts of the Spirit is found what Paul calls the 'more excellent way' (1 Cor. 12. 31) of charity.

7   If we try to address the Holy Spirit by separating it mentally from the person of Christ, in some way it seems to retreat and vanish. The Spirit is sent to us by the Son, the Son is revealed to us by the Spirit. The Holy Spirit is not a substitute for Christ, but prepares us for Christ, forms him in us, makes him present to us. In this way, one could say that the Son, our model, is the 'object' towards which our spiritual life reaches. The Spirit, working in us, is the 'subject' which strains towards that object and carries us towards him.

8   In the absence of prayers addressed directly to the Holy Spirit, we must practise what the Apostle Jude, in his epistle (v.20), calls 'praying in the Holy Ghost', which could either mean that the intention and words of our prayer are given to us by the Spirit, or that our soul unites itself in silence to the unknown prayer that the Spirit never ceases to form. It is the true Supplicant in us. As Paul says: 'the Spirit itself maketh intercession for us with groanings which cannot be uttered' (Rom. 8. 26).

9   When we say that the Holy Spirit dwells in us, we 'appropriate' (as theologians say) to the third Person of the Trinity an action in which the two other Persons are themselves included, for the Trinity as a whole shares in the outgoing movement of each of its members. But it is very much in accordance with Scripture to speak of an indwelling of the Spirit in the human creature, which is its temple.

10   Unlike the Roman or Anglican Churches, the Churches of the Byzantine rite do not have a Sunday specially dedicated to the Holy Trinity other than Pentecost.

11   It would be very instructive and fruitful for us, for example to read the Gospels not from the point of view of Jesus's mission to men, but from that of the Son's relationship to the Father. We would then see how much this relationship is the very essence of the mystery of Jesus. The Greek Fathers were well aware of the importance of this disinterested contemplation of the divine life. However, dating from Luther, one part of Christianity has wished only to know about 'Christ for us', in his redemptive action. This has entailed great loss.

12   Without wishing to give a theological outline here – even a very brief one – of the mystery of the Trinity, we would like to indicate the general lines that the human spirit has followed in order to approach this mystery. We shall eliminate immediately the modalist heresy, which sees in the three Persons simple aspects or modes of the activity of God. We can then consider the Trinity on the ontological, the metaphysical plane: in the divine Being, three 'substantial' relationships – of fatherhood, sonship, and spiration are distinguishable; these

relations are called 'substantial' because, in contrast to the relations that exist between created beings which are 'accidental', and somehow detachable from the essence which sustains them, the divine relations are what constitute each of the three Persons; the Father is inasmuch as he is Father, the Son is inasmuch as he is Son, the Spirit is inasmuch as it is Spirit. Such is the line of approach of Thomas Aquinas and his followers. One can look at this from the psychological plane, and make analogies between the divine Persons and what takes place in the human soul: the Father is the first principle — power, memory; the Son is the intellect; the Spirit is will, love. Such is the line taken by those who follow Augustine. Whereas the Latin Fathers have, on the whole, started with the divine unity and moved from there to the three Persons, the Greek Fathers have preferred to consider first of all the Persons and then attain to the divine unity. Their thinking was followed in the West by Richard of Saint-Victor, who conceived of the Trinity as consisting of three personal loves; the Father is the first lover, the Son the first beloved, and the Spirit the 'co-beloved' whose existence is necessary to the two other persons, for a perfect love desires to share what it receives and multiply what it offers. The mystery of the Trinity can obviously not be comprehended by human intelligence. But, in being an object of faith and not of rational understanding, it can be approached and sensed by our soul, thanks to the harmonies which it arouses.

13   The Roman Church celebrates the same feast on the 1st November. The feast of the first Sunday after Pentecost began being celebrated in Antioch during the fourth century. To begin with, it was a feast of all the martyrs, then other saints were gradually added. We have a sermon of St Ephraim's which dates from 373, and a sermon of St John Chrysostom's, dating from 407, in honour of this feast.

14   One must not think of sainthood as an 'extraordinary' state, nor identify it with extraordinary ascetic exploits or with rare mystical graces. There are indeed superior — heroic — degrees of saintliness, but in the sense given in the New Testament, saintliness is simply the state of a soul united to God through the operation of the Holy Spirit. This state of union exists in every Christian whom sin has not separated from God. Saintliness is therefore a normal state for a Christian, and the call to saintliness is addressed to all.

15   See ch. II.

16   See ch. IV. The length of the portion of the epistle is not always exactly the same on these different occasions.

17   From this Sunday, the Church stops using the liturgical book called the *Pentekostarion* which has been used since Easter. The usual practice is resumed and the services for Sundays are taken from the *Oktoechos*, those for ordinary days of the week from the *Paraklitike*, and those for the variable feasts of the saints from the *Menaion*.

18   A rich Church is in a state of danger: a Church which desires riches is going down the slope of scandals and disasters. Ecclesiastical history is often the history of a terrible judgement of God directed at the human element of the Church.

19   This error has sometimes been committed in some of the Protestant Churches, especially some of the Lutheran ones. Wesleyan Methodism and Fox's Quakerism were reactions in favour of sanctification, which had been neglected by some interpreters of justification by faith. Many Roman believers may have heard sanctification spoken of more than justification. The notion of justifica-

tion is not sufficiently thought about by the Orthodox, but, with them, above all it is ritualism and a certain 'externalism' which are the obstacles to a real concept of sanctification.

20 See. ch. I.

21 Deut. 30. 14.

22 See. ch. IV.

23 John 6. 34.

24 Apollos was an Alexandrian Jew who brought the Gospel to Asia Minor and to Greece with success, and whose collaboration Paul appreciated. References to him are found in Acts 18 and 19, Cor. 3, and Titus 3. 13.

25 The Apostle Peter. *Cephas* is the Greek form of the Aramaic *Kepha* 'stone', the surname given to Simon by Jesus.

26 Mark 9. 16-30.

27 We do not dispute the possibility that such phenomena can be linked with spiritual causes. We do not know what part the Spirit has played in, for example, the great geological events, but we do not doubt that these events have, in the final analysis, served the cause of the Spirit. The relationship between the divine organising power of the physical universe and the divine tenderness towards individual souls is strikingly expressed in Revelation 1. 16-17, where the same divine Person, out of whose mouth went a sharp two edged sword and who held in his right hand seven stars, places this *same* right hand on the Seer, when in terror he has fallen at his feet, and says to him: 'Fear not'.

28 See the gospel for the fourth Sunday after Pentecost.

29 1 Cor. 13.2.

30 The sum is enormous.

31 Luke 18. 18-27.

32 See. ch. III.

33 This passage is of great historical importance. Paul can write, without anyone denying it or contradicting him, that the resurrected Jesus had been seen by the twelve and by more than five hundred brethren, of whom the greater number were still alive at the time when he was writing. When he visited Jerusalem, Paul had made contact with them. Could the apostle have made such an assertion if he laid himself open to being immediately refuted by the Jewish polemicists? Even if we did not have the gospel accounts of the Resurrection, Paul's reference (which is earlier than the texts of the gospels) to numerous witnesses of the Resurrection who were still alive is sufficient to provide the historian with a problem of the first order – the greatest of all historical problems. The negative solution given to this problem is dictated not by history, but by *a priori* philosophical concepts. But the faith of those who believe in the Resurrection of Christ is remarkably reinforced by Paul's phrase, which is all the more impressive in that it seems a passing comment, for he does not go on to discuss the fact of the Resurrection at this point.

34 The first six ecumenical councils were those of Nicaea (325), Constantinople (381), Ephesus (431), Chalcedon (451), Constantinople (553), Constantinople (680). It is surprising to find that the seventh ecumenical council, that of Nicaea (787), is not mentioned here. But, when the commemoration of the Fathers was established, the council of 787 had not yet acquired a status of complete equality with the previous ecumenical councils. Moreover, this council, which was the final episode in the iconoclast dispute, and which decided on the place of images in worship, had not formulated theological principles which

were as fundamental as the Christological and Trinitarian definitions of the other six councils.

35 Sixth Sunday after Easter. See ch. VI.

36 Elijah, although he wrote nothing, became the most venerated of the prophets of Israel. He lived in the ninth century before Christ. He probably came from Tishbe, in the territory of Gilead, and stood out against the worship of Baal, as well as against the evils of the king, Ahab, and of his queen, Jezebel. Like Enoch, he was mysteriously lifted up to heaven, leaving his disciple Elisha to inherit his mantle and his power.

37 The Arabs call Mount Carmel 'Mount Elijah'. Muslims, as well as Palestinian and Syrian Christians, venerate various places that legend associates with the history of the prophet. A 'Revelation of Elijah', which is, however, of doubtful authenticity, seems to have influenced two passages in the writings of St Paul (1 Cor. 2. 9, and Eph. 5. 14). The claim by the Latin Order of Carmelites to have been founded by Elijah, and to have an unbroken line of descent from him, cannot be upheld historically.

38 1 Kings 19. 11-13, following the Hebrew text. This book corresponds, in the Septuagint and the versions that derive from it, to the 3rd book of Kings. Our references follow the Hebrew.

39 1 Kgs. 18.

40 2 Kgs. 2. 11.

41 1 Kgs. 17. 17-24.

42 See ch. V.

43 See ch. VI.

44 This feast originates in Constantinople. On August 1st, a relic of the Cross was solemnly carried from the chapel of the imperial palace to the cathedral of Haghia Sophia; it was brought back to the palace on August 14th.

45 See ch. I.

46 See ch. IV.

47 This commemoration of the 'Beheading' of John the Baptist was celebrated at Constantinople and in Gaul before being adopted by Rome. It is a day of fasting. The feast of June 24th, however, seems to be of western origin; it is mentioned in the sermons of St Augustine.

48 It is Herod Antipas, before whom Jesus appeared, who is concerned. Antipas, the tetrarch of Galilee, was the son of King Herod the Great, during whose reign Jesus was born. Although he was married to the daughter of King Aretas of Arabia, Antipas lived with Herodias, the wife of his half-brother, Philip; this Philip was the father of Salome, the young girl who danced before Herod and who, at her mother's instigation, asked for the head of John. According to the Jewish historian, Josephus, it was in the fortress of Machaerus, near the Dead Sea, that John was executed. Antipas, disgraced by the Roman Emperor Caligula, was banished to Lyons, in Gaul, in the year 39 of the Christian era; Herodias went with him into exile.

49 Matt. 17. 12, 13.

50 The feasts of these two apostles have been combined into one because of the very ancient tradition according to which they were both martyred in Rome, on the same day. Peter's execution would have taken place near the Vatican hill, and Paul's on the Via Ostiensis, during Nero's persecutions round about the year 68. We have no precise information about either Peter or Paul's activities after the period covered by the Book of the Acts. This ends with the arrival of Paul in

Rome, where he was to be judged. We do not know where Peter was at this time. The stay and the death in Rome of the two apostles is not a question of dogma, but of history, and must be treated with full objectivity and the freedom of science. All the same, the literary documents and the topographical traditions concerning the apostolate and martyrdom of Peter and Paul in Rome are old enough and important enough for us to attach a considerable weight of probability to the constant opinion of the Church on this subject. From the fourth century, the feast of the apostles Peter and Paul was celebrated on June 29th in Rome; by contrast, Constantinople and the East celebrated it a few days after Christmas, on December 28th. The Roman custom eventually became universal, but we do not know precisely when.

51   Paul was not with the eleven at the time of Pentecost, but Ananias conferred the Holy Spirit on him by the laying-on of hands, straight after his conversion (Acts 9. 17).

52   John 21. 15-17.

53   The ancient Roman formulae, *servus servorum Dei* 'servant of the servants of God', and *sollicitudo omnium ecclesiarum*, 'concern for all the Churches', express an entirely admirable ideal. It will be for history to say to what extent the reality has lived up to this ideal.

54   The authenticity of these words has been denied by certain critics. From the fact that they are not found in the gospels of Mark and of Luke, and that several Fathers of the second century did not seem to know of them, these critics have concluded that they form a later, 'romanising', interpolation. There are strong arguments against the hypothesis of an interpolation. Naturally, we do not pretend to settle this problem, which the Orthodox can and must approach in a spirit and through methods which are purely scientific. The interpretation of the words themselves is a classic 'area' of divergence. Is the Church founded on the very person of Peter, in so far as he is distinct from the other apostles? Or on Peter, in so far as he represents, and is the mouthpiece for, the whole apostolic body? Or on the faith which Peter has just confessed? The Fathers of the Church have given very different answers to these questions. St Augustine, after having adopted several interpretations in succession, ends by declaring (in his *Retractationes*) that he leaves the question open. All agree in recognising that, amongst the apostles, Peter had a certain ascendancy and certain privileges and prerogatives granted him by Jesus. But was he vested with genuine governmental authority? And was this perpetually transmissible? These are the points on which opinions are divided. It is on the answer given to such questions that the attitudes of the Roman Church, on the one hand, and of the non-Roman Churches, on the other, are based.

55   See. ch. I.

56   Gal. 2. 11.

57   Vespers service.

58   It might be useful here to go into the historical and theological significance of the word 'apostle' in some detail. An apostle was someone sent by Christ. His calling and his mission were not of human but of immediate divine origin. The Twelve had been chosen by Jesus during his earthly life, Paul by the glorified Jesus, Matthias (who succeeded Judas) by the Spirit — who was consulted by means of drawing 'lots'. Moreover, the apostles had to 'have seen the Lord', have been with him (Mark 3. 14). Matthias fulfilled this condition; Paul, though he lacked knowledge of the historical Jesus, had that of the eternal Christ. (In this,

there is an idea which is of great practical importance for whoever dreams of 'mission' and 'apostleship': one cannot be sent by Jesus if one has not first lived — in our day, spiritually — with him.) The apostles were not so much the preachers of a doctrine (which any Christian could be) as the direct witnesses of the life, the person, and above all, of the Resurrection of Christ (Acts 1. 22). The apostles did not have the government of a local Church. Each apostle exercised an absolute and universal jurisdiction. The Fathers of the Church attribute to them the privilege of personal infallibility and that of being confirmed in grace (that is to say, preserved from voluntary sin). It can be seen from all this that one cannot simply and unreservedly identify the concept of episcopacy with that of apostolate. Bishops — in the same way, moreover, as priests and deacons, and even the laity — are partly what the apostles were, but they are not all that the apostles were. When one speaks of 'apostolic succession', it is necessary to understand precisely what it is about. We may also note the fact that some men who are in no way successors to the apostles through the hierarchic line of succession do still participate in their succession through the line of sanctity, whilst other men to whom the imposition of hands has meant participation in 'apostolic' jurisdictional power may remain completely foreign to the sanctity of the apostles. Few terms today give rise to as much confusion of ideas as that of 'apostolic succession'. If it is used, what is involved must be stated precisely.

59   The feast of the Transfiguration began to be celebrated in Asia during the fourth century, probably by the Armenians. They celebrate it with special solemnity, preparing for it by a six-days' fast and making it last three days. Like several other Christian feasts, the Transfiguration seems to have replaced a pagan 'nature feast': the blessing of the new fruits on the day of the Transfiguration is perhaps a remnant of this origin. Though it was adopted very soon by the Greek Church, the feast was not introduced into the Roman Church until the ninth century, and, even so, it was not until the fifteenth century that it was generally adopted in the West.

60   See the feast of the prophet Elijah (20 July), in the section entitled: Some Minor Feasts of the Summer (p. 232).

61   This mountain is not given a name in the gospels. The liturgical texts speak of Thabor, though it has been pointed out that Mount Hermon corresponds better to the facts known from the gospels. Nevertheless the tradition connected with Thabor was current in Palestine as early as the fourth century.

62   Matt. 17. 8.

63   A certain contemporary school of Orthodox thought would like to place the Transfiguration at the centre of the whole Christian mystery, and lays excessive emphasis on the transformation of the cosmos. The essentially Christological character of the Transfiguration, and its link with messianic suffering is thereby ignored. Also, some Byzantine mystics of the middle ages attached an importance to the "light of Thabor" which neither the Scriptures nor the Fathers of the Church give it. Orthodoxy cannot be reduced to the Transfiguration and to Easter night, as some of its apologists would have one believe. One must admire the wisdom with which the Church, in its liturgical cycle, gives to everything its place and true proportion, and endeavours to maintain a harmonious balance between the various aspects of the unique mystery.

64   The origins of this feast are rather obscure. In Palestine, from before the year 500, it was celebrated on August 15th. The Egyptians celebrated it too, but

on January 18th. Its observance on January 18th passed from Egypt to Gaul during the fourth century. With the Greeks, some followed the Palestinian and some the Egyptian custom. In the seventh century, the Byzantine Emperor Maurice fixed the feast definitively on August 15th.

65   See. ch. I.

66   We know neither when nor where Mary died. Two traditions exist in regard to this: according to the one, Mary died in Jerusalem, according to the other, at Ephesus.

67   Some writings attributed to the apostle John, to Meliton of Sardis, and to Dyonisius the Areopagite proclaim the Assumption of Mary. However these writings are apocryphal and they cannot be earlier than the 5th century. Some sermons of St Andrew of Crete and of St John of Damascus also speak of the Assumption. But these products of the early Byzantine middle ages, though interesting and edifying from the spiritual point of view, have no historical authority. In connection with the Assumption of Mary, we do not have what we have in relation to the Resurrection of Jesus — knowledge derived from contemporary testimony which is direct and concurring.

68   Rom. 6. 23.

69   Mary was a unique creature, as close to God as is possible for a created being. Jesus's flesh was entirely and solely the flesh of Mary.

70   The time after Pentecost continues until the first Sunday of preparation for Great Lent. But the start of the liturgical year, in September, which is followed by Advent, Christmas and Epiphany, leads us into an atmosphere which is so different from that of Pentecost that we feel we can stop here with the time of Pentecost, at the same time as the liturgical year itself draws to an end.